Studies in Women Writers in English

Studies in Women Writers in English

VOLUME–V

Edited by

MOHIT K. RAY
RAMA KUNDU

ATLANTIC®

PUBLISHERS & DISTRIBUTORS

Published by
ATLANTIC®
PUBLISHERS & DISTRIBUTORS
B-2, Vishal Enclave, Opp. Rajouri Garden,
New Delhi-110027
Phones : 25413460, 25429987, 25466842

Sales Office
7/22, Ansari Road, Darya Ganj,
New Delhi-110002
Phones : 23273880, 23275880, 23280451
Fax : 91-11-23285873
web : www.atlanticbooks.com
e-mail : info@atlanticbooks.com

ISBN 81-269-0635-9 (Vol. V)
ISBN 81-269-0338-4 (Set)

Printed in India
at Nice Printing Press, Delhi

Preface

The new series—*Studies in Women Writers in English*—is a grateful acknowledgment of the contribution and public recognition of the emerging voice of women in the arena of literature during the last few centuries, and especially in the latter half of the twentieth century. Women writers across the globe have made their distinctive mark, with their own perception of life—be it feminine, or feminist or female.

The critique of work by women writers introduced in the present volume, the fifth in the series, bears evidence to the growing critical attention towards authors writing outside the mainstream, in America, Canada, and especially in India.

The eighteen essays included in this fifth volume of the series cover a wide spectrum. The women writers discussed in this volume include one from Britain, i.e., Mary Shelley, one from America, i.e., Toni Morrison, the Nobel Laureate for Literature in 1993, one from Canada, i.e., Margaret Laurence, and a host of Indian writers—from an early pioneer like Krupabai Satthianadhan to the partition novelist Bapsi Sidwa, as well as contemporary avant-gardes like Shashi Deshpande, Anita Desai, Shobha De, Manju Kapur, and Arundhati Roy—in addition to the émigré Indian writer Bharati Mukherjee.

Dr Santwana Haldar in her scholarly essay on the celebrated work of Mary Shelley shows how surprisingly relevant Mary Shelley's *Frankenstein* continues to be. While underscoring Mary Shelley's radical notion of 'transgression' as defiance of the laws of nature which was involved in scientific pursuits, Dr Haldar brings out Mary Shelley's ethical stand in this regard which becomes particularly important in today's context.

Ms Devika discusses Toni Morrison's novels with particular reference to their existential dimension and builds her thesis that Toni Morrison's characters are formulated by an essential alienation, insecurity, and angst.

Dr Binod Mishra, again, takes up one particular novel of Toni Morrison, *Jazz,* and focuses on the existential angst as it informs the characters going through their fears and frustrations; Mishra, however, also notes a positive element in these characters' aptitude for extending mutual support.

Dr Rashmi Gaur and Rano Ringo offer a post-feminist reading of Margaret Laurence's most well-known Canadian novel, *The Stone Angel.*

Dr Madhu Joshi examines *Saguna,* which started as serial in 1886, as an early reflection of the aspirations of the 'New Woman' in India at the turn of the nineteenth century, and places the work in the historical-cultural context of the late nineteenth century India.

Dr Mallikarjun Patil studies Bapsi Sidwa's *The Ice-Candy Man* as a partition novel which, according to Patil, appears to suffer in comparison with some other major partition novels, and particularly Khushwant Singh's *Train to Pakistan.*

Dr Binda Sharma and Dr G.A. Ghanshyam make an in-depth study of Bharati Mukherjee's *Wife* and analyse the way Bharati Mukherjee captures the psychological displacement that follows in the wake of cultural displacement and the resultant alienation in an immigrant woman's life.

Dr Binod Mishra sensitively responds to the 'intricacies' that arise out of the lack of communication among the various characters in Anita Desai's *In Custody.*

Sadhana Agrawal offers a fine sensitive response to Anita Desai's unique novel, *Journey to Ithaca,* as 'a saga of multiple journeys,' including outward journey to a land, and inward journey within oneself.

Dr G.A. Ghanshyam, in his paper on another novel of Bharati Mukherjee, *Jasmine,* approaches the work as 'a novel of cultural transplantation,' although he notes that *Jasmine* seems to represent a more positive response to the challenges of a new life than the earlier work of Bharati Mukherjee.

S. Ambika, in her long discussion of Shashi Deshpande's novel, *The Dark Holds No Terrors,* hits upon the 'basic question' as well as the 'basic paradox' of Deshpande's novel, which she finds revolving round the issue of the identity of an Indian woman *vis-à-vis* family, society, and self. Ambika also shows Deshpande foregrounding a balanced approach that is constituted neither by victory nor by defeat but by harmony and understanding.

Ram Sharma, on the other hand, examines Shashi Deshpande's *That Long Silence* by relating the novel to the feminist discourse regarding the woman in the role of a writer—her problems and obstacles, aspirations and frustrations as involved in the challenge.

Dr Narinder Kumar Neb pleads a case for Shobha De's 'readability,' and laments that De's writings, in spite of their popularity, have not received the kind of critical attention that they deserve.

Dr G.A. Ghanshyam, in yet another article on Bharati Mukherjee, analyses Bharati Mukherjee's exploration of the theme of alienation and assimilation with particular focus on *The Holder of the World.*

Dr Shubha Tiwari claims the title of "An Excellent Word-Weaver" for Arundhati Roy, and also holds that 'much is to be forgiven to those who write well.'

Binayak Ray makes a thematic study of Roy's canonized novel *The God of Small Things*.

Devika examines Manju Kapur's *Difficult Daughters* and brings out the continuing threads of parity between different generations in spite of the obvious generational gaps and fissures.

Dr Mallikarjun Patil makes a brief overview of some concepts of feminism from theoretical perspective.

Since most of the authors discussed in these articles are prescribed in the English syllabus in the universities of India, both the teachers and the students will find them extremely useful, and the general readers who are interested in literature in English and/or women writers will also find them intellectually stimulating.

We thank all the contributors to this volume for their learned papers which have enriched the anthology.

Our heartfelt thanks go to Dr K.R. Gupta, Chairman, Atlantic Publishers and Distributors for the confidence evinced in us and also for seeing the book through the press.

Mohit K. Ray
Rama Kundu
Editors

Contents

1

'Transgression' in Mary Shelley's *Frankenstein* and Some Debates on Human Cloning

SANTWANA HALDAR

Mary Shelley's *Frankenstein* (1818) had been thrown into negligence and near-oblivion by her contemporaries and by the Victorian moralists, and it came into the limelight only towards the end of the twentieth century, thanks to the various readings of the book by the feminists, structuralists, post-colonial theorists and others.[1] Surprisingly, the title of the novel "Frankenstein," which is also the name of its protagonist, was mistakenly attributed to the demonic figure created by Frankenstein who is ultimately crushed by his own creation and "Frankenstein" became a metaphor for the potentially disastrous results of scientific invention.[2] Undoubtedly, the metaphor suited the traumatic experience caused by the Hiroshima-Nagasaki holocaust. With the fear of a nuclear war hanging overhead, the sensible people all over the world began to express their concern for the scientists' disregard of potential human consequences of their pursuit, and found in *Frankenstein* a readymade metaphor. Mary Shelley's story of a scientist who created a demon-like figure out of an assemblage of the parts from dead bodies and was fated to be totally doomed by his creation, fitted into the general atmosphere of doubt and concern for unmindful scientific inventions. The present paper seeks to highlight Mary Shelley's scientific views as revealed in the novel, as well as her ideas on the limitations of science and technologies which are particularly relevant in the twenty-first century.

In an age when Percy Shelley's rebellious Prometheus was hailed by the Romantics. Mary levelled the charge of transgression against her modern Prometheus (subtitle of her novel) and it was wrong to interpret this transgression in terms of overreaching God. Frankenstein transgressed not the law of God but the law of Nature that takes steps against the lack of concern for potential human consequences of scientific pursuits. Mary evolved an ethical stand of her own out of this concern.[3] Victor Frankenstein, the central character of her novel is found guilty from this standpoint. Notwithstanding his fascination towards the 'philosopher's stone' and the 'elixir of life' (the twin objects of alchemic quest—the first for its purported capacity to turn other metals to gold, the latter for defying death), Victor is projected as a scientist from the very beginning. As Victor said,

> The natural phenomena that take place every day before our eyes did not escape my examinations. Distillation, and the wonderful effects of steam, processes of which my favourite authors were utterly ignorant, excited my astonishment; but my utmost wonder was engaged by some experiments on an air pump, which I saw employed by a gentleman whom we were in the habit of visiting.
>
> I eagerly inquired of my father the nature and origin of thunder and lightning. He replied, 'Electricity,' describing at the same time the various effects of that power. He constructed a small electrical machine, and exhibited a few experiments; he made also a kite, with a wire and string, which drew down that fluid from the clouds.[4] (Vol. I, Ch. I)

As Victor went to the university he met several professors including M. Krempe and M. Waldman. The latter left a deep impression on him. It was M. Waldman who told Victor that the labours of man of genius, however erroneously directed, scarcely ever fail in ultimately turning to the solid advantage of mankind. M. Waldman supplied Victor with the necessary informations regarding the history of chemistry. He told how the modern masters of science, with their eyes fixed on the microscope, have discovered the process of blood circulation and of the breathing system.[5]

> They have acquired new and almost unlimited powers; they can command the thunders of heaven, mimic the earthquake, and even mock the invisible world with its own shadows. (Vol. I, Ch. II)

He also put emphasis on learning different branches of science all together. As he said to Victor,

> A man would make but a very sorry chemist, if he attended to that department of human knowledge alone. If your wish is to become really a man of science, and not merely a pretty experimentalist, I should advise you to apply to every branch of natural philosophy, including mathematics. (Vol. I, Ch. II)

Though Victor attempted to reanimate a collection of the parts of corpses, and the attempt seemed to have connections with medieval alchemy, Mary Shelley tried her best to show that Victor's attempt was based on the advanced scientific research on chemistry and electricity which flourished in the early nineteenth century. Victor said to Walton,

> I doubted at first whether I should attempt the creation of a being like myself or one of simpler organization, but my imagination was too much exalted by my first success to permit me to doubt of my ability to give life to an animal as complex and wonderful as man. The materials at present within my command hardly appeared adequate to so arduous an undertaking; but I doubted not that I should ultimately succeed. I prepared myself for a multitude of reverses; my operations might be incessantly baffled, and at last my work be imperfect: yet, when I considered the improvement which every day takes place in science and mechanics, I was encouraged to hope my present attempts would at least lay the foundations of future success. (Vol. I, Ch. III)

Mary's vision of the isolated scientist discovering the secret of life is no more a fantasy.

That the scientists have already been successful in 'cloning' animal bodies, the fantasy has turned into prediction. Mary Shelley's imagination foreshadowed the specific scientific inventions that she had dealt with, and so her novel is rightly hailed as the first legitimate example of the genre called 'science fiction.' According to the critic Anne Mellor, science fiction as a genre has three characteristics: it is to be grounded on valid scientific research, it gives a prediction about the future of that research, and lastly, it offers a humanistic critique of either specific technological inventions or the very nature of scientific thinking. All these characteristics may be found in *Frankenstein*. It is grounded on the specific research, namely, that of creating life in the laboratory without a mother's womb. Secondly, it predicts the modern researches on cloning, and more than any thing else, *Frankenstein* criticises the way some scientists have been trying to control nature. Mary Shelley was well versed in the main currents of contemporary science just as she was well versed in the literary, political and social conditions of England, thanks to the frequenters of the Godwin household and her own interest in study. Percy Shelley was also much interested in Science, particularly in electricity. In his 1818 preface to *Frankenstein* Percy Shelley referred to Erasmus Darwin, and commented that:

> The event on which this fiction is founded has been supposed, by Dr. Darwin, and some of the physiological writers of Germany, as not of impossible occurrence. (Preface to the anonymously published 1818 ed.)

Percy himself assumed the work to be based on fancy, but does not think it "a series of supernatural terror." Humphry Davy, Luigi Galvani and Erasmus Darwin were at the forefront of the late 18th and early 19th century scientific debates and Mary Shelley who had a hold on their works, drew much from their writings. Victor's education in chemistry and the teachings of M. Waldman are modelled on Davy's *A Discourse, Introductory to a Course of Lectures on Chemistry* (1802) which Mary Shelley had read in 1816, before she started writing the novel. Giving all this information, Anne Mellor finds in Mary Shelley's novel a feminist critique of Science itself. It is because Victor sought a creative process based on chemical know how, eliminating the women's role, he was to be punished for opposing the process of gradual development through sexual reproduction. Anne Mellor has it:

> Mary Shelley's novel implicitly invokes Darwin's theory of gradual evolutionary progress to suggest both the error and the evils of Victor Frankenstein's bad science. The genuine improvement of the species can result only from the conjunction of male and female sexuality. In trying to have a baby without a woman, Victor Frankenstein has failed to give his child the mothering and nurturance it requires, the very nourishment that Darwin explicitly equated with female sex. Victor Frankenstein's failure to embrace his smiling creature with parental love, his horrified rejection of his own creation, spells out the narrative consequences of solitary paternal propagation.[6]

In her Introduction to the 1831 edition of *Frankenstein* Mary referred to Dr. Darwin. Mary remembered that while talking about the various philosophical doctrines, Lord Byron and Shelley commented on Dr. Darwin.

> They talked of the experiments of Dr. Darwin, (I speak not of what the Doctor really did, or said that he did, but as more to my purpose, of what has than spoken of as having been done by him) who preserved a piece of vermicelli in a glass case, till by some extraordinary means it began to move with voluntary motion. Not thus, after all, would life be given. Perhaps a corpse would be reanimated; galvanism had given token on such things: perhaps the component parts of a creature might be manufactured, brought together, and endued with vital warmth. (Mary Shelley's Introduction to the 1831 ed. of *Frankenstein*)

In 1791, Luigi Galvani published his *Commentary on the Effects of Electricity on Muscular Motion*, in which he told that animal tissue contained a neglected innate vital force, and he called that force animal electricity. Later, this force became known as galvanism. Galvani argued that 'animal electricity' is produced in brain, and that it is different from both the 'natural electricity' produced by lightning or by electric eel, and the 'artificial' electricity produced by friction. According to Galvani, the 'animal electricity' could be used for activating both nerves and muscles if they could be connected by an arc of metal wire connected to a pile of copper and zinc plates. Anne Mellor has described how Galvani's theories became famous in Britain when Prof. Luigi Aldini, Galvani's nephew and defender, publicly showed that with the use of a Voltaic pile connected by metallic wires, the eyes, ears, tongues and nostrils of a recently killed ox-head could be moved and swelled.[7] These incidents were likely to have been discussed by Byron and Shelley in the course of their conversations to which Mary alluded in her Introduction.

While Anne Mellor's feministic objection to Victor's scientific research was that it was a 'bad science,' Marilyn Butler reduced it to just a 'backward' science.[8] Butler reads the novel in the background of what is known as 'vitalist debate,' a debate between Abernethy and Lawrence who represented opposing viewpoints in a contemporary debate. Butler has dragged Victor, who was so far enjoying the status of mythical Prometheus, to the position of a "humble Sorceror's Apprentice," who has insignificant knowledge of science. In her well researched article Bulter has linked Victor's method to the views of Abernethy whose vitalist theories have been superseded by the materialistic views of Lawrence. Butler offers a new perspective through his suggestion that the monster allegorically displays the growth of the human race over millenia.

It becomes clear from the different perspectives taken up by the critics that *Frankenstein* is still able to offer fresh ground for criticism. Taking the novel for a science fiction it may be observed that, be the scientific research of Victor a 'bad science' or even 'no science,' Mary Shelley's emphasis is not so much on the research itself as on some ethical issues that emerge from that research. And those ethical issues are more relevant these days than they were in Mary's age. Those issues may be stated one by one. First, if a new species is at all created by the scientists in the laboratory, what will be the social, psychological and moral status of that species in the modern world? Secondly, would not such creation of life in the laboratory disturb the ecological balance? The third issue which is more poignant than the others for its direct attack on the investigator, may be as follows: Is not a modern scientist often disturbed by his/her conscience for inventing something the use of which hardly lies within his/her control? In that case the scientist becomes, as Victor becomes in the novel, a slave to his own creation. What is the use of one's intellect and hard toil, then, if one is destined to be a slave, being unable to exercise one's free will?

These issues have become more relevant these days because the idea of creating life without sexual intercourse is no more a fantasy. Modern science has made a lot of progress in this respect. In February 1997, a sheep was successfully cloned from an adult sheep cell at the Rostin Institute in Edinburgh, Scotland. Many scientific and popular books have been written on cloning, specially on the dangers of cloning from human beings. Among others, the books written by Robin Cook and Ken Follett raise those ethical issues which emerged from *Frankenstein*. In Robin Cook's novel Chromosome6 imaginary fear is created through the successful cloning of human organs in animal bodies. In *The Third Twin*, Ken Follett describes eight clones being prepared from one embryo. The horror created by such books is the same kind of horror that was released by Mary Shelley's *Frankenstein*. People all over the world were so horrified after the successful cloning of a lamb, that a global debate on the potentiality of human cloning was fuelled. Scientists who argued against human cloning, observed that sexual reproduction alone can give rise to diverse offsprings. The genetic variation that arises from sexual reproduction alone, can enhance the ability of a species to adapt to new and complex changes in the environment.[9]

It is now discovered that the simplest organism may have millions of base sequences as constituents of hundreds of thousands of genes, and changing a few codons of a single gene may bring about distinct changes in the genetic expressivity of the organism. The millions of years of organic evolution involving changes in genetic complements would be totally ignored by human cloning. And therefore the scientist should hardly deserve any credit for human cloning. It is argued that just giving a touch here and there to an already existing 'universal' edifice should not entitle one to personal ownership. Scientists all over the world almost agree that biotechnology, if not wisely applied, can be black hole down which valuable resources of manpower can disappear without any positive benefit. In this way the debate that was first introduced with *Frankenstein* has been continuing. Mary Shelley chose such a subject for her novel as has been more relevant than ever in the present Global scenario. The ethical issues that emerge from *Frankenstein* are basically the same that emerge from the debate on human cloning. The great advancement in biology, medicine and agriculture has raised the ethical issues into the forefront. In his book *Bio Ethics for the People by the People*, Darryl Macer has surveyed the world-view on the ethical issues raised by the modern science and technology. Though there are demands for researches on biotechnology and genetic engineering, most of the respondents want only a restricted use of these two branches of science. Only the therapeutic value of these two branches is needed, and except this value the risks underneath have been cited by the respondents. According to Macer, this public concern is one indicator of the bioethical maturity in the society.[10] We are reminded of Victor's exclamations,

> "... What glory would attend the discovery, if I could banish disease from the human frame and render man invulnerable to any but a Violent death!" (Vol. 1, Ch. I)[11]

If Victor were engaged only in finding ways to banish disease from human frame, there would be no cause for his misery. Victor became a slave to his creation and could not even exercise his free will. Victor's mission thus highlights some ethical questions the type of which are raised at the end of the 20th century.

In his book *Daedalus or Science and Future*, J.B.S. Haldane observed that unless our ethical outlook evolves to keep pace with the development of science and technology, social chaos and disaster would result. What Haldane speaks in the field of biotechnology and genetic engineering, was already conceived by Mary Shelley when she could successfully imagine the egoistic nature of a modern scientist engaged in creating life without a mother's womb.[12] The success of *Frankenstein* as a science fiction, the first of its kind in English literature, owes much to Mary Shelley's ethical concerns expressed in her novel. The writers of the twenty-first century almost echoe Mary Shelley when they express their concern that artificial creation of life may create a chaos in the world and that there should be a limit to the interference with Nature. *Frankenstein* has become a cultural myth of the modern world and has provided us with a metaphor for the potentially disastrous results of unmindful scientific aims.

NOTES AND REFERENCES

1. The review of the novel published in *Edinburgh Magazine* (March 1818 issue) praised the description of nature in the novel, but found fault with the epithet 'Creator' applied to a mere human being. The *Quarterly Review* (January 1818) raised the moral issue complaining the author's refusal to moralise about Frankenstein's blasphemous act. The novel was then supposed to be written by P.B. Shelley. With the 1823 edition it was however disclosed that the writer was Mary Shelley, the second wife of P.B. Shelley. During the first eight decades of the twentieth century the novel was considered interesting, but not of much literary value. In 1938, R. Glynn Grylls described *Frankenstein* as a 'period piece' which is "historically interesting, but not one of the living novels of the world." *Mary Shelley: A Biography* (O.U.P. 1938), 320. The novel began to attract more critical attention as newer ideas developed in the field of literary criticism. In 1979 George Levine and U.C. Knoepflmacher edited a collection of essays. *The Endurance of Frankenstein* which marked a turning point in Frankenstein criticism. The articles collected in this volume incited further research on new topics. For example, Lee Sterrenburg's essay 'Mary Shelley's Monster:

Politics and Psyche in *Frankenstein*' traces the genealogy of the monster metaphor to the conservative polemics of Edmund Burke and the Jacobin tradition of Godwin and Wollstonecraft. The last two decades of the twentieth century saw a significant reassessment of *Frankenstein* within broader cultural context. A serious feminist criticism of the book is found in *The Madwoman in the Attic: the Woman Writer and the Nineteenth Century Literary Imagination* by Sandra M. Gilbert & Susan Gubar (New Haven: Yale University Press, 1979). Gayatri Chakravorty Spivak's study of the novel as a critique of Imperialism is another noted work. [Three Women's Texts, and a Critique of Imperialism *Critical Inquiry*, 12 (Autumn, 1985): 243-61.]

2. York Notes on *Frankenstein* (by Glennis Byron. London: York Press, 1998) informs us that "Most dictionaries now define a 'Frankenstein' as an agency that proves uncontrollable, a creation that slips from under the control of, and ultimately destroys, its creator. We have played our own variations on this modern idea of 'Frankenstein,' with, for example, HAL 2001, *A Space Odyssey* and the replicants of *Bladerunner*. To reduce the meaning of Shelley's own tale to our twentieth century dictionary definition, however, would be a mistake" (9).
3. Critics including Anne Mellor have suggested that Mary distinguished between that scientific research which attempts to describe accurately the functioning of the physical universe and that which attempts to control or change the universe through human intervention. Mary celebrates the former, which she associates most closely with the work of Erasmus and Darwin. She also draws the readers' attention to the danger inherent in the latter, found in the work of Davy and Galvani. It is possible to show with reference to the text that Mary Shelley liked Walton's process of investigating nature without interfering with it, and that she protested against any attempt to control or to overreach nature.
4. Benjamin Franklin's *Experiments and Observations on Electricity* (1751) refers to this experiment.
5. The circulation of blood was discovered in 1628 by William Harvey. Robert Boyle experimented on air, attacking in 1661 the theories of Aristotle and Paracelsus. By the early 1800s, the advent of air balloons, harnessing of electricity, and the

invention of explosives and the Zoetrope, had opened new horizons.

6. Anne Mellor: *Mary Shelley: Her Life, Her Fiction, Her Monsters* (New York & London; Methuen & Routledge, 1988) 101.
7. *Loc. cit.*, 105. The exact words quoted by Mellor were as follows:

   "... the eyes to open, the ears to shake, the tongue to be agitated, and the nostrils to swell."
8. Butler, Marilyn: 'Frankenstein and Radical Science,' *Times Literary Supplement* 4 April 1993. Reprinted in The Norton Critical Edition, 302-13.
9. Science and technology have already achieved the miracle of conception outside the mother's womb. But the result of such inventions are not accepted in the society. As one scientist writes, "Sexual reproduction keeps recessive mutations from being expressed. Every embryonic cell carries two copies of each gene, one from the mother and one from the father, of the organism. The protein making machinery of the cell often requires just one good copy of a gene to make the requisite protein. So if the copy of the mutated and dysfunctional gene has been inherited from one of the parents, the body usually does not succumb totally to the disorder. The trait then manifests in a milder way and there is fair chance that such heterozygote will survive" *Cloning* by P.D. Gupta (National Institute of Science Communication; New Delhi, 1999) 33.
10. Macer: *International Bioethics Survey: World View,* 1994.
11. The scientists in the twenty-first century are also hopeful of producing organs using embryonic stem cells which hold great promise to treat diseases like diabetes, Parkinson's disease etc. But some scientists still hold negative views and observe that human organs are far too complicated to be produced in a laboratory. To quote Harry Griffin, Asst. Director of Roslin Institute in U.K. which cloned Dolly, the lamb, "Chances of producing organs using embryonic stem cell are almost impossible. It can only be used to treat diseases where the root cause is a detective cell. (Moreover) removing a malfunctioning organ that has transplanted is quite easy, it is not so in the case of cells. This is because it will be difficult, if not impossible, to identify and recover mutated cells,.... Cloning

should not be restored to in the case of human even if it is for a therapeutic purpose" quoted by R. Prasad in 'Making Human Organs—a mirage.' *The Hindu* (Madras; Jan. 31, 2002).

12. Victor Frankenstein's egoistic nature is reflected in his words. He said,

    Life and Death appeared to me ideal bounds which I should first break through and pour a torrent of life into our dark world. A new species would bless me as its creator and source; many happy and excellent natures would owe their being to me. No father could claim the gratitude of his child so completely as I should deserve their's (Vol. I, Ch. III).

Note: All references to *Frankenstein* have been taken from the 1818 ed. of the novel printed at Finsbury Square, London.

Existential Concerns in Toni Morrison

2

DEVIKA

Life has fascinated the sublime souls of this planet to disinter its secrets, which mystify all who strive hard to explore its unknown realms but are left more intrigued and entangled because of the subtlety of its perpetual continuity. Questions like "What does it mean to exist?," "Why do we live?," "What is life?," etc. have left them bewildered and befuddled. This curiosity to unearth the enigma of this unending process has always prompted the writers all over the world to penetrate into this much-gnawed affair to come up with something substantial in describable terms. Amidst this coterie of male and female writers, Toni Morrison has carved a niche for herself because of her chiaroscuro delineation of the esoteric affairs of life sans any lopsided view of the reality. Though Toni Morrison, during the course of her literary journey, has established herself as a distinguished writer, the terra firma of her works chiefly consists of universal concerns of humanity and rests mainly on the principal query of relevance of human existence in an indifferent universe.

Toni Morrison's several novels show the influence of existential thinking in a very discriminating way probing all the delicacies of human sensibility. The novelist achieves a remarkable feat as she chooses to probe the dilemma of human beings against a realistic social backdrop, a tactic, that renders her work all the more plausible and convincing. Das, a prominent critic on Toni, voices a similar opinion as she records:

> The Black-power movement of the 60s and 70s wielded the weapons of protest. Black writers like Wright,

> Howe, Ellison, Hurston, *et al.,* chronicled sagas of protest. But Morrison does not merely do so. Conscious as she is of the dilemmas of the black people, her novels reflect the tension between protest and transcendence; between suffering and strength, and between collective and individual identity.[1]

Her works like *Beloved, Song of Solomon,* and *Jazz* leave an indelible impression on the mind of the reader because she explores human life through the themes of existentialism within the territory of society itself. She weaves the gossamer web of life in her exquisite *Beloved,* which is the story of Sethe—an ex-slave, Denver—her daughter, Beloved—the spirit of her dead daughter and Paul D—her lover and the friend of her husband. The scars of atrocities bestowed on her back are imprinted on her mind in such a way that it is hard to erase them. Her exposure to horrendous streaks of life has dismayed her so much that she thinks it better to relieve her younger daughter off the burdens of life. This assessment, however, shows her another side of life when the spirit of her daughter comes back.

Projection of life flanked by death makes it pellucid that death provides no escape from the labyrinthine puzzle of life; in *Beloved* the circle of life is ventured in such a way that a spirit, that is, Beloved is allowed to participate in the novel. Inclusion of a specter as the central figure against the broader canvass of life and death highlights Toni as an artist who gives us the picture of life in its true colours sans distorting its originality and hence charm. To enact the drama of life and death, the backdrop of society is the perfect podium. In *Beloved,* Morrison implies that it is not mandatory to show the existential dilemma without society; it can be inextricably intertwined within the society. Utterly disillusioned Sethe, entangled in an inexplicable routine of life, finds death more befitting for her daughter:

> She come back to me of her free will and I don't have to explain a thing. I didn't have time to explain before because it had to be done quick. Quick. She had to be safe and I put her where she would be.... I'll explain to

> her, even though I don't have to. Why I did it. How if I hadn't killed her she would have died and that is something I could not bear to happen to her. When I explain it she'll understand....[2]

Sethe chooses not to let the pockmarks make a tree on the back of her daughter as it has done on hers whose burden she will have to bear throughout her life. Though, Toni cajoles her characters to make choices, act accordingly and ultimately reach at some sort of realization yet feels uneasy to allow them to take decisions for others as in the case of Sethe. Toni, after a hiatus, brings Beloved comes back into the life of her mother to make her realize the transgression.

Integrity of life and death reflects Toni Morrison's vision of an unending continuity. Sethe seems convinced that death puts a full stop to the absurdities of life and it is the only solution to combat them but return of Beloved in her life crystallizes her thinking that death is no answer to the mind-boggling affairs. Everybody has to undertake a personal journey to find out for oneself what exactly life is and why is it the way it is. Undergoing multitudinous experiences her characters envisage life accordingly. Beloved fails to get to the hub of life as she is denied the right to live and feel it on her own.

It is the individual journey of Sethe, Paul D, Beloved, and Denver. They cannot afford to understand life just by listening to the tales told by others; to get to feel life on their own they are forced to inch towards the essence. Being an objective observer is not sufficient because it doesn't demand detachment; it expects involvement into it to get to the crux that is nowhere to be found until one gets immersed into it. That is why neither Paul D nor Sethe can tell Denver what life is or how to live it. Denver has to embark on the journey on her own to understand its complexities. When experience helps her sense the presence of realization only then she is able to save her mother out. Similarly, Beloved's comeback is an indication that life may be indescribable or shallow but it cannot be escaped; it has its fascination and magnetic charm. Even Sethe has wished to live life along with her kids, but only after making the choice:

> Up till then it was the only thing I ever did on my own. Decided. And it came off right, like it was supposed to. We was here. Each and every one of my babies and me too.... I was big, Paul D, and deep and wide and when I stretched out my arms all my children could get in between. I was that wide. (162)

But she forgets that she cannot shield and deprive her kids from the experiences of life—her two sons leave home never to return and her murdered daughter comes back to grab her right to live. Denver cannot help crying when she finds herself isolated from all and her anguished soul outpours her desire to be a part of society. Acceptance for her is as important as for Beloved, Sethe, Paul D and all others. The pain of anguish is very acute when she utters her piece of mind:

> "I can't no more. I can't no more."
> "Can't what? What can't you?"
> "I can't live here. I don't know where to go or what to do, but I can't live here. Nobody speaks to us. Nobody comes by. Boys don't like me. Girls don't either." (14)

Thus, the question of human beings confronting reality and choice haunts all the characters of the novel. Irrespective of victories or defeats Toni sandwiches all her characters in the situation of choice; some turn out to be ultimate losers with nothing substantial in their lap and some get to the core with regal éclat. Sethe tells Paul D about her predicament of making choice and then getting nothing but losing whatever little she has had. On her account, it brings forth the absurdity of making choices and losing whatever little they have in their grasp:

> I got a tree on my back and a haunt in my house, and nothing in between but the daughter I am holding in my arms. No more running—from nothing. I will never run from another thing on this earth. I took one journey and I paid for the ticket, but let me tell you something, Paul D Garner; it cost too much! Do you hear me? It cost too much.... (15)

"Slowly, methodically, miserably" (19) she continues eating

the forbidden fruit of life. The realization on her part "Freeing yourself was one thing; claiming ownership of that freed self was another" (95) makes the sordid condition all the more unbearable. Mikhail Sholokhov's words from his story *A Different Breed,* "Morning—a pallid weakling—brought a feeble dawn from the blue-grey east,"[3] seem to highlight Seethe's bleak future. The agony of the character is emphasized as the novelist attempts to highlight her helplessness in the presence of the cryptic process of making choices to get nothing but arriving at such nook of life where "drabness looked drab; heat was hot" (39). "She was shocked to see how small the big things were" (245). "Seethe's eyes bright but dead, alert but vacant" (242-43) say it all through the deadening silence without any words, emotions, gestures or movement.

The barren tree shorn of leaves and verdure, imprinted on her back expounds the infertility of human life; she gets nothing in her life, no shade, no breeze, no fruits, and no fuel to keep it warm. When lived this way she finds it outrageous to exist but with no way out; the spirit of her daughter Beloved comes as a whiff of fresh air only to remind her ultimately that it is equally painful to die. The tree though it is there shows no sign of life. It is quite clear that like this tree Sethe wields nothing to bestow on others and even Paul D who appreciates her finds her ugly and avoids looking at her when they have sex for the first time; indubitably, nothingness is there in her repertoire and every body is more than welcome to share it. She justifies her achievements quite convincingly, "There's nothing to rub now and no reason to. Nothing left" (272). Nothing seems to catch her attention, "No question. And no matter, for the sadness was at her center, the desolated center where the self that was no self made its home" (140).

Allowed to choose and act Sethe decides to put her daughter to death, she decides to live along with Paul D, and when Beloved is back she decides to give all the love and care which she thinks should be showered on her. All choices in her life aggravate her anguish. The dilemma of choosing and failing, however, torments not only Sethe but also other characters who have to suffer due to the choices they make. Even Paul D's decision, first to live with Sethe and Denver, and then to walkout of that relationship when he comes to know about the heinous crime Sethe has committed, makes him a victim of anxiety and dread.

For some characters, though, the proposition of choice turns out to be rather auspicious. This can easily be asserted in the case of Denver who remains a non-entity till she chooses to remain passive; the moment she changes her choice of remaining passive there is a change in the track of her life. When she herself undertakes her journey instead of scrutinizing it as an outsider, she comes to know of life with its boons and banes. The journey may provide any sort of result—positive or negative—it gives a kind of satisfaction to Denver when she manages to save her mother from the spirit of Beloved, her sister.

In her *Beloved* thus, Toni Morrison paints in words the life of Sethe, Paul D, Denver and Beloved caught in jumble of twigs. Convincingly, she puts them into the pale of her world and shows them struggling against the seemingly invincible forces to find out the mainstay of their existence. Her dexterous delineation helps her adumbrate how do they lead their life enshrouded with "nothing. A bleak and minus nothing. More like absence" (270). She makes her character memorable with the consummate touch of her artistic skill. This trend is not limited to *Beloved* only it is evident even in *Song of Solomon,* yet another story of family drama.

Song of Solomon, revolving around the complexity of the eternal continuity, is the story of Milkman Dead who glides from the effulgence of darkness to the sheen of knowledge. He commences his odyssey as a jejune and ends as the descendant of Solomon realizing the inevitability of making choices. He does take time but eventually descends on the podium of realization to unburden his soul and spirit off the contrite choices producing nil aftermaths.

Along with Milkman Dead, Pilate also makes choices to have the bite of the fruit of life producing acrid taste of absurdity. Through her, Toni Morrison delineates the outlandish process of making choices and landing nowhere. The very issue of *belongingness* looms like an apparition face to face always demanding some sort of answer to the befuddling queries. Loss of a navel that could provide the testimony of her *belonging* triggers her to obviate any unpleasant confrontation by making a choice of going against the established mores of society. "And she holds the opinion very firmly that it is proper that her own ideas should be considered."[4] She dares to set her own priorities without giving a thought to the norms of society. Her concern for choice is so strong, though loser by the standards of society, she prefers not to hinge on the norms blindly followed by people like her brothers; she feels satisfied to lead life not according to the currents and crosscurrents of society but by her own whims and wishes. Her throbbing existential angst goads her to lead an anonymous life than to reveal the missing navel. Her plan to get the baby outside wedlock without disclosing her secret of rootlessness succeeds and she refuses to get married because of the apprehension of losing her identity "all on account of the fact that she had no navel."[5]

Pilate's way of living, taking decisions, and abiding by them to face the consequences of whatever she does in her life, makes her a lady of substance who dares lead life the way she feels comfortable. Since she doesn't lead life to make others happy, she refuses to tread on the trodden path; her crystallized goals help her do whatever she feels like. Her brother, though, secretly cherishes the desire to live like her yet prefers to remain away manacled by the restrains of society. In one of his short stories "Miss Harriet" Guy De Maupassant "felt that there was laid upon that human creature the eternal injustice of implacable Nature!"[6] Pilate feels in the same way for her nephew. Going by the standards of society, somehow he realizes that it is not society that will find out why he exists, it is his job to do so and greatly influenced by her aunt's way of living, leaves the apron of her mother and sisters.

The awakening that he is *dead* not because now he no longer lives physically but because he cannot make any choice is though slow yet sure. Only after taking a plunge in the arena of action he gets acceptance from the members of society. Now, the truth stands in front of him and it dawns on him that "there was nothing you could do with a mooring except acknowledge it, use it for the verification of some idea you wanted to keep alive" (13). Action is required to exist and gradually, he comes to know why "I'm a Dead! My mother's a Dead! My sisters" (38).

His money minded father, instead of leading a normal life with his wife and kids, parodies the middle class way of living of the whites. His negation of richness of originality tames him to lead a mechanical life marked by stringency, indifference and falsification. His unadulterated love for money, artificial ways of living, and his much-acclaimed fame make him curb his impulses. His wife, daughters, and son simply do not exist for him; his proclivity for his son increases not to sustain his son's love and affection but help him maintain his money and false airs. No wonder, he lives a life dominated by symbolic death and the strange part of life for him is that "Everything had improved for Macon Dead during the war" (63) when the place has been filled with the heap of scattered cadavers. That is why throughout his life "Death always smiled. And breathed" (136).

His father's insensitive treatment of his mother makes her stop behaving like a normal lady and start behaving like a child to get the attention. Crushed by smashed sensibilities, she turns to her son for attention. In a desperate effort to be loved she loses her power to assert and just manages to remain her natural self when she is in the company of Pilate, her sister-in-law. Likewise, his sisters live the life of a shade without any identity of their own because in the outside world they are supposed to behave the way their father wishes and inside the house their brother remains the center of attention. The sisters, fully aware of their puppet like existence, manage to live the way they feel like within that orb. Milkman, somehow, finds it quite pitiable that they have no choice but to lead complacent life. He senses that it is happening because they have got attuned to lead a passive life and finds his father the worst victim. For Milkman nothing is queer but the fact "He dead.

A dead man ain't no man. A dead man is a corpse. That's all. A corpse" (81). The process of living death suffocates him and he flutters to come out of these fetters.

Toni Morrison, here, seems to propose that they are dead not because of the fault of somebody but because they lead a vegetative life. Their sterility is the corollary of their smugness. Morrison revels in revealing the history of the process of living death of human beings making Milkman their representative:

> ...who had a name that was real. A name given to him at birth with love and seriousness. A name that was not a joke, nor a disguise, nor a brand name. But this lithe young man...could never be known. No. Nor his name. ...this heavy name scrawled in perfect thoughtlessness by a drunken Yankee.... A literary slip of pen handed to his father on a piece of and which he handed on to his only son, and his son likewise handed on to his; Macon Dead who beget a second Macon Dead...and beget ...Lena Dead...Corinthians Dead and...another Macon Dead, now known...as Milkman Dead. (17-18)

An effort on his part to move from ignorance to illumination makes him realize that existence requires efforts on his part to have an identity of his own on which he can bank. He finds himself a misfit because "deformity was mostly in his mind. Mostly, but not completely..." (62). Now, nonplussed by the intricacies "finding peace nowhere and in nothing" (127) to reach somewhere to get out of this feeling of stagnation, "he questioned them. Questioned everybody" (79). The agony keeps torturing him and he simply blurs out, "My name is Macon, remember? I'm already Dead" (118). This punching sense of alienation sets him on his journey to find out the meaning of his own existence and he starts roaming to discover where he belongs. Though he has never been on his own earlier, the awakening "You by yourself ain't nobody" (67) triggers him on and he comes to know about himself, his position in this society, and about his ancestors. For the first time in his life he gets the feeling of living and being part of something big which assuages all his turmoil. Now, clarity settles in that like everybody he also has to take decisions on his own, stick to them, and move ahead on this path of realization which none else can explore for him.

Toni Morrison always gives the impression to set her characters find out on their own their real self. If a relationship is running smoothly but consciousness of life is not there then she snaps those ties and makes her characters find out where exactly they stand on their own without being somebody's wife, husband, son, or daughter. Hence, Toni Morrison projects the concept of the value of human personality very prominently with the meticulous touch of her skill and likewise *Jazz* is no exception. Here, she places her characters against the fast life of city and shows that city life corrodes their natural enamel making them nothing but hollow and sterile.

It is the story of a couple who decide to lead life as it suits them but find it hard to live outside society and ultimately become a part of it. Morrison weaves the pastel pattern of their life. Joe Trace and his wife "awfully skinny, Violet; fifty, but still good looking"[7] are madly in love with each other only to be estranged by the forces of life when their platform of love gives way to cracks. The delicate dreams for idyllic life simply vanish at the mere touch of cold reality, "where blasé thing takes place" (7). Joe goes ahead on his path of life so does Violet "in Violet and Joe Trace's apartment, the rooms are like the empty birdcages wrapped in cloth" (11) but now they realize that it is not served at silver plate instead they have to be a part of that system to understand it, "Nobody says it's pretty here; nobody says it's easy either" (8).

Deeply immersed in love he "just go(es) like a leaf down the wind"[8] to find solace in the arms of another woman. His love for Violet has been no less than his attraction for Dorcas, the difference is only of attitude and the veer of time. He has been true to his self when in love with his wife; even in his relation with Dorcas he remains true to his self. He discards the norms of society not to be a maverick but to do whatever he feels right and appropriate to remain true to his notions of righteousness, "He *knew* wrong wasn't right, and did it anyway" (74). Life provides him with the opportunity to "Choose. And he did" (86). The question of choice always haunts human beings and it remains their privilege to choose. Thus, in Toni Morrison, it is almost a recurrent tale of people rediscovering their own reality and meaning as the novelist sets them on a journey from unawareness to awareness. Frequently, we find her characters are either lost in their smugness or drowned in their intellectual or spiritual stupor.

Toni, as a quintessentially contemporary writer, whose emphasis is to depict the torn psyche of individuals in the wake of an existential challenge, prods her characters and we see time and again, her characters embark on their spiritual voyage, with some sinking deep and others emerging alive and even invigorated by the experience. With Joe as always with Toni Morrison's characters, life comes with a proposition to choose and he goes ahead and makes a choice. Nothing, therefore, on the earth can stop Joe from choosing Dorcas as his beloved, "I *chose* you. Nobody gave you to me. Nobody said that's the one for you. I picked you out.... But the picking out, the choosing.... I talk about being new seven times before I met you..." (135).

In this work of musical elegance and assonance, Morrison seems to suggest that like the music composition of jazz, life is an amalgam of cacophonous and mellifluous notes displaying disparate and mellow notes simultaneously, exhibiting the unique nature of life. Present slot of generation is the victim of society; they are not what they want to be but what society has made them by constantly battering them and bruising their psyches. No wonder Violet mumbles, "I don't have no evil of my own" (80). The very spirit of life for Violet is throttled by the person who "never hurt nothing" (81) and who has been ready to give his everything to marry her, has married her and showered his love on her and then drifts away on his own because it is the journey where you are supposed to move on your own. With the passage of time "old crazy Violet" (133) gives it a tough fight and tries to come out of this "Nothing, Joe. Nothing" (24) and this "nothing but persistent" (6) nothingness. Violet has no illusion regarding anything and is a down to earth woman who knows "Fancy soap is fancy. Not meant to last" (45). But Life has made her so barren she cannot think of something creative, "Oh." Violet blinks rapidly. "Nothing. I mean...nothing" (24).

The liberty on the part of individuals to choose ignites Toni so much she bestows them with the power to choose and live "He had chosen; so would she" (86). Like Joe Violet also exercises her right to choose. "Seeing bleak truth" (101) has ossified her to such an extent that she wishes to spoil the face of a dead girl who has taken away her husband and intends to make up for the loss by doing deleterious harm to her. Acutely suffering from the guilt of not being a mother, Violet sees in Dorcas her "daughter who fled her womb" (109) and now she realizes that by not being a mother she has been deprived one of the greatest blesses of nature. She goes to see Dorcas's aunt and pleads to know more about her own husband, "I'm fifty and I don't know nothing.... I want some fat in this life" (110).

Morrison universalizes oppression; it is not that only slavery, apartheid, or gender discrimination can be the only cause of sufferings. Black may torment black, men may be foes instead of friends, and ladies may cheat ladies irrespective of being black or white. Social forces may or may not be there and inner turmoil may vary in intensity. Despite innumerably varied causes depiction of life seems quite effortless and natural. The loss of identity, the echoes of void, feeling of insecurity, oppression, etc. are not new to humanity; only the intensity has increased. Alienation has galvanized human beings to find their own identities.

Consequently in *Jazz* it is the desire to lead life according to her comforts that makes Violet uneasy. Human life, bound by norms set out by others, gets devoid of its charm. The life of Violet is no exception, "the City took away the back and arm power she used to boast of" (92). Now surprisingly and subtly victimized by the norms of society she just remains a shadow of her real self, "a not me at all" (97). Bemused, she continues gyrating where "...nothing was safe—not even the dead" (9) and circle of life moves "From freezing to hot to cold" (51) involving beings of "freezing faces" (58).

Against the setup of love and betrayal, Morrison shows the aftereffects of dejection and alienation. The characters, lucidly projected by Morrison's realistic strokes, are no naives unaffected by the corruption of life, but quite mature persons fully aware of their precincts. Outside violence is not new to them. Violet, completely aware of destructive side of city life, remains unaware of the harm and pain that can be inflicted by dejection until she feels alienated from her husband. Her husband Joe, on the other hand, is quite contented the way his life goes on. Acceptance from one and all makes him negligently unaware of the alienation of his wife. Realization befriends him only after he is ditched by Dorcas, his girlfriend. Feeling humiliated by rejection, Joe "insecure" and "unrooted"[9] goes to the extent of murdering the poor girl whereas Violet tries to spoil her face.

The denizens of this barren land are wrapped in emotions. "Chief among them was fear and—a new thing—anger" (75). They react to happenings in their peculiar ways; it gets clear from the dialogue between Violet and Dorcas's aunt regarding the death of Dorcas.

> "I don't understand women like you. Women with knives...."
> "I wasn't born with a knife."
> "No, but you picked one up."
> "You never did?..."
> "No, I never did. Even when my husband ran off.... You picked up a knife to insult a dead girl." (85)

Dorcas's life comes to an end before she starts understanding the concept of life and death. Being a genuine product of youth she does not want to spoil her life by doing nothing. She wants to be alive and kicking, tries every possible way to remain happy and engaged but when she is at the threshold of her youth life becomes unbearable for her. "It is terrible when there is absolutely nothing to do or worth doing..." (63) at the same time it is "ridiculous and delicious and terrible" (70-71). Morrison is very assertive in her stance that not only life but death also is an integral part of this complete circle. The novel ends with True Belle's acknowledgment, "Thank God for life," True Belle said, "and thank life for death" (101).

To conclude, Toni Morrison puts her characters against the backdrop of society. She keeps on changing the background from brutalities of slavery to the open violence of city life. She makes it lucid that existential concerns are always there to torment the human beings, as escape from the affairs of life is next to impossible. These concerns are not particular to a specific class or community but are scattered everywhere in society. The ubiquitous existential concerns in her works set her characters to initiate their journey to unearth the realities related to them. They are torn apart by the inner trauma which is further accentuated by the alienation prevalent in their lives. The greatness of Morrison helps her set her characters in outstanding circumstances but she never lets her hold get loose and turn her work into a loose piece of literary work. Thus, what characterizes her works is a sense of insecurity, rootlessness, alienation, dread, anxiety, angst, and void embedded with immaculate craft. Her works and her characters are also moulded in a convincing cast increasing her worth as a writer.

NOTES AND REFERENCES

1. Das, Shruti. "A Critique of Toni Morrison's Feminism." *Feminist English Literature.* Ed. Manmohan K. Bhatnagar. New Delhi: Atlantic Publishers and Distributors, 1999. 214-21.
2. Morrison, Toni. *Beloved.* Great Britain: Pan Books Ltd., 1988. All the subsequent references for *Beloved* have been taken from the same edition, hereafter cited, within the text along with page numbers in particular.
3. Sholokhov, Mikhail. *The Fate of a Man and Early Stories,* Trans. Robert Daglish. Union of Soviet Socialist Republics: Raduga Publishers, 1989, 106.
4. Meares, Ainslie, *The New Woman.* London and Glasgow: William Collins Sons & Co. Ltd., 1974, 31.
5. Morrison, Toni. *Song of Solomon.* Great Britain: Vintage, 1998. All the subsequent references for *Song of Solomon* have been taken from the same edition, hereafter cited, within the text along with page numbers in particular.

6. Maupassant, Guy De. *The Best Short Stories*. Hertfordshire: Wordsworth Editions Limited, 1997, 106.
7. Morrison, Toni. *Jazz*. Great Britain: Vintage, 2001. All the subsequent references for *Jazz* have been taken from the same edition, hereafter cited, within the text along with page numbers in particular.
8. Lawrence, D.H. *Sons and Lovers*. New Delhi: UBS Publishers' Distributors Pvt. Ltd., 2003, Reprint, 405.
9. Lessing, Dorris. *The Golden Notebook*. New York: Granada Publishing Limited, 1977, 31.

Existential Angst in Toni Morrison's *Jazz*

3

BINOD MISHRA

The curiosity to unravel the enigma of perpetual and perplexing continuity of life has tempted the sublime souls throughout the globe. This much-gnawed affair has prompted these authors to use their ingenuity to dent something substantial in describable terms. Among these pronounced authors, Toni Morrison also radiates because of her immaculate touch. The terra firma of her much acclaimed novel, *Jazz* consists of universal concerns of humanity focusing on the relevance of human existence in an indifferent universe. Existential thinking, which is liberally scattered in her work, is all set to probe delicacies of human sensitivity. The remarkable feat to put her protagonists *vis-à-vis* dreary reality makes them react spontaneously sans hinging on any garb.

The laceration of soul by the inside as well as the outside forces turns out plausibly with exquisite focus on details. The calm and poised lifestyle is brutally smashed to embark them upon a peregrination to get a vestige of their relation to this bigger reality. Rest is denied unless they tread on.

The present paper aims to trace existential angst in Morrison. She delineates the issues of the protagonists in such clear terms that the question of survival becomes vital. If there is no discord and disagreements in life, the subtleties of living become humdrum. The way Morrison's characters solve the intricacies of life, speak volumes about their potentialities.

Tony Morrison is primarily an African-American novelist writing for the black women whose colour is only a camouflage to their bright souls in perpetual struggle. A novelist, whose province, as the critics say, is purely black female experience, is not devoid of the vital questions like class, community and colour conflicts. Fomenting vehemently her fulminations against America's treatment of blacks in general and black women in particular is a reflection of Morrison's existential angst. She considers novel as a framework for answering various challenges and bringing some solace to the African anguish. The African-American oppression and exploitation of man by man has been a continuing theme in Morrison's novels. Her deep understanding of African people and the wounds of their souls find echoes in one novel after another. Beginning with '*The Bluest Eye*.' Morrison has adroitly adumbrated the agony and oppression that can strengthen individuals and the community to reach the state of ecstasy and esteem on the ladders of struggle.

Most of Morrison's novels have brought her award and acclaim. Considered a feminist by critics the world over, Morrison weaves a variety of strains mixing memory with desire and desire with denunciation. All her major novels namely *The Bluest Eye (1970), Sula (1973), Song of Solomon (1977), Tar Baby (1981), Beloved (1987)* and *Jazz (1992)* have facilitated our understanding of multi-cultural plurality of her voices. Her first novel *The Bluest Eye* is a beautiful delineation of her emphasis on racism. *Sula* reflects the author's focus on gender, taking in its stride her advocacy of woman's individual rights. *Song of Solomon*, which won National Book Critics Circle Award, describes the exploitation of the African women by the African men. The novel discusses at large the African-Americans struggle to sustain their prosperity and integrity without risking their black identities. Racial pride and reputation colour Morrison's *Tar Baby*. One finds in this novel an implicit hint on capitalism, which undeniably gives rise to racial and class-consciousness. *Beloved*, widely acclaimed as Morrison's masterpiece won the famous Pulitzer Prize in 1988. Morrison in this novel integrates all her ennui, envy and puts an end to nausea by fomenting her furies. The novel is a queer blend of heroism and villainy and a consummation of journey from confinement to manumission.

Morrison was awarded the *Nobel Prize* in literature in 1993. She also received *National Book Foundation Medal* for her distinguished contribution to American letters, *Pearl S. Buck Award* in 1994 and the title of *Commander of the Order of Arts and Letters* in 1994. Various honorary degrees have also been conferred upon Morrison by many reputed universities.

Morrison's novel *Jazz* is named after a musical style. The Oxford Advanced Learners Dictionary describes it as a type of music with strong rhythms, in which the players often improvise. This genre of music was originated by African-American musicians. The music reflects the lively and carefree way of life. The novel, like this musical variety, is suffused with abrupt beginnings and abrupt developments. The novel starts with the struggling married life of Violet and Joe but it takes different routes with different people steering their course of life convoluted albeit with the lone problem of survival in a fast changing world with multi-layered narrow domestic walls. Like the musical mode of *Jazz*, the novel establishes a contact between the characters and the readers by using familiar material to express various sentiments. Here, the novelist, according to Robert Roth, avoids 'authorial dominance' and in stead allows the readers to be "engaged in a productive dialogue in which their own purposes and practices come into play, often taking the foreground."[1]

Jazz is the story of a happy married couple, who starts from the village to the towns and try their best to ensure security, sanguinity and sublimity in their lives by taking various jobs and changing their roles frequently. They manoeuvre to bring betterments in their life but seem to have lost the meaning of living. Taxed with the hardships of life, they move to the New York City. But the city life brings them more discomforts than comforts and allows a vacuum in their life. The novel has many other characters that also experience the tedium of life in death. The major characters being Violet, Joe and Dorcas, the minor characters, too bear the testimony of existential angst yet their appearance in the background is like the holy water that purges people of their crimes. These characters in *Jazz* live in hiding but help the major characters in finding their real selves out. The novel, despite its hide and seek settings provide enough succour to recover the endangered and encumbered nuptial bond of Violet and Joe.

Most of the characters of *Jazz* oscillate between their present and past and *vice versa*. They are dissatisfied with their present condition and seem to relish either in their past or their impending future. Their insides enkindle them and the outside forces bring them repulsion. In a world, which they claim to be theirs, they are treated as aliens and their present threatens them. They cry within to attenuate their apprehensions. Their inside journey brings them close to their own community where each brings solace to the other by bandaging their bruises. This fear of insecurity breeds unity and a clarion call to take on all onslaughts faced by Africans in America. Morrison has been successful in making her characters realize this fact in *Jazz* as well in her previous novels. The collective consciousness, an output of individual awareness, is the only cementing force, which can bring a solution to all sorts of maladies.

Moreover, the characters in Morrison's novel dissatisfied with their present belongings do a sort of self-searching. Their peripheral existence drives them to seek refuge either in past or in their unpredictable and unbelievable future. This propensity of Morrison and her characters has tempted critics to recognize the characteristics of the term magical realism in many of her fictions. According to critics, novels with such labels have a distinct narrative technique. The language in such works is racy, self-conscious and it comprises superb style and a studied detachment of tone. The great German critic Franz Roh, who innovated this term in 1925, traces a blend of unrealistic and realistic events in this literary practice. The practitioners of this term especially in 1920's and 1930's took liberties with unities of time, space and characterization in their dramas. These dramatists created an atmosphere, which was angst-ridden and magical. Like the expressionist plays of August Steinberg, magical realist novels, too have these attributes. The novels of Toni Morrison, to a great, extent have these elements.

Morrison's personal life, both early and in developmental stage has various ups and downs. We find too much of flexibility and displacement in her early days. Her birthplace, Ohio was a conglomerate of African-American experiences. It had a mixed culture and was a fusion of industrial and rural history. Her family history also was not without rootlessness. Her forefathers had migrated to Ohio from the Deep South. Morrison graduated from Howard University and did her masters from Texas Southern Texas University. The change of her name from "Chole Anthony Wofford" to Tony is also not devoid of her revolutionary propinquity. Her marriage with a Jamaican architect and later her divorce hints at her experimental ways and her penchant for settling things in her own stride.

An in-depth analysis of the characters *of Jazz* can help us in understanding the fact that despite the flux and fluidity of time most of Morrison's characters are individuals suffering from existential angst. They are unique in the sense that they try to re-discover their selves and bring a recuperation to keep life agog. Our understanding of this existential anguish will become overt if we categories them into two sets. We have several male characters in the novel with Joe Trace as the main and Golden Gray, Henry Lestroy, Victory, Gistan, Stuck, Action as supplementary. Likewise Violet is the most powerful female character with Dorcas, Rose Dear, True Belle, and Alice Manfred as her complimentary selves.

Violet, the heroine of the novel is an embodiment of persecution perpetrated on her by none other than Joe Trace, her husband. Violet met Joe in Palestine while working on a landowner's farm. Violet's young and powerful physical features made more powerful by handling mules, baling hay and chopping wood, used to rest on Joe's chest, which she claimed as her own smooth pillow. They married because they had much in common. Joe worked gins and lumber and cane and cotton and corn. He was adept at doing all sorts of job. He butchered when needed, plowed, fished, sold skins and game. After thirteen years of their marriage, they decided to move to the city for a luxurious life. Having had many miscarriages, some because they wished and others because they wanted, had an adverse effect on Violet's body and mind. Her wilful abortions remind us of T.S. Eliot's masterpiece *The Waste Land* where the poet puts a very genuine question and ridicules at the modern life's awareness virus which has entered their lives amid the fun and frolic of unreal existence. The poet asks, "What for you married if you don't want children?"[2] Reluctance of one time becomes a repining in coming days and results in a failure of communication between the wife and the husband where one may ask the other:

> Speak to me. Why do you never speak. Speak.
> What are you thinking of? What thinking?
> I never know what you are thinking. Think.[3]

This failure of communication is to a great extent responsible for the gap through which Dorcas enters their lives and invites troubles for herself and for Joe and Violet.

City life made living comfortable and heart longing for infants. Violet started a hairdressing job in houses and as a result, she started cursing her past, imagining 'how old that last miscarried would be now.' Her lullaby enabled her to sleep with dolls in her arms. Her agony grew to such an extent that she shut herself up and started speaking less except living with a flock of birds, including her parrot that said, "I love you." We can find Violet's angst in the following lines when the narrator says, "Violet is still as well as silent over time her silences annoy her husband, then puzzle him and finally depress him. He is married to a woman who speaks mainly to her birds. One of whom answers back: 'I love you.'"[4]

Life for Violet loses hold when she comes to know about Joe's shooting a girl whom he loved and kept crying afterwards. Violet goes to the funeral and cuts the dead face beyond repairs. The dead girl, Dorcas created a desire in Violet and she goes to every nook and corner to get further details. Violet, in a bid to take the revenge on the girl who took her husband away is shocked to see Joe pining for the dead girl whom Violet cannot rival. Violet is full of angst when she tells one of her customers about Joe, "He thinks about her all the time. Nothing on his mind but her. Won't work. Can't sleep. Grieves all day, all night."[5]

Violet's investigations about Dorcas take her to Alice Manfred, Dorcas' aunt. Embittered though in the beginning. Alice develops sympathy for Violet on hearing her predicament. She had been reading in the newspapers about the atrocities on women and Violet's malaise was not an exception to that. Violet's insistence to know everything about Dorcas is to recognize the part, which she lacked, and Dorcas possessed. The twist in Violet's tale converts Alice, who wonders, "At fifty-eight with no children of her own, and the one she had access to and responsibility for dead, she wondered about the hysteria, the violence, the damnation of pregnancy without marriage ability."[6]

Alice traces her own anguish also in Violet's heartening and horrendous act. Violet grows apprehensive and burns with jealousy to think about Joe's runaway with Dorcas, the heifer she calls her. The thought of the two in Indigo on Saturday with all sorts of blandishments in the dark tears her and Violet grows disdainful to imagine how:

> under the table drumming out the rhythm on the inside of his thigh, his thigh, his thigh, thigh, thigh and he bought her underwear with stitching done to look like rosebuds and violets, VIOLETS, don't you know, and she wore it for him thin as it was and too cold for a room that couldn't count on a radiator to work through the afternoon, while I was where?[7]

Violet's angst grows to such an extent that she destroys Dorcas' funeral and she feels her act justified. When she thinks about her other self, who struck the Knife on Dorcas' corpse, she is full of envy, ennui and anxiety, "And that's why it took so much wrestling to get me down, keep me down and out of that coffin where she was the heifer who took what was mine, what I chose, picked out and determined to have and hold on to."[8]

Having unloaded all her agony before Alice Manfred, Violet feels relieved. She also tells Felice, Dorcas' friend that she 'Killed the me that Killed her.' Violet gets a picture of Dorcas from Manfred and puts it on the mantel over the fireplace. Violet has developed a love for the girl and we find her existential angst at worst when she tells Alice, "All my troubles be over if I could get my body sick stead of my head."[9]

The readers are touched to the core when Violet tells Alice:

> We women, me and you. Tell me something real. Don't just say I'm grown and ought to know. I don't. I'm fifty and I don't know nothing. What about it? Do I stay with him? I want to, I think. I want...well, I didn't always...now I want. I want some fat in this life.[10]

What Violet says may be very particular but is also general in the sense that it was women's fate in America, especially black women. Violet wants to come out of it and she throws out the birds whose 'wings grown stiff from disuse and dull in the bulb light of an apartment with no view to speak of.'[11] This act of Violet is a preparation for a life, which has to be lived. Violet's fight seems to have come to an end and she has to live with Joe and the living presence of the dead unsmiling girl who waked Violet from her agonized and agitated state of mind.

Dorcas, an eighteen-year girl is a beautiful link in Joe-Violet relationship. Dorcas' arrival in Joe's life is the arrival of an enigma that solves and dissolves the tranquility terrifying the tumultuous and once tenacious marital bond of the Violet. Dorcas opens the door of communication for Joe but makes grapevine more active. The communication between Dorcas and Joe receives a severe jolt since the common frame of reference is very elusive. Their temporary union was a meeting of youth and age. Dorcas' longings are the reveries of an orphaned girl who wanted to 'wear silk' hose and a pair of silk stockings.

Dorcas was initially fascinated by Joe because she had some secrets to be shared with someone. Her ruined childhood, because of the riot, which claimed her parents' life and her box of dolls, are quite symbolical. Dorcas longed to be with Joe in clubs and parties where people could see them and she could giggle in Mexico. Dorcas and Joe had secrets to be shared but quite in contrast, as Joe wanted to hide his secrets in Dorcas. Dorcas is better than speechless Violet to Joe. But for Dorcas, her association with Joe was only an encouragement. Dorcas was sick of her choice and she wanted to live her own life free from her aunt. The trouble started when Dorcas' eyes fell on Acton who was of her age and who could fondle her as a young man and could tell her when she didn't like the way she fixed her hair. Dorcas expresses the reasons of her boredom with Joe and is full of anguish, "He didn't even care what I looked like. I could be anything, do anything—and it pleased him. Something about that made me mad. I don't know.[12]

Dorcas grows impatient to know that Joe was coming to search her. But she has taken her decision not to be with him. She feels more vitality and vigor in Acton and wants to forget her association with Joe. What she says is full of her anxiety for a better future and a better vibration, which Joe lacked. She admits, "With Joe I pleased myself because he encouraged me to. With Joe I worked the stick of the world, the power in my hand."[13]

Dorcas was also a victim of her black colour. She along with her friend, Felice hated 'this bunching off according to their skin' in their schools. Dorcas finds Acton more warm and intimate and discovers that Joe's cologne didn't have the provocation and the intensity of love that the young Acton offered. She's disgusted with Joe and wants him to relinquish her. She longs for freedom, be it from her aunt Manfred, from the parochial conditions of her surroundings and even from Joe who failed to give her an unbelievable sky. Full of grief and hatred, Dorcas bursts out to Joe, "I want you to leave me. I don't want you inside me. I don't want you beside me. I hate this room. I don't want to be here and don't come looking for me."[14]

And Dorcas is freed from everything when Joe shoots her that night in the party. Dorcas refused to go to the hospital and bled to death. She didn't reveal the name of the killer and had said, "Leave me alone. I'll tell you tomorrow."[15] And that tomorrow never came. Dorcas died in angst but before her death she remembered Joe. That also suggests Dorcas' tribute to Joe who loved and shot her only to 'keep the feeling going.'

For some black people jazz meant claiming their bodies. The longing to be free and having their own choice of making and marring their lives is not without the ping of existential anguish. Violet, Joe and Dorcas have their yearning and hence they suffer as a result. Violet's happiness and harmony suffer blatantly to know about Joe's nestling with Dorcas who could be of their daughter's age. Her barren life pines for some occasional relief when she takes Dumbfrey women's baby in her arms. She is mistaken for stealing the baby. Violet defends herself yet what she says is an outburst of an uproar within, "Would I leave my bag, with the stuff I make my living with if I was stealing your baby? You think I'm crazy?"[16]

Existential angst in *Jazz* arises not only out of many geographical displacements but also because of the split in the characters. Joe and Violet are husband and wife yet they often fail to understand the emptiness in their conjugal life. Their physical union suffers because of their mental partition. The emergence of a wall of separation goes unnoticed since both of them want to re-discover their own lives. Their marriage based on their true love admits several impediments as the years roll and prosperity makes way in their lives.

The main cause of Joe's agony is that he has no identity of his own. His childhood memories pester him since his parents left him without any trace. His upbringing by Mr. Frank and Mrs. Rhoda along with their six children falls heavy on Joe. He decides to call himself Joe 'Trace' and this reflects his concern for his self-esteem. The crisis of his identity sparks off his quest and this journey continues wherever he goes and with whosoever he comes across.

Joe Trace feels ashamed and guilty of his injustice done to his wife Violet, who had been with him in both good and bad times. His fancy for an eighteen-year-old girl, Dorcas and later his disgust for her compels him to shoot her. Unable to withstand the stings on his soul, Joe tries to discover what tempted him to substitute Violet by Dorcas. He finds himself at war and is left with a blurred consciousness. Not convinced with his own arguments, Joe seems torn between belief and despair and awareness is on way. His reminiscence of his past is not repentance but an acceptance of his individuality, which can give him some solace. He does not want to fall in his own eyes. He wanted everything to be shared and whom could he share with, none but with his one-time friend, Victory. But no, he would not do so. He raves and rebels with his own self:

> Dorcas, girl, your first time and mine. I chose you. Nobody gave you to me. Nobody said that's the one for you. I picked you out. Wrong time, yep, and doing wrong by my wife. But the picking out, the choosing. Don't ever think. I fell for you, or fell over you. I didn't fall in love; I rose in it. I saw you and made up my mind. My mind.[17]

Joe's unhappy life becomes worst after Dorcas' death. His escape route to Dorcas looks like his being a peccant but he's conscious of his self-esteem and integrity while arranging a nest for Dorcas, he tells Malvonne, "I don't want nothing ornery, and I don't want to be hanging out in clubs and such. I just want some nice female company."[18]

Joe is unable to bear Violet's silence. No doubt, he even kills Dorcas, the great talker yet he's acutely conscious of what he has done to Violet. He's full of shame and he admits, "That I treated Violet like a piece of furniture you favor although it needed something every day to keep it steady and upright. I don't know."[19]

He did not know and in his blindness he was always trying a way out. All his roles had given him complicated anger and deadened his consciousness. His search for his mother whom they called 'wild' continues and he wonders how a once responsible person erred so errantly. He is full of guilt and exhibits his angst when he tells Felice why he killed Dorcas, 'Scared. Didn't know how to love anybody?'[20]

Nothing can be a greater proof of his angst than to understand his flexible nature. He had changed himself several times and now after Dorcas' death, he stares at Dorcas' photograph. He is full of despair, "It is the face of a sneak who glides over to your sink to rinse the fork you have laid by her plate. An inward face—whatever it sees is its own self you are there, it says, because I am looking at you."[21]

Other male characters also share a disjointed identity and their existential journey too is full of deprivation and despair. Golden Gray, the illegitimate son of Miss Vera Louise, also wants to know who his father was. Amid several hindrances and with the sound advice of True Belle, he comes to discover Henry Les Troy who fled because of his colour. Gray is so desperate to meet his father that he says:

> What do I care what the color of his skin is, or his contact with my mother? When I see him or what is left of him I will tell him all about the missing part of me and listen for his crying shame. I will exchange then; let him have mine and take his as my own and we will both be free, arm-tangled and whole.[22]

Having discovered Henry as his father, Golden Gray is not shocked to know that he was black because his father, a nigger was protected by Vera Louise. Golden Gray's desire to be a free man is badly injured when Henry asks and wonder, "Don't we all. Look be what you want—white or black. Choose. But if you choose black, you got to act black, meaning draw your manhood up—quick-like, and don't bring me no whiteboy sass."[23]

Henry Lestroy's outcry gives us an outlet of black people's exploitation at the hands of white people. It also implies that racism became a concomitant reason for oppressing African people. We agree with what Walter Rodney observes, "Oppression of African people on purely racial grounds accompanied, strengthened and became indistinguishable from oppression for economic reasons."[24]

Apart from Violet and Dorcas, other women characters also suffer from existential anguish. Rose Dear, Violet's mother, True Belle, Violet's grandmother, Alice Manfred, Dorcas' aunt and Felice, Dorcas' friend also bear and wear the rough and tumble of times. Rose Dear jumped in the well and ended her life because her husband couldn't live his real life and the Readjuster party wanted him to transfer his self to some other place. True Belle sacrificed her life only to help a white man's daughter, whose illegal relationship with a nigger shouldn't divulge. Alice Manfred's husband ran off with another lady. Alice was starving for the woman's blood. Alice's search brought her nothing but the man's suit, the tie and the shirt he liked best. Felice also had a troubled time and she had to remain quiet at school. She had some relaxed moments in Dorcas' company but her death was a personal loss to her. Dorcas' untimely death opens Felice's eyes and she does not want to be like her. Malvonne, Joe's neighbour rents her house to Joe but she does not bear any ill will with Violet. Finally before agreeing to rent her house, she puts many questions to Joe. What she tells Joe is soaked with existential angst not about Violet in particular but about women in general, "What kind a person you think I am? Okay there's no love lost between Violet and me, but I take her part, not yours, you old dog."[25]

Miller Sisters, who run a crèche for watching the children of mothers who worked out of the house, also have a woeful ballad in their eyes. These hapless sisters tell their charges moral stories and also advise them to respect themselves. One of Miller sisters, Neola, a one-armed deserted lady had her frozen arm curled over her heart made more poignant with the refusal of her could be groom who left the state.

It is of great importance that the characters in *Jazz* help each other reveal their past and discover their hidden selves. They not only sympathize with each other but also soothe their wounds. They become friends and validate the truth that friendship is a sheltering tree where they rest and relax and bandage their bruises. They become a 'mama' for each other. Mbalia observes, "What Violet, Alice, Dorcas and Felice have in common is the need for 'mamas.'"[26] One can find that the male characters too help each other in soothing. Joe and Victory, Gistan and Stuck, Henry Lestroy and Golden Gray conceal each other's secret, share each other's fate and help in revealing themselves.

The characters in *Jazz* bring to our minds another Nobel Laureate, V.S. *Naipaul's Half A Life (2001)* where most of the characters live a borrowed life. They lead a life, which is full of fear and frustration. Willie and Ana episode is much like Violet-Joe episode. In Naipaul's novel, Ana provides a sheet anchor to Willie and after sixteen years, Willie deserts Ana to return to his homeland. Ana boils within but does not stop Willie. The other characters also suffer the same fate. Willie has a borrowed name and his thoughts are drenched in despair:

> It was not easy to imagine. Just as no man can truly wish to be some body else, since no man can imagine himself without the heart and mind he has been granted, so no man can of a later time can really know what it was like to live on the land those days.[27]

Thus, we find that most of the characters in Morison's *Jazz*, despite the occasional breaks come out of it successfully. Their mantra for life is to fight till they can. Life is more important than youth, which can bring some sweet or sour moments. There may be some warm glimmerings at times but the beauty and benignity of life lies in facing the onslaughts of time since everyone's choice does not get voice. Life has every chance of bringing improvement and improvisations. What the novelist says in the last section of the novel is the *summum bonum* of what human being can do, just like jazz music to keep life going:

> That the past was an abused record with no choice but to repeat itself at the crack and no power on earth could lift the arm that held the needle. I was so sure, and they danced and walked all over me. Busy, they were, busy being original, complicated, changeable—human, I guess you'd say, while I was the predictable some, confused in my solitude into arrogance, thinking my space, my view was the only one that was or that mattered.[28]

REFERENCES

1. Robert Roth, "Deconstructing Audiences: a poststructuralist re-reading," *Sense of Audience in Written Communication*, Ed. Gesa Kirsch & Duane H. Roen. London: Sage, 1990, 181.

2. T.S. Eliot, "Game of Chess." *The Waste Land.* Line 164.
3. *Ibid.*, Lines 12-14.
4. Toni Morrison, *Jazz.* Vintage Books: New York, 1992, 24.
5. *Ibid.*, 15.
6. *Ibid.*, 76.
7. *Ibid.*, 95.
8. *Ibid.*, 95.
9. *Ibid.*, 84.
10. *Ibid.*, 110.
11. *Ibid.*, 93.
12. *Ibid.*, 190.
13. *Ibid.*, 191.
14. *Ibid.*, 189.
15. *Ibid.*, 213.
16. *Ibid.*, 21.
17. *Ibid.*, 135.
18. *Ibid.*, 48.
19. *Ibid.*, 123.
20. *Ibid.*, 213.
21. *Ibid.*, 12.
22. *Ibid.*, 159.
23. *Ibid.*, 173.
24. Walter Rodney, *How Europe Underdeveloped Africa* (Dar es Salaam: Tanzania Publishing House, 1972), 100.
25. *Jazz,* 46.
26. D.D. Mbalia, "Women Who Run Wild," The Need for Sisterhood in *Jazz, Modern Fiction Studies*, 634.
27. V.S. Naipaul, *Half a Life*. London: Picador, 2001, 150.
28. *Jazz,* 221.

Towards a Woman's World: A Post-Feminist Reading of *The Stone Angel*

4

RASHMI GAUR AND RANO RINGO

The consciousness of feminism is the consciousness of victimization. As a philosophy of life it seeks to discover and change the subtle and deep-seated causes of women's oppression. Feminism raises the consciousness of an entire culture by revealing to women how their values, their education, their culture have worked against them because they are all 'man-made' and have excluded the voice of women. Toni Morrison uses the term 'master-narrative' to describe the expectations, values, concerns and ideas which are perpetuated by the dominant culture. Simone de Beauvoir says of woman's position in man's world, "She is defined and differentiated with reference to man and not he with reference to her; she is the incidental, the inessential as opposed to the essential. He is the Subject, he is the Absolute—she is the Other" (De Beauvoir 16).

In this world of binary oppositions there are boundaries separating victim from predator, male from female, mind from body and good people from bad people. Bifurcation of reality into hostile opposites permits patterns of subordination and domination, which Atwood refers to as 'power politics' (Atwood 23). Alienation is the direct outcome of the 'self-versus-other' consciousness. As opposed to this is the feminine self-and-other' consciousness. The feminist thinkers perceive masculine psychology as a primary factor in female subjugation and all destructive activities. The situation can be countered when women turn their world into a subject and a cultural ideological source (Singh 41). But in binary oppositions, the feminine has been viewed as something negative and repressed. The present paper intends to show how patriarchal society has smothered joy in the lives of both men and women by its repression of femininity and how a world based on feminine sensibilities can provide a positive alternative to the masculine one. This paper does not identify biological man and biological woman with masculine and feminine respectively. The paper is a post-feminist reading of Margaret Laurence's *The Stone Angel* (1964), supported with Jungian psychoanalysis and Existential arguments. Toil Moi has used the term 'post-feminism' to cover the different configurations of feminism and post-modernism present today (Moi 15). Derrida talks of liberating our thoughts from binary oppositions This rejection of a single truth is important to an understanding of post-feminism. Post-feminism is the ultimate acceptor of diversity. Multiple truths, multiple roles, multiple realities are part of its focus. Post-feminists believe that women are already as valuable as men and assert the value of women as women. Equality and difference are not antithetical for them. Alice Jardine has propounded the concept of genesis to deliberately valorize repressed femininity. Helene Cixous, Luce Irigaray and Julia Kristeva have been instrumental in the establishment of post-feminism as a philosophy. Jung's psycho-analytic framework has been used as an ideological support as his concepts are neither gender-specific nor context based. Archetypal factors transcend time and space and Jung's method demonstrates the fact that 'inner' and 'outer' realities are intertwined.

In *The Stone Angel* some autobiographical strains can be easily perceived. Margaret Laurence (1926-87) was born in the small town of Manitoba, Canada to Robert Wemyss and Verna Simpson. Like Jason Currie, Hagar's father in 'The Stone Angel,' Laurence's father was of Scottish protestant ancestry. The stifling influence of Puritanism is reflected throughout the novel. And just as Hagar is raised without a mother, Laurence's mother died when Laurence was four. She stayed in several countries—England, British Somaliland, Ghana and finally returned to Canada. She is best known for her Manawaka novels.

The Stone Angel (1964) is a compelling journey seen through the eyes of a woman nearing the end of her life. From her childhood, as the daughter of a respected merchant to her rebellious marriage, Hagar has fought a long battle for independence and respect. In the course of examining and trying to understand the shape her life has taken, her divided feelings about her husband, her passionate attachment to one son and neglect of another, she is sometimes regretful but rarely penitent. Asking forgiveness from neither God nor those around her, she must still wrestle with her own nature. The feminist dimension of 'The Stone Angel' can be described as a kind of background only because there is almost no overt consideration of its philosophy in the novel. The novel avoids polemics by this fortunate circumstance, that Hagar cannot herself articulate (because historically she doesn't know) the feminist view of her case. On the first reading, the novel appears to be the story of an old woman consumed with pride. Laurence cites patriarchal society as a kind of instigating culprit for it, and she argues that men and women alike have been injured by the forces which lead to Hagar's intractable, compensatory pride. *The Stone Angel* is told in the first person so that Laurence must do all her pleading behind the scenes.

Margaret Laurence attaches great significance to titles. 'Titles,' she says, "are important as they should in some way express the theme of the book in a rather poetic way" (Vauthier 11). The title which she chose for her first Canadian novel certainly fits her definition. Solid and ethereal, opaque and spiritual. *The Stone Angel* confronts the reader with a challenge because of the oxymoronic quality of the phrase. The stone angel is a monument to Hagar's dead mother. What other characters in the novel do to or about it, how they respond to it reflects their personality and the values they stand for. Jason Currie, Hagar's father and the Manawaka store-owner, bought her in pride to mark [his wife's] bones (3). He claims that she (the stone angel) is 'pure white marble.' She was the first, the largest and certainly the costliest (*Ibid.*). The stone angel proclaims Jason's status as one of the foremost citizens of the Puritan Manawaka society. The statue serves the weak wife as well for having fulfilled her reproductive role. In the words of his daughter, it is 'his monument,' "more dear to him, I believe, than the broodmare who lay beneath because she'd proved no match for his Stud" (43). Hagar says about the stone angel on her mother's grave, "I wonder if she stands there yet, in memory of her who relinquished her feeble ghost as I gained my stubborn one..." (3). She is consistently identified with the stone angel. To Hagar, the associations of the stone angel are necessarily double. It is linked with the mother whose weakness Hagar openly despises and is a reminder of mortality. But her 'mother's angel' is also her father's monument. To the extent that it embodied paternal and societal values which she still shares, and to the extent that it is a symbol of Currie superiority, difference and triumph over oblivion, the monument has a positive dimension is Hagar's mind.

The association of angel and mother requires a careful attention, for it is obscured by our knowledge that the stone angel is essentially a monument to Jason Currie's pride. In the shadow of the stone angel Hagar becomes another angel, ministering and mild—the kind of woman we take her mother to have been. To trace the development of Hagar's personality from Jason Currie's stone angel to her mother's angel is of primary interest in this paper.

Hagar's quest for self-actualization or individuation should be understood within the psycho-analytic framework of Carl Gustav Jung. According to Jungian psychologists, the 'ego' is merely the centre of the conscious personality while the 'self' is the unifying centre of both the conscious as well as the unconscious personalities. The 'self' incorporates within its paradoxical unity all the opposites embodied in the masculine and feminine archetypes. Western civilization has emphasized masculine rational faculties to the exclusion of the feminine faculties of intuition. The separation between the conscious and unconscious psyche is unhealthy from the psychological point of view as like the body, the unconscious psyche too has an instinctive wisdom which can correct the faults and excesses of consciousness provided one is open to its messages. One factor which obstructs understanding of the conscious and unconscious is the *persona* which is a term used by Jung to designate the role played by an individual in accordance with the expectations of society (*Collected Works*, Vol. 7: 156). The first step in the quest for individuation is the attempt to break the total identification with persona. The next step is the confrontation with the shadow or the repressed part of one's psyche. Jung defines 'shadow' as an archetypal figure—"the negative side of the personality," the sum of all those we like to hide (*Ibid.*, 160). The third step involves the understanding of the archetypes of the collective unconscious like the Wise Old Man and the Great Mother, the animus and anima (a person's experience of the opposite sex). While the magical, prophetic and healing powers of the Wise Old Man enable a genuine development of personality, the Great Mother has infinite capacity for loving and understanding, helping and protecting. The final step of the individuation process involves a successful reconciliation of the consciousness, shadow, complexes and archetypes. Further, the four stages mentioned above find a parallel in Carol Christ's classification of women's spiritual quest as consisting of four stages—*viz.*, 'nothingness, awakening, insight, naming' (Carol xv).

Commenting on the opening passage from *The Stone Angel* that describes the Manawaka cemetery, Dennis Cooley perceptively remarks that Laurence "opposes what is foreign and what is native, what is imposed and what is discovered, what is artificial and what is natural. In psychological terms she contrasts conscious and unconscious experience" (Cooley 29). Early in the novel, Hagar is seen walking only 'on paths.' This is an early indication of the repression of natural instinct by Hagar who is totally subsumed by the patriarchal values of the Currie household upheld by her father. The image which Jason Currie seems to have imported from Britain is the Victorian image of woman as 'The Angel in the House' Jason shares the Victorian belief in male superiority and accepts its notions of what behaviour and what education is appropriate for a lady. Hagar's education has been as close as possible to that of a Victorian young lady. 'I knew embroidery, and French, and menu-planning for a five course meal, and poetry, and how to take a firm hand with servants, and the most becoming way of dressing my hair' (42-43). Very little of what Hagar learns serves her in life. We see that an education which aims at making woman decorative will keep her dependent upon men. Later Hagar will envy young women like the nurse who have been better equipped for autonomous survival (284). In her article 'Did Women Have a Renaissance?' Joan Kelly voices similar views. She concludes, "Renaissance ideas on love and manners, almost exclusively a male product... served to justify the removal of women from an 'unlady like' position of power and erotic independence" (Kelly 137-64). Kelly identifies the humanistic education of the Renaissance noble woman as one of the reasons she lost power to create culture and the corresponding power to shape society.

Jason also encourages the male virtues in Hagar and neglects feminine virtues. Hagar perceives femininity only as weakness which is unacceptable to her sense of self. Proud of her refusal to cry in the scene where he beats her with a ruler, Jason remarks that she has a 'backbone' (10) and takes after him. So Hagar is courageous, proud, brainy—everything that her father admires, and she is also female, so that these virtues are perceived as useless. Jason wants the angel of his house to be proud, requires per social arrogance as an extension of his own-although he naturally expects obedience within doors. Thus, Jason Currie is the material signifier of the 'double standards' that are prevalent in an andocentric world. It is this paradoxical ideal which Hagar readily accepts and which later poses problems. Possessed by a fierce animus, Hagar 'wraps herself in her sanitary persona' (Cooley 33) and quickly denies thoughts and feelings from the unconscious areas of her self. She forgets that a lady is first of all a woman. Such an attitude alienates her from her husband and children. Her pride is ancestral derived from the Currie class. The patriarchal society appeals covertly to a sense of class in women, an eminence which they achieve through the standing of their fathers and husbands. In his way women are reconciled to the subservience which is allocated to them as a sex. A closer look reveals that her pride is nothing but a mask (persona) she unconsciously wears to conceal her numerous fears—fear of what people might think, fear of being different, fear of being isolated. At ninety, Hagar surfaces with the liberating though painful realization that she has never been able to 'rejoice' due to her animus—bound pride. Hagar is a remarkable instance of a psycho-analytical study on neurotic frontiers of fears and anxieties due to an unhealthy stifling environment of androcentrism.

It is through her rebellious marriage to Bram that Hagar takes her first step to 'individuation.' Though she derives pleasure from being with Bram, she never lets it out. Such a repression cancels her rebellion against her father for she has internalized his value system. The sum of Jason's teaching is that 'Men have terrible thoughts' (46), a notion which explains in part the Victorian allocation of chastity to women, as angels they must compensate for the bestiality of man. This illustrates the degree to which women can be willingly subjected to the ideological terms of the masculine discourse. Such women conform to what Luce Irigarary calls 'La Mascarade,' a false femininity that allows a woman to experience desire only in so far as it is prescribed by the desires of men (Irigaray 20). Commenting on her pride. Helen Buss comes to the conclusion that Hagar translates her Eros into Logos—her body into head—refusing to accept her womanhood.... To show response would be to accept some part of the feminine (Buss 55). Bram looks like freedom but even after marriage, freedom eludes her. This is partly because she does not accept Bram as he is, but tries to reform him into something more like what her father has in mind. Thus, she luxuriates in his savagery—'he looked like a bearded Indian'—and in the next instant imagines him 'rigged out in a suit of gray soft as a dove's father' (45). Bram is cast in her imagination as the primitive man who would miraculously prove to be a gentleman. The lady is still in harness, blind to the rough plebian life outside her sphere. Then again, Bram is not so different from Jason as Hagar thinks. Thus, he gives her the elegant decanter as a wedding gift, and so like Jason wants sons (not daughters) to create a dynasty. Hagar's response to this ambition in Bram is 'the nerve of him' (101). Precisely because she is a woman, part of her self-discovery is that she has had to live 'alone and against' in order to preserve her autonomy in a male-dominated society.

Another problem which Hagar faces is her inability to accept her motherhood and maternal instincts. This is seen in Hagar's rejection of her feeble dead mother, her weak effeminate brothers, her sharp tongued attacks on Doris, a daughter-in-law who literally mothers Hagar, and her contempt for Clara, Bram's first wife. Stephanie Demetrakopoulas describes Hagar's problem as 'animus-bound' pride that makes her reject feminine relatedness and describes Hagar herself as a 'Persephone trapped forever underground with the depressing, disconnecting masculine values of Hades' (Stephanie 42-59). The theorization of the theme of motherhood has generated several shifts even within feminist thought. On the one hand, radical and socialist feminists, including Simone de Beauvoir, Shulamith Firetone and Juliet Mitchell foreground the oppressive aspects of motherhood, on the other, theorists like Nancy Chodorow and Dorothy Dinnerstein focus on the pre-Oedipal bond between mothers and children and treat 'motherhood as a source of pleasure and ambiguous power,' (Paulina Palmer 96). Emphasizing the pre-Oedipal bond, Helene Cixous links the 'ecriture feminine' (Cixous 245-64) to the mother's voice and Julia Kristeva detects in 'maternal jouissance' (Kristeva 48) the potential for disrupting phallocracy. Using the pre-Oedipal bond, Adrienne Rich makes a distinction between motherhood as an institution and motherhood as an experience. While the former 'highlights the control which patriarchy exerts on women's reproductive capacities, the latter affirms the potential for pleasure and self-fulfilment offered by motherhood (Paulina Palmer 97). Women like Hagar's mother are locked into a conception of themselves as mothers to the race. Hagar despises such an attitude. She approaches the birth of her first son reluctantly. Often in the novel images of the birth process seem repulsive as when Hagar observes the 'mammoth matriarchal fly labouring obscenely to squeeze out of herself her white and clustered eggs' (170). Hagar instead of feeling compassion or anger on her mother's behalf, merely shares her father's contempt for the biological slavery of woman. As Simone de Beauvoir says, "The term 'female' is derogatory not because it emphasizes woman's animality, but because it imprisons her in her sex" (Beauvoir 10). Hagar describes her mother as a "spindly and anxious girl ... [who] peers perplexed out of her little frame, wondering how on earth to please" (59). That little frame is, of course, the strait-jacket which Hagar wishes to avoid in her own life. It requires of women that they live to please others. But Hagar reacts two extremely, distancing herself from all feminine tenderness and becoming hidebound in pride. Hagar is not what she seems to be to those around her. Repeatedly we see her on the point of relenting, of acknowledging despised feminine sentiments within herself—feelings which are there, and which are needed badly; repeatedly she retreats into that pride which based on her rejection of the mother's image. Hagar's unconscious prompts her to think about her 'lost' men but her conscious self rejects the thoughts. She wants to hold Doris' hands and beg forgiveness for acting churlish, wants to 'mother' Dan and the dying chicks but her social self, i.e., persona exercises rigid control over her emotions. Hagar's alienation from her true self and from others is on account of her uncritical acceptance of the life denying values of the town and of her father. Freedom, acting out of one's 'own self-definition,' is denied to women; in fact, "the history of women parallels the history of imperialism, of being defined in others' terms, not our own" (Fulton 108). Hagar's tragedy lies in the fact that for ninety long years she has lived an amputated life keeping her inner self securely apart from her socially conditioned self.

Patriarchal ideological structures such as capitalism and Canadian Presbyterianism are responsible for Hagar's alienation. A product of masculine mode of questing and conquering, they impose alien abstractions upon the environment or use implements that subdue it intellectually or physically. Successful

Manawakans like Jason Currie believe implicitly in the need for order. By imposing their will upon the land, such 'fledgling pharaohs' (3) hope to deny all that is chaotic, native and natural. While Jason Currie resembles Prospero, Bram can be compared with Caliban. Bram fails as a farmer because he is temperamentally not suited for farming. He loves the land and rejoices in all things wild and beautiful but possesses no inclination to corrupt or work on nature. Hagar strongly believes in the gospel of individualism handed down to her by her father, Jason Currie, who has known hard times as a pioneer. Clara Thomas notes that Jason's unremitting drive for financial success to the exclusion of tender virtues and his pride in it is linked to religion. Canadian Presbyterians believed that "the elect of God, the saved, were shown forth by their works, and therefore, that the man who succeeded in the world's terms by his own labours had also succeeded in God's terms, his outward success the sign of his favoured status among the elect" (Thomas 24). Personal effort, hard-work, order, respectability, self-control, propriety, wealth and social position were seen as absolutely necessary to ensure election. The Protestant work ethic does not take kindly to weakness in any form among the individuals. Hagar contemptuously dismisses weakness and eulogizes strength. She feels that Regina Weese, "a flimsy gutless creature, bland as an egg custard" (4) deserves nothing but scorn for 'caring with martyred devotion for an ungrateful fox-voiced mother year in and year out (4).

Hagar associates death with weakness as in the case of her mother, Henry Pearl's baby sister, Dan, Matt and later, even Bram. She does not desire to hasten her death "by as much as a span of breath" and cannot believe that she has grown weak enough to die (192). It is only after she enters the hospital that she comes to terms with her imminent death. Unfortunately, Hagar sees love too as a kind of weakness. She nags Bram for his manners and speech and does not reveal even a trace of tenderness. One night however, she walks over to the grieving Bram "without pausing to ponder whether I should or not or what to say (87)" and consoles him for the loss of his horse. That night Bram behaves very gently with her. This event clearly shows that their marriage would not have ended the way it did had Hagar chosen to reject her socially-conscious ego and act spontaneously, in tune with her inner self. Though ninety years old, Hagar cannot tolerate tears or any other manifestation of weakness from herself. In the hospital when she petulantly tells the nurse that she hates being helped, all that the nurse says in response is, "Haven't you ever given a hand to anyone in your time? It's your turn now. Try to look at it that way. It's your due" (276). Only then does Hagar realize that by acknowledging weakness one is in no way diminished and that at some time or the other in life we all need to help and to be helped.

The religion practised by Jason Currie and by most Manawakans is based on fear; not on love. In this connection Hugh Mc Lennon says, "Calvinism as understood by many of its practitioners, shifted the balance of the Christian gospel from a message of hope, love and redemption, to one of guilt, death and damnation, backwards from the Christ of The New Testament to the Old Testament God of wrath and retribution" (Elapeth, Hugh 289). Brought up on homilies, Hagar learns to see God as a punishing unmerciful father figure on the one hand, and his son as an ineffectual sacrificial victim, like her mother, on the other" (Buss 92). "The death of the mother principle in the protestant religious and secular ethos" (Maeser 153) is what accounts for the rigidity of Hagar's nature. She sees the deity as an old man in the sky and rebels against God the Father all her life till she is able to find God in the form of the woman energy within herself.

Hagar's alienation from others, though largely of her own making, is also due to the fact that all those around her are caught up in parallel captivities and are engaged in divergent flights. In "The Female Eunuch," Germaine Greer says that in modern times we live in a state of conformism without community, of proximity without communication. True to what she says, the Manawakans are an alienated lot for while conformists like Jason Currie, Matt, Dan, Marvin, Mr. Oatley, Mr. Troy, Lottie and Doris are trapped within their persona and live by it, non-conformists like Bram, Arlene, John Murray and the Tonnerre boys live exclusively by their shadow. Hagar who is both a conformist and a rebel, finds herself tragically isolated from both the groups. Marvin and his younger brother John, are externalisations 'of the split within Hagar between the Currie past and the Shipley present' (Hutcheon 56). By an irrational belief, Hagar holds that Marvin is a Shipley, whereas John is a Currie. It turns out to be just the reverse. As John once puts it succinctly, "you always bet on the wrong horse. Marvin was your boy, but you never saw that..." (237). Linda Hutcheon provides a psychological reading of the whole issue:

> In preferring John to Marvin, Hagar had revealed her double allegiance to the passionate flesh and the repressive will...her motherly devotion to her Shipley son was an acceptable social sublimation of her denied passion for Bram. Similarly, her secret despising of the hard-labouring, prosaic, but Currie like Marvin is an unconscious rejection of her father's values and inhibitions. (Hutcheon 59)

Hagar's alienation from non-conformists like Bram, John and Arlene proves to be far more disastrous than that from the conformists. It leads to her rejection of the feminine which has disastrous consequences for her younger son. 'Maternal thinking' grows out of 'maternal practice,' which requires responding to the reality of the child, an other who demands preservation and growth. To recognize excessive control as a liability sharply distinguishes the maternal from the scientific practice (Ruddick 350). But Hagar's patriarchal conditioning makes her perceive the feminine passiveness of motherhood as weakness. Unlike Marvin who suffers rejection, John is smothered by his mother's possessive love. From the moment of his birth Hagar takes to him and labours to make him resemble her father, Jason Currie. John finds in Arlene the naturalness and spontaneity he has missed in his 'prissy Pippa' of a mother. Unlike Hagar, Arlene does not attempt to 'change' John. She accepts him as he is and helps him overcome his alcoholism by merely being beside him. Then Hagar conspires with Lottie to separate their children; an act which symbolically and literally stamps out their lives. John kills both Arlene and himself in a car crash. Hagar, in need of water at Shadow Point, quotes Coleridge and asks, "What albatross did I slay for mercy's sake?" (186). Hagar's albatross, the guilt she feels for John's death, will be appeased only when Hagar in the role of the ancient mariner can look into her heart and admit the failure of love.

The futility of John's rebellion against Hagar is evident from his struggle with the stone angel in the Manawaka cemetery. When attempting to set right the 'bloody marble angel' (179) which has taken a header among the peonies, John sweats and grunts angrily and contrary to Hagar's wish does not look at all like Jacob trying to wrest a blessing from the angel. Towards the end of her life, Hagar compares her other son Marvin as well with Jacob. But in John's case, the analogy reveals that like her father and husband she is not without dynastic hopes. Though John seems to identify symbolically the stone angel with his mother, he is not trying to wrest a blessing from her. Only the overthrow of the angel would be liberating, but he complies with the wishes of the phallic mother and restores the phallic statue. While the first occurrence of the motif displays Hagar's disappointed expectations and reveals her self-deception, the second signals a moment of understanding, consequent upon the recognition of the destructiveness of her pride. This time the son (Marvin) is "gripping with all his strength and bargaining," not grunting, not yielding, he is wrestling with the messenger of God. Hagar is again the angel. No longer the stone angel, but the angel of God, and therefore able to release and be released (Vauthier 20).

This transformation in Hagar's personality is the result of the integration of Hagar's ego and shadow at Shadow Point. Her descent and her rebirth are described in Jungian terms. During her flight to Shadow Point, Hagar is dressed bizarrely out of necessity, for probably the first time in her life. It is at Shadow Point that Hagar gradually begins to realize that her insistence on proper appearances, correct speech and decorous behaviour have prevented her from enjoying herself by participating in life fully. The steps to Shadow Point lead 'down and down' indicating the plunge Hagar must take into her unconscious self (148). Hagar's fear of the night sea, an archetype of the unconscious, and her fear that her descent may not be followed by an ascent are typically Jungian. Murray, whom Dennis Cooley regards as the Jungian figure of the Wise Old Man, communicates openly with Hagar, tells her of his fears, needs, frustrations and guilt over the death of his son and unwittingly prompts Hagar to do the same. Hagar's quest 'is away from a tradition that offers her the values of light, logic and paternal godhead and towards the values of darkness, emotion, instinct and maternality' (Buss 27). Thought and sensation, she realizes, must be balanced by feeling and intuition. It is again at Shadow Point that Hagar is helped in her identification of womanhood through the Keatsian figure of Meg Merrilies. Meg is 'brave as Margaret Queen and tall as Amazon,' thus representing a womanly strength based on a female tradition rather than a denial of femininity. The fact that Meg's bed is the brown heath turf connotes not only the earth-mother aspect of the figure, but also indicates the old gypsy's connection with the mother as the archetypal final figure that welcomes the individual to death.

Having accepted her shadow and achieved union with the positive animus, Hagar finds support in a fuller life as is seen from the way she relates with the old women, particularly Elva Jardine, in the hospital ward and with the young half-Chinese girl, Sandra Wong. Her awakening reaches the conscious part of her mind and gets verbalized only when she hears Mr. Troy sing the first verse of the Doxology in a firm and sure voice. The last line of the first verse—'Come ye before Him and rejoice'—ushers in a vital moment of insight and Hagar acknowledges the destructiveness of her self-conscious pride; "Pride was my wilderness, and the demon that led me there was fear. I was alone, never anything else, and never free, for I carried my chains within me, and they spread out from me and shackled all I touched" (192).

At ninety, Hagar accepts her humanity and wonders if she is partly responsible for the deaths of John and Brain. Trying to think of the free acts performed by her in ninety years, she can think of only two 'recent' acts—one, 'a joke' in fetching the bed pan which she ironically refers to as the "shiny steel grail" (301) for Sandra and the other, a lovingly spoken 'lie' to Marvin telling him that he has been a better son than John. Though Hagar does not realize it, her free acts after the night in the cannery (Shadow Point) are more numerous. She forgives Murray for breaking his promise to her by leading Marvin and Doris to her hide-out, tries to console Mr. Troy by saying that the hymn has not upset her, tells Doris that the hymn sung by her clergyman did her good and gives Doris her mother's sapphire ring for Tina.

Hagar's quest for self-realization can also be viewed from Existential perspective. Existentialism emphasizes freedom of choice and responsibility for the consequences of one's acts. But woman discovers herself and makes choices in a world where men oblige her to accept herself as the other. She must challenge the existing order by asking how a woman can attain full humanity and what circumstances limit her freedom. Only then will she be able to attain selfhood. Self may be defined as an individual, an 'I' with an urge to know itself. At the precise moment of awareness, the 'I' reflects itself as both the subject and the object. This brings us to the question of true and false selves, which may be differentiated as the idea of what one is according to oneself as opposed to the idea of one by society. In his book, 'Existentialism,' John Macquarrie refers to this distinction as the gap that exists "between existence and essence, or between facility and possibility, or between the self one is and the self that one is projected" (Macquarrie 203). He further points out that it is this 'gap' which brings in a sense of alienation as also sets the process of self-realization going. Hagar's own thoughts after listening to Mr. Troy Sing best illustrate this point; "Every good joy I might have held, in my man or any child of mine or even the plain light of morning, of walking the earth, all were forced to a standstill by some brake of proper appearance—Oh, proper to whom? When did I ever speak the heart's truth?" (293). Hagar Shipley's moment of self-realization occurs when she confronts willingly her past deeds and confesses and accepts the responsibility for the deaths of Brain and John to Murray Lees.

Carol Christ, in her discussion of women's spiritual quest, describes existential 'nothingness' as a spiritual experience which necessitates "a stripping away of the façade of conventional reality that allows us to confront our own depths and to see the world without illusion" (Carol 80). Hagar meets Lees at a cannery when she runs away from home to escape going to an old age home. She drinks wine with him who is a perfect stranger and also sinks into sleep close to him. As Andre Dommergues points out, "The fastidious lady is not ashamed of herself. For the first time may be, she has established a genuine relationship with a man and understood the meaning of human solidarity" (Dommergues 63-71). Also, for the first time Hagar outwardly shows her emotion when she openly cries for the deaths of her husband and her son. She forgives Murray for informing Marvin about her whereabouts and also reaches and touches his wrist in an open show of affection and regard for a fellow human being and acknowledges the enslaving nature of her pride. Another feature that the quest for self-realization has in common with existentialism is to choose for oneself and accept total responsibility for one's actions. As J.M. Kertzer puts it, "responsibility, freedom and guilt are three of the terms by reference to which Hagar must judge her life (Kertzer 499-509). Hagar's freedom is linked to her acceptance of responsibility and guilt for the deaths of Bram and John.

Another criterion of importance is suffering or angst. The major hurdle in realizing the self is the incapacity or the refusal to see oneself squarely as one is. Suffering, by its very intensity, forces this insight and awakens awareness. On her deathbed, Hagar realizes that her Currie-pride has led to self-denial and self-deception and has prevented her from rejoicing. She cannot undo the past. She will not deny the person she has been, but in the act of giving her mother's ring to Doris for her grand-daughter, Hagar succeeds in linking four generations of women with some faith that whatever plagues continue of pride or other oppression, there will also be increasing joy.

Although she does not remember her mother in these last hours of life, Hagar as she approaches her own grave, has achieved something like a reconciliation with that other angel. So it is that Hagar's last thought, as she holds the glass of water triumphantly in her own hands, is 'There, There' (308). These are the mother words, which she has failed to supply for others in their deepest need and which should have been free as water. In these last words, she appears as a mother to herself: it is a beautiful resolution of her independence and need. This phase of Hagar's life can be called the 'female' phase. Elaine Showalter has described the female phase as the phase of affirmation when women reject both the feminine phase (phase of imitation) and the feminist phase (the phase of protest) as two forms of dependency. They turn instead to female experience and revel in being women. If Hagar's mother uncritically accepted the norms of male-dominated society, Hagar went to the other extreme of dissociating herself from femininity completely. Only when she learns to value and respect her femaleness is she freed from the patriarchal bonds.

NOTE

All the textual references are from *The Stone Angel*, Toronto, Ontario: McClelland &Stewart Inc., 1964.

WORKS CITED

Atwood Margaret. Power Politics. Toronto: House of Anansi, 1971.

Buss, Helen M. *Mother and Daughter Relationships in the Manawaka Works of Margaret Laurence*. University of Victoria: English Literary Studies, 1985.

Christ, Carol P. *Diving Deep and Surfacing: Women Writers on Spiritual Quest*. Boston: Beacon P, 1980.

Cixous, Helene. "The Laugh of the Medusa," Trans. Keith Copen and Paula Cohen. *New French Feminisms*. Ed. Elaine Marks and Isabella de Courtviron. New York: Schocken Books, 1981.

Cooley, Dennis, *Anti-massacred in the Wilderness: Art and Nature in The Stone Angel.* Mosaic XI.3 (1978).

De Beauvoir, Simone. *The Second Sex*. New York: Penguin Books, 1984.

Demitrakopoulas, Stephanie A. "Laurence's Fiction: A Revisioning of Feminine Archetypes," Canadian Literature 93 (1982).

Dommergues, Andre. "Order and Chaos in *The Stone Angel*,' *Etudes Canadiens* (1981).

Elapeth Cameron, Hugh Mac Lennon. *A Writer's Life*. Toronto: University of Toronto Press, 1981.

Fulton, Keith Louis. "Feminism and Humanism': Margaret Laurence and the Crisis of Imagination," *Crossing the River Essays in Honour of Margaret Laurence*. Ed. Kristjana Gunners. Turnstone Press.

Gross, Konrad. "Margaret Laurence," *Essays on Contemporary Post-Colonial Fiction*. Ed. Hedwig Book and Albert Wertheim. Munchen: Max Hueber Verlag, 1986.

Hutcheon, Linda. "Pride and Puritan Passion," *Etudes Canadiens*, 11 (December 1981).

Irigaray, Luce. *This Sex Which is Not One*. Trans. Margaret Waller. New York: Columbia University Press, 1984.

Jung, Carl Gustav. 'Two Essays on Analytical Psychology," *The Collected Works of C.G. Jung* Vol. 7. Trans. R.F.C. Hull. Eds. Sir Herbert Read, Michael Fordham and Gerhard Adler. London: Routledge and Regan Paul, 1953.

Kertzer, J.M. "*The Stone Angel*: Time and Responsibility." *Dalhousie Review* 54 (1974).

Kelly-Gadol, Joan. "Did Women Have a Renaissance?" *Becoming Visible: Women in European History*. Ed. Renate Bridenthal and Claudia Koonz. Boston: Houghton Mifflin Company, 1977.

Kristeva, Julia. *Desire in Language: A Semiotic Approach to Literature and Art*. New York: Columbia University Press, 1988.

Macquarrie, John. *Existentialism*. Harmondsworth: Penguin Books, 1982.

Maeser, Angelika. "Finding the Mother: The Individuation of Laurence's Heroines," The Works of Margaret Laurence. Ed. John Sorfleet, *Journal of Canadian Fiction*.

Palmer, Paulina. *Contemporary Women's Fiction: Narrative Practice and Feminist Theory*. Jackson and London: University Press of Mississippi, 1989.

Ruddick, Sara. "Maternal Thinking," *Feminist Studies* 6, 2 (Summer 1980).

Singh, Sushila. *Feminism: Theory, Criticism, Analysis*. Delhi: Pencraft International, 1997.

Thomas, Clara. "Pilgrim's Progress: Margaret Laurence and Hagar Shipley," *A place to stand on: Essays on and about Margaret Laurence*. Ed. George Woodcock. Edmonton: Ne West Press, 1983.

Vauthier, Simone. "Images in Stones, Images in Words Margaret Laurence's *A Stone Angel*," *Critical Approaches to the Fiction of Margaret Laurence*. Ed. Christien Riegel. Vancouver: University of British Columbia Press.

New Women in Transition: Krupabai Satthianadhan and Her *Saguna*

5

MADHU JOSHI

> "...what a world of untried work lay before me, and what large and noble possibilities seemed to open out for me! I would now throw aside the fetters that bound me and be independent. I had chafed under the restraints and the ties which formed the common lot of women, and I longed for an opportunity to show that a woman is in no way inferior to a man. How hard it seemed to my mind that marriage should be the goal of woman's ambition, and that she should spend her days in the light trifles of a home life, live to dress, to look pretty, and never know the joy of independence and intellectual work! The thought had been galling. It made me avoid men, and I felt more than once that I could not look into their faces unless I was able to hold my own with them. So, like a slave whose freedom has just been purchased, I was happy, deliriously happy. Some of my readers may be inclined to say that in recording these experiences I have given way to exaggeration. Let me assure such that this is not the case." (*Saguna* 131),

declares *Saguna*, the teenage heroine of Krupabai Satthianadhan's autobiographical novel *Saguna*—categorically and confidently. The words that she utters would surely gladden the heart of every staunch true-blue feminist. Furthermore, Saguna's emphatic assertion assumes added importance when we realize that Krupabai Satthianadhan had started writing *Saguna* as early as 1886, that it was serialized in the Madras Christian

College Magazine in 1887-'88 and was posthumously published as a book in 1895.

Viewed in the light of the passage quoted above, *Saguna* seems to be the very epitome of the New Woman, a breed that had first made its appearance in Indian literature during the second half of the nineteenth century. This New Woman was self-assured, assertive and ambitious; she was also invariably, unashamedly and uncompromisingly conscious of her individuality, her dignity and her independent identity that was not dependent on any man, whether he was related to her by birth, by marriage or by virtue of emotional ties. At first sight *Saguna* and her creator Krupabai Satthianadhan appear to be New Women to the very core; indeed, Satthianadhan, whose *Saguna* is the first autobiographical novel in English by an Indian woman, is credited with being the pioneer of the tradition of New-Woman writing in the English language in India. However, a closer reading of *Saguna* highlights the fact that both its heroine and her creator, although "deeply committed to contemporary women's issues... [were merely] an integral part of an evolving, albeit conservative Indian feminism" (*Saguna* xii).

However, that is not the impression that the reader gets at the beginning of *Saguna*. Satthianadhan begins the book by stating that she plans "to present a faithful picture of the experiences and thoughts of a simple Indian girl, whose life has been highly influenced by a new order of things which at the present time is spreading its influence to a greater or lesser extent over the whole of her native land" (*Saguna* 19). She goes on to tell us of the little girl Saguna whose mother would often admonish her for being far too fond of books saying, "What is the use of learning for a girl? A girl's training school is near the *chool* (the fire over which everything is cooked) and however learned a girl may be she must come to the *chool*" (*Saguna* 21). Saguna's brothers, too, would rejoice when they found her doing menial chores about the house but, with her elder brother Bhaskar supporting her and encouraging her quest for knowledge, the spirited young girl would have her revenge on them by solving the sums that they were unable to solve. As she grows older Saguna talks earnestly about issues such as the practice of *suttee,* child-marriage, the wretched lot of Indian widows, the prohibition on women's education and the tendency of Hindu wives to think of their husbands as their lords and masters. It is obvious that Saguna is deeply aware of the fact that there is something radically wrong with a society that smugly refuses to treat its women at par with men and heaps on them all manner of indignities and abuses.

Saguna's dissatisfaction with the current state of affairs is underscored when she starts telling the story of her mother Radhabai, a child-bride who comes in for some rough treatment at the hands of her cruel sister-in-law and stern mother-in-law. Talking of these young wives Krupabai writes, "Poor girls! What can we expect from such impoverished, stunted minds?... No wonder then that they grow vain, flippant, inordinately fond of money or stupidly proud of their hoarded gold and jewels...and yet these are the daughters of India whose lot is considered as not needing any improvement by many of my countrymen who are highly cultured and who are supposed to have benefited by western civilization" (*Saguna* 37). These are certainly the sort of words, spoken with a great deal of conviction and fervour, that we would expect from a fervid New Woman.

However, it is when Satthianadhan is recounting the story of Radha and her husband Harichandra, i.e. Saguna's own father, who virtually kidnaps his wife in order to convert her to Christianity against her will, that the reader first realizes that there seems to be an inherent contradiction in Saguna's views about the right of a woman to chart her own destiny. As Saguna deals with her father's "Struggle with his natural self (*Saguna* 57) at the forced conversion and with her mother's prolonged agony at being deceived, coerced and "polluted" (*Saguna* 59) in this manner, not once do we find Saguna objecting to the fact that her helpless mother was forced against her will to take a step that would change the whole course of her life. It is obvious that she feels very strongly for Radha and Harichandra's plight but the sort of vehemence that can be detected when she comments on the hapless Hindu wives inextricably caught in the web of *pativratadharma* is nowhere to be seen when she talks about Radha being treated as a mere object by Harichandra, however well-intentioned he might have been.

Thus, Saguna grows up in a Christian home and every now and again we find her resenting the fact that, as a girl, she is expected to live her life within the confines of the home and hearth. Each time someone makes an attempt to domesticate her she flares up and declares, "And am I not as good as a boy? I can do as many sums as they, ...and I can read and write too" (*Saguna* 76). The individualistic streak that she invariably displays leads her sister to say to Bhaskar, "She is a strange girl, is she not?" (*Saguna* 77). This 'strange girl,' after Bhaskar's death, boards for a while with two European ladies Miss Roberts and Miss D and then moves on to a larger European *zenana* school. This, incidentally, is when she goes to school for the first time where, she fears, she "would become public property, ...and be watched by girls of my own age, laughed at and freely criticised by all" (*Saguna* 124). Yet, she informs us, "my old rebellious spirit rose within me" (*Saguna* 125) and she manages to take all the ups-and-downs that she encounters in her stride. When, for example, she is wrongly accused of staying away from the girls' prayer union and Miss P's holy lesson because she is too conceited and self-opinionated to want to attend them, she, at once, defends herself: "I have not done any wrong, and I don't deserve this treatment" (*Saguna* 134). Later on, she exhibits the same sort of spiritedness in giving a piece of her mind to three presumptuous young men who dare to think that she will unquestioningly jump at the chance of accepting their respective proposals of marriage.

It is in this school that Saguna comes in contact with the lady doctor whose strong personality has a decided effect on the young and impressionable girl in search of something which will fulfil her as-yet-undefined desires. She starts studying medicine with this unconventional lady and when the latter returns to America she makes arrangements for *Saguna* to continue her medical studies in England. It is at this stage that the hand of conformity once again intervenes in the form of an old family friend Mr. A, the missionary in charge of making arrangements for Saguna's visit to England. He refuses to give her permission to study abroad as he is convinced that she would not be able to "stand the climate and the hard strain" (*Saguna* 150). Even though Saguna insists that the missionary's words dealt a "death blow" (*Saguna* 150) to her hopes, she accepts his decision without protesting too much and readily accepts his suggestion that he will make arrangements for her to study medicine in India. The picture of *Saguna* that emerges at this point is certainly not that of a woman who would brook no obstacles along the path that she has chosen for herself.

However, once Saguna has accepted the decision that was made by others for her to pursue her medical studies in India she shows exemplary courage in the manner in which she tries to achieve her goal. In an age when travelling by train was very inconvenient and even fraught with dangers for a young girl travelling by herself, she sets off towards an unknown and unfamiliar destination "shuddering at... [her] own loneliness" (*Saguna* 151). In spite of the innumerable adjustments that she has to make, she works very hard and at the end of the first year she stands first in her class—everything is as it should be in the life of this New Woman. Here it must be stressed that studying to be a doctor was certainly not a commonplace vocation for a young Indian woman in the nineteenth century; indeed, the first Indian woman to qualify as a doctor, Anandibai Joshi, acquired her medical degree as late as 1886.

Then, once again, another crucial development takes place in Saguna's life and this puts an end, once and for all, to her plans of becoming a doctor. At the end of the first year in medical college, in spite of her exceptionally brilliant results, "a feeling of complete prostration" (*Saguna* 155) comes over her and she is unable to go on with her studies. Here it must be pointed out that, even though Saguna clearly regrets the fact that she is unable to complete her studies, once again, the readers do not encounter the sort of sorrow and desperation that one would expect from an ambitious and focused young woman who finds herself being thwarted just as she is setting out to fulfil a long-cherished dream. To use her own words, when she finds her "hope of achieving great things with my own power" dashed to the ground due to her feeble health she feels her "helplessness keenly" (*Saguna* 158). Indeed, we cannot help noticing a contradiction between the two Sagunas that we encounter at some very critical junctures in her life. On the one hand is Saguna, the New Woman, full of hopes and aspirations, determined to chart the course of her own destiny, and, on the other, there is Saguna, the pliable and even somewhat irresolute young lady who seems to belie all the avowals of grit and determination about "those golden dreams of work and independence" (*Saguna* 155) that she had made just a short while ago. Whenever such a glaring contradiction catches our attention we cannot help agreeing with the opinion expressed in *The Encyclopedia Americana* that, "In general, established laws, customs, attitudes and habits of thinking were slow to change, specially when they involved the acceptance of new ideas about women and their place in society" (Americana 103).

While she is recuperating at her sister's house in Poona, Saguna meets a young man (Samuel Satthianadhan, Krupabai's husband in real life) who finally changes the course of her whole life. His entry into her life and the growing closeness between the two of them leads to a great deal of agonising self-examination on Saguna's part—she finds herself being pulled in one direction by her "restless untamed spirit" (*Saguna* 157) and in a very different one by a desire that now begins to rear its head: "Oh! That I had somebody to guide me" (*Saguna* 160). Due to this divergence of desires, Saguna finds herself on the horns of a dilemma and for a long time she is in two minds about the path that she should follow. This dichotomy reminds us of Mary Anne Ferguson's views about the stereotypes regarding the images of women in literature and her opinion that "A person who deliberately departs from a socially approved stereotype by playing a new role—developing a new lifestyle—usually must pay a heavy cost in guilt, alienation or psychosis" (Ferguson 4). This is precisely what happens to *Saguna*. After some intense introspection she finally and, might one add, tamely decides to throw in her lot with the England-returned young man, who turns out to be the son of her mentor in medical college (Rev. W.T. Satthianadhan, Krupabai's father-in-law in real life). All talks of independence, a career and an identity of her own are forgotten henceforth and we cannot help remembering William Blake's "mind-forged manacles" (Murdoch 18) and regretting that such manacles are the hardest of all to break. Susan J. Rosowski hits the nail on the head when she says that, "for a woman... [acquiring and deciding on] an art of living is difficult or impossible: It is an awakening to limitations" (Rosowski 313).

It is interesting to note that throughout their lives Saguna and—since Saguna is an autobiographical representation of an author who adheres very closely and faithfully to facts from her real life—her creator Krupabai have found refuge under the patriarchal umbrella. To begin with, there is a dead father who is hero-worshipped to the point of idolatory; then there is Bhaskar, the brother who urges his doting sister Saguna to "be as your sister was, modest, gentle, and kind, a real woman" (*Saguna* 25). After Bhaskar's untimely death Saguna meets the American lady doctor who, incidentally, is the only woman who has a marked influence on Saguna's life. Indeed, we cannot help wondering if, perhaps, Saguna's life might not have followed a different course had the lady doctor—an inveterate non-conformist and a New Woman, if ever there was one—not returned to America at the time that Saguna was denied permission to travel to England to study medicine. When she goes to medical college at Madras, Saguna comes across another strong patriarchal figure, a clergyman and missionary, her future father-in-law who once actually asks her: "I wish you would work with me.... Will you leave your studies?," to which Saguna replies, almost bucolically, "Yes,...I will work with you." Finally she meets her husband under whose powerful influence she shelves her plans for an independent career along with all her reformist zeal, once and for all. We cannot help remembering that this is the same

Saguna who had once castigated one of her suitors, 'the student,' and told him in no uncertain terms, "Marriage is not the goal of every girl's ambition.... It is really disgusting to see how many of you imitate the English in manners, dress and other superficial things without imbibing their liberal spirit which gives to a woman equal privileges with man" (*Saguna* 149). As Chandani Lokugé puts it, "after unsuccessfully attempting to fly to the skies..., Satthianadhan comes to terms with hopping at ground level" ("Introduction," *Saguna* 9). It is ironical that in doing so she is merely lending weight, albeit inadvertently, to the smug declaration of another suitor, 'the doctor' this time, who had pompously assured her, "It is not necessary for all girls to earn their own living and devote their lives to study. It is only those who cannot get husbands who must do this" (*Saguna* 148).

To be fair to Saguna and to her creator Krupabai Satthianadhan, it must be mentioned that they are beings who are caught in the crosscurrents of the Indian-British as well as the Hindu-Christian encounters in the second half of the nineteenth century. Both of them had Hindu parents who had converted to Christianity and the questions of nationality and religion played a major role in shaping their personalities and their notions about themselves, in particular, and the world around them, in general—and these, in turn, had obviously affected the way in which they viewed themselves as women. In this context it should be noted that it is her belief in God which always gives Saguna the strength to bear the greatest tribulations with courage and dignity—when she is wrongly accused of being disrespectful in school she turns to God for solace and says, "Him I needed, and He came and I found joy" (*Saguna* 135), and, again, when she finds herself all alone on her way to medical college she prays and tells us that "I felt a presence beside me, in those dark lonely hours and it brought light and joy" (*Saguna* 152). It is interesting that it is her belief in the same omnipotent God and her desire to serve him that finally helps her in making up her mind about her future husband—clearly a case of one patriarchal figure, even though it is God almighty himself, furthering the cause of a fellow patriarchal figure!

When *Saguna* was first published Krupabai Satthianadhan was hailed as an "object lesson to her sisters in Southern India" (*Miscellaneous Writing* 119). Today, when we think of her we are reminded of Ellen Glasgow's words, penned in 1913, that, "Ages of false thinking about her on the part of others have bred in woman the dangerous habit of false thinking about herself, and she has denied her own humanity so long and so earnestly that she has come at last almost to believe in the truth of her denial" (Glasgow 656). It is a great pity that Saguna, who makes numerous courageous and praiseworthy attempts to be her own person throughout her life, unfortunately ends up being just another "man's womanly woman" (*Ibid.*) at the end of the novel. At this point it must be emphasized that, unlike her creation Saguna whose story ends with her betrothal, Krupabai Satthianadhan had a successful literary career even after marriage. Moreover, before her untimely death at the age of thirty-two, she played an active role in the area of the education of girls, whenever her failing health permitted her to do so. To be fair to her, it must also be recorded that, although she did abandon her medical career, she remained deeply committed to contemporary women's issues throughout the short span of her life. Furthermore, her continuing to write even on her death-bed, in order to complete her second novel *Kamala*, provides ample proof of the indefatigability and determination that we would expect from a New Woman.

Krupabai Satthianadhan had portrayed her life in *Saguna* during a time of great social strife and dislocation when the issue of women's empowerment was at a nascent stage. This was a time when "different behaviour patterns... [were automatically] expected" (*Britannica* 906) of men and women. It is, therefore, not surprising that the final image that we have of Saguna and her creator Krupabai Satthianadhan is that of New Women in transition—women who are courageous and ambitious but who, at the same time, are "bewildered about their identity; ... [and who, therefore,] feel damned it they do and damned if they don't" (Ferguson 2).

WORKS CITED

1. *The Encyclopedia Americana International Edition.* V. 29. (Connecticut: Grolier Incorporated, c 1984).
2. *The Encyclopaedia Britannica: Macropaedia.* Volume 19. (Chicago: University of Chicago, c 1983).
3. Ferguson, Mary Anne. *Images of Women in Literature* (Boston: Houghton, 1973).
4. Glasgow, Ellen. "Feminism," *New York Times* (Nov. 30, 1913).
5. Murdoch, David, Ed.. *The Siren's Song (An Anthology of British and American Verse).* (New Delhi: Orient Longman, 1971).
6. Rosowski, Susan J. "The Novel of Awakening," *Genre* [1979 Fall 12(3)].
7. Satthianadhan, Krupabai, *Miscellaneous Writings of Krupabai Satthianadhan* (Madras: Srinivasa, Varadachari and Co., 1896).
8. Satthianadhan, Krupabai, *Saguna: The First Autobiographical Novel in English by an Indian Woman.* Ed. Chandani Lokugé (New Delhi: Oxford University Press, 2002).

Bapsi Sidwa's *The Ice-Candy Man* as a Partition Novel

6

MALLIKARJUN PATIL

India having been ruled by the British for nearly 200 years got its freedom only in 1947. But the losses it incurred out of its struggle for independence are innumerable. Obviously one of them is partition. The country was broken down in 1947 because of Muslim League's misguided efforts and India lost its territories on both its sides.

Indeed, Lord Mountbatten implemented his plan of partition and Gandhis and Nehrus nodded to it. But the fanatic Hindu-Muslims misused the genesis of partition and saw that a river of blood drained on either side.

The partition horror accompanying the transfer of population has been a major theme in India-Anglian writings. Even many Pakistani writers have, like their Indian counterparts, written much about the partition theme. Although the treatment different writers make use of, differs from one another, the subject is the same and the same is ably exploited by writers.

Even though many Pakistani and Bangladeshi writers have written about the horrible event of partition in the Indian subcontinent, Indian writers have an edge upon them. The fictional works by Raj Gill, H.S. Gill, Kartar Singh Duggal and others focus upon the theme of partition very vividly. Even G.D. Kosla's *Stern Reckoning: A Survey of the Events Leading upto and Following the Partition of India* (1949) is a useful work.

A deep understanding of these novels drives home the point that a persistent pattern runs through the novels by

Sikhs. The principal characters in these novels are all Sikhs and each novelist shows a romance between a Sikhs boy and a Muslim girl. Even these novels show historical evidence abundantly.

Let us examine some of these novels. Raj Gill's *The Rape* (1974) opens in 1947 in a village in West Punjab, now a part of Pakistan, where Dalipjit, a Sikh boy rapes Leila, a Muslim girl whom Dalipjit's father has already molested. H.S. Gill's *Ashes and Petals* (1978) has a similar theme. His novel is about Ajit, a cavalry officer who tries to marry a Muslim girl in spite of the ongoing Muslim-Sikh disturbances. *Twice Born Twice Dead* (1979) by Kartar Singh Duggal covers much the same period as Gill's. Duggal's novel, in the wake of massacre, is a cry for compassion.

The next best novels on partition are Khushwant Singh's *Train to Pakistan* and Bapsi Sidwa's *The Ice-Candy Man.* However the treatment of the subject differs, the substance of these two novels is akin to each other. If Khushwant Singh writes about communal troubles that broke out in Mano Majra, an India border village, Bapsi Sidwa writes about the same, that broke out in Lahore, a big town in Pakistan. In other words *Train to Pakistan* and *The Ice-Candy Man* appear to be complimentary to each other. One striking thing in them is their conclusions.

Now let us examine the characteristic comparisons in these novels in so far as the theme of partition is concerned.

Just like Khushwant's *Train to Pakistan,* the Pakistani Parsi writer Bapsi Sidwa's *The Ice-Candy Man* explores the horrors of 1947's holocaust. However Bapsi Sidwa's novel is from Parsi angle, it depicts the bloody event succinctly. But unlike Khushwant Singh, Sidwa elaborates the cataclysm indirectly.

The Ice-Candy Man is divided into several chapters and it runs into 279 pages. It is quiet bulky. Bapsi Sidwa's elaboration of the plot and lengthy characterization has lent the novel an epic dimension. But along with this go the qualities of prosiness, redundancy and monotony. Too much about a few characters does not make the novel eminently engaging.

The Ice-Candy Man deals with the partition horror and the life of Lenny, a limping girl, an Ice-Candy man, a Muslim and an ayah, a Hindu. Lenny, the Ice-candy man and ayah's lives are governed by the event of partition and its consequences. Still a number of characters are affected by the 1947's communal troubles. Bapsi Sidwa succeeds in elaborating the intercommunity life from Parsi angle.

The novel begins with a quotation from Mohammad Iqbal's poem 'Complaint to God':

> With dust in my mouth, I am abject: to God I make my complaint.
> Sometimes You favour our rivals then sometimes with us You are free,
> I am sorry to say it so boldly. You are no less fickle than wee. (1)[1]

The poem is man's complaining to god about the Latter's whimsicality in creating the world and in not maintaining it. The protagonist cries, "I am sorry to say it so boldly. You are no less fickle than we" (1). This reminding Hardy's protagonists, makes us remember Lenny's opinion that human existence is miserable. Man has to suffer for every pleasure. One's joy is another's pain as much as one's gain is another's loss. Besides, disasters add much suffering to human existence. The partition is one of such unprecedented events, which worsted people's lives in the Indian sub-continent.

Lame Lenny is the narrator of the novel. Her troubles start with her health. She is hospitalized because of a handicap. Even the Lahore hospital's horrifying smells and stench weaken her.

> I am held captive by the brutal smell. It has vaporized into a milky cloud. I float round and round and up and down and fall horrendous distances without landing anywhere, fighting for my life's breath. I am abandoned in that suffocating cloud. I moan and my ghoulish voice turns me into something despicable and eerie and deserving

> of the terrible punishment. But where am I? How long will the horror last? Days and years with no end in sight.... (6)

Lenny undergoes an operation and writhes in pain. But she is still optimistic. Lenny's parents are an ordinary lot—illiterate and ignorant. They had a bad luck in Lenny's contracting of polio. This ill feeling is seen in their private lives. The family is known for its Parsi way of life.

An interesting character in the novel is Shanta, an eighteen-year-old ayah—who silently bears the pains of tending a limping Lenny. Ayah is a memorable character possessing Ruth's qualities.

Lenny's other childhood memories include the company of her cousin and an eclectic aunt. Joys and pains of her environment lurk in her bosom continually. Lenny has a brother called Adi and the comparison and contrast between them end there. Lenny's house being in a lush and densely populated area of Lahore gives her a chance to befriend many big people and derive maximum news about partition.

One day when Lenny and Ayah go out for an outing, we are introduced to a peculiar character called an Ice-candy-man—a reencounter. He is a Muslim peddler and an absorbing gossipmonger. The Ice-candy-man is a sort of hawker. He works at Lenny's alongside Ayah. He is a smoker representing a shoddy, almost disreputable type. But one thing that makes him an attractive figure is his familiarity with the national affairs. He knows about the British, Jap and Bose. It is through him Lenny tells us about Partition troubles. Her friends like Dost Mohammed and Runna brief her on Hindus' massacre in Bengal, Bihar and the English's neutrality over it.

Later the villagers—Sikhs and Muslims—erupt in protest and massacre people and the scene is akin to the ones depicted in Khushwant Singh's Mano Majra:

> When it was discovered that the train had brought a full load of corpses, a heavy brooding silence descended on the village. People barricaded their doors and many stayed up all night talking in whispers. Everyone felt his

> neighbour's hand against him, and thought of finding friends and allies. They did not notice the clouds blot out the stars nor smell the cool damp breeze. When they woke up in the morning and saw it was raining, their first thoughts were about the train and burning corpses. The whole village was on the roofs looking toward the station. (103)[2]

Bapsi Sidwa writes:

> Late in the evening three military lorries had lumbered into Pir Pindo gouging deep ruts in the fields and laying waste swathes of sugar cane. They were Gurkha soldiers come to evacuate them.
>
> 'Those Muslims who want to go to Pakistan had better go into the truck,' a soldier shouted through a megaphone. He was short and stocky like most of his race. 'We will leave at dawn.'
>
> 'What?' the puzzled villagers asked. 'Is Pakistan already there?'
>
> 'Who knows,' said the Gurkha. 'I'm telling what I'm told to say.'
>
> The villagers gathered in the open yard of their masque. They squatted in a tight arc round the mullah and the choudry. I imagine their faces: obstinate, dazed. And the choudry's as, smiling wryly, attempting with sarcasm and wisdom to mask his panic, he says: 'Do you expect us to walk away with our hands and feet? What use will they serve us without our lands? Can you evacuate our land?' he asked cunningly. (110)

Everyone belonging to Hinduism, Islam and Sikhism starts arguing, siding, conspiring and quarreling with others. Masseur, a hardcore speaks to his Sikh counterpart Sher Singh something for solution:

> 'The only way to keep your holdings, Sardarjee, is to arrive at a settlement with the Muslim League,' intervenes Masseur, smoothing the quarrel with his voice. He dusts the rice from Sher Singh's beard, if you don't, the Punjab will be divided.... That will mean trouble for us all. (129)

As in Khushwant Singh's *Train to Pakistan,* so in the *Ice-Candy Man,* Bapsi Sidwa projects the 'Kaliyuga.' During this age coincided with modern times, along with promotion of science, the degeneration of values crop up. The two world wars or the partition of India are some of the issues that create a widespread devastation. A gardener very close to Lenny talks of Kalyug in which the so-called brave or good people are compelled to yield to the evil and wicked.

The partition event sends wrong signals everywhere. It is fierce in the India-Pak borders. People in Lahore, Amritsar, Sialkot and Pathankot get devastated due to Hindu-Muslim feud and in between the Sikhs though once a buffer state suffer as well. Not to speak of, Sher Singh who has married an American lady flees away to India in spite of his dare-devilry. The scene in which a load of Muslim corpses, especially bags of Muslim women's breasts come maddens the Muslims. As a result, Muslim goondas indulge in communal atrocities. Even Shankar and Geeta go away. Hari, Lenny's servant as he does not have a place to go away becomes a Muslim, while the low castes like Moti and his tribe get converted to Christianity. Even the Ice-candy-man turns communal.

Lenny with her mother meets Gandhi after the horrors of partition heard. She says Gandhi is a myth of the time. He is small, shriveled and old looking. But he is ahead of the times. She is happy over her little talk with the Mahatma.

But one day there is an alarm:

> It is sudden. One day everybody is themselves—and the next day they are Hindus, Muslim, Sikh, Christian. People shrink, dwindling into symbols. Ayah is no longer just my all-encompassing Ayah—she is also a token. A Hindu.
>
> There is much disturbing talk. India is going to be broken. Can one break a country? (92)

So immediately all people become aware of their caste, religion, race and nation. Lenny's family is reduced to irrelevant nomenclatures—Parsis.

Later there appears a strange box in Lenny's house. The littleuns wonder at it. With similar mystery it disappears later.

Lenny and people go to Pir Pindo where in a conversation with Dost Mohammed and Imam Din, she finds more news about India to be broken down. Not much later the marauding Muslims attack Lenny's house and run berserk for Ayah. Indeed, she is molested. In turn, Massuer, a Muslim is killed by the Sikhs. The horror multiplies in villages and towns. Pir Pindo and other villages around Lahore lay devastated. Dost Mohammed reports a few things later:

> Sikhs have attacked at least five villages around Dehra Misri to their east. Their numbers have swollen enormously. They are like swarms of locusts, moving in marauding bands of thirty and forty thousand. They are killing all Muslims. Setting fires, looting, parading the Muslim women naked through the streets—raping and mutilating them in the center of villages and masques. The Bias, flooded by molten snow, and the monsoon, is carrying hundreds of corpses. There is an intolerable stench where the bodies, caught in the bends, have piled up. (197)

The old Lahore city built by the Moguls is burned. Even Amritsar is burned. Millions of people—Hindus, Muslims, Sikhs lose their lives. Runn's story illustrates this phase of man-made horror. Characters like Lenny and the Ice-candy-man deserve a special attention. The Ice-candy-man, a sort of vendor and sadhu turns a pimp-like poet-turned ascetic on being turned by ayah. A small quote establishes their positions:

> He is a deflated poet, a collapsed peddler—and while Ayah is haunted by her past, Ice-candy man is haunted by his future: and his macabre future already appears to be stamped on his face. (165)

When the communal troubles break out, we find these persons thriving at Hira Mandi, a red district where all people—poets, pimps, prostitutes, singers and dancers live a jolly life. Bapsi Sidwa alludes to this locale often with a degree of acumen.

But one day, some Sikhs beat the Ice-candy-man for his illegal trafficking of Ayah. Even the Ice-candy-man tries to marry her in vain. The police succeed in extraditing the bedraggled lady from Hira Mandi. Still the Ice-candy-man follows her singing a love-song:

> My passion has brought me to your street—
> Where can I now find the strength to take me back? (277)

However, what is most interesting is the conclusion Bapsi Sidwa makes with an apt touch:

> Until, one morning, when I sniff the air and miss the fragrance, and run in consternation to the kitchen, I am told that Ayah, at last, has gone to her family in Amritsar.... And Ice-candy-man, too, disappears across the Wagah border into India. (277)

Like *Train to Pakistan, The Ice-Candy Man* is well wrought out. Although it does not evince that kind of technique as in *The Crow Eaters,* still it reads well. Like Mano Majra, Lahore is a locale here. People inhibit this work of fiction are as wide as people from Parsi to that of all major religions. The only difference between the community compositions in these novels is communities in Singh's novel are small. In fact, Mano Majra is a small village in the border between India and Pakistan. Whereas in *The Ice-Candy Man*, the locale is a big city as old as 1000 years and the communities are complex both in customs and following. A kind of diversity creeps in every part of the novel. Besides, the novel is quite realistic and comic. It is full of jokes sustaining readers' interest. What else the presentation is neat and clean. The archaic use of language and Sidwa's vulgarity in certain usages are formidable. The dialogues are apt.

Another important thing to be observed is that the theme of partition in Khushwant Singh's novel is best delineated and the same is not seen in the *Ice-Candy Man.* Singh vividly describes the whole community troubles. In fact, Singh's major concern is description of Partition horror. Bapsi Sidwa's main concern is to show Lahore life through Lenny's eyes. Partition theme is not domineering. Even the title of the novel is inappropriate. Singh is strong even in terms of language. In just 157 pages he narrates one of the major tragedies of the 20th centuries world, whereas Bapsi Sidwa though wishes to deal with it even in 279 pages does not succeed. *The Ice-Candy Man* is full of gossip, loquacious talk, family matters discussed bizarre. Lenny is surely a headache to refined readers. Her boastful stature, pride and verbatim makes the novel dull and dry.

REFERENCES

1. All the references to Bapsi Sidwa's *The Ice-Candy-Man* are taken from the Penguin edition published in 1989.
2. All the references to Khushwant Singh's *Train to Pakistan* are from the Penguin edition published in 1996.

Wife: A Study in Psychoanalytical Conflict

7

BINDA SHARMA AND G.A. GHANSHYAM

> I have no pride-no pride, no name; no face, no country. I don't belong anywhere.
>
> —Jean Rhys
>
> The Narrator in *Good Morning Midnight*

Bharati Mukherjee's novels portray the traumas and tensions, probing and pining of the contemporary man through an exploration of the lacerated psyche of the characters. Isolated from the self as well as the society, Bharati's characters are forlorn and lovelorn. They are so obsessively and neurotically involved in the affairs of life that they fail to decide the tenor of their life. She grapples with the psychic moments the psyche to unveil the hidden and mute motives and impulses behind the individuals mental odyssey. Her novels are existential in tone, for they deal with the contradictions and predicaments faced by the individuals in the struggle of life.

Her novel *Wife*[1] stands out as a unique fictional work by virtue of its insight and probing into its heroines psyche. Surfacially *Wife* is the simple story of Amit and his wife. Dimple newly married Bengali immigrants to the USA. Dimple the protagonist stands as a unique character. She is an escapist lost in her world of fantasy she is alienated and aloof. She is recessive, socially disinterested and socially ineffective. Lonely and confused she wants to break through the traditional taboos of wife. She aspires for love and freedom in marriage. This aim brings out her indignation, grief, resentment, peevishness, spite and sterile anger. Dimple appears to indulge in masochistic suffering in order to lull the pain of disappointment with life, especially with married life:

> She fantasized about young men with moustaches, dressed I spotless white, peering into opened skulls. Marriage would bring her freedom, cocktail parties on carpeted lawns; fund-raising dinners for noble charities marriage would bring her love. (3)

The dreams come crashing down as she is married into a middle class Bengali family where very often we see her obsessively measuring her husband against her ideal man and her life against her dream and finding both of them wanting in many respects and despairing as a result. Dimple virtually has nothing to look forward to. Life with Amit both in India and America is a big disappointment for her.

It is necessary to understand and study the character of Amit to understand Dimple. A simple middle class professional having dreams and aspirations to move higher in the social ladder he is unsentimental and unresponsive to the emotional needs of his young wife. Cautious and meticulous he is the very embodiment of an Indian male, paradoxical, who would advocate of female education but is lacking in a complementary progressive attitude to accept and digest the awareness and changed ideas of their womenfolk regarding their place and position in family and society.

Isolated, lonely and unable to communicate with others we find Dimple obsessively thinking about 'Death' which for her is the final and logical goal. Dimple's neurotic disposition and sado-masochistic impulses are revealed twice in the earlier part of the novel. Firstly when she almost hysterically kills a rodent imagining it to be pregnant:

> I'll get you! She screamed. There's no way out of this my friend! She seemed confident now, a woman transformed. And in an outburst of hatred her body shuddering, her wrist taut with fury, she smashed the tip of a small grey head. (35)

This is the first instance when she unleashes her pent up violent rage. The aggression leads to self-destruction, unable to interact with the outside world she looses contact with herself and her own desires.

In the second instance forlorn and lonely she inflicts violence on herself and her unborn child and terminates her pregnancy in the most bizarre manner:

> If she had planned it for months she would have used something flashy—a red-hot poker from the kitchen or large sewing scissors—but if she had planned it, she knew her anger would have chilled to inaction. She would have become discreet and adaptable as usual. Certainly she would not have picked a skipping rope as her weapon who would have thought you, could skip your way to abortion? (42)

Her masochism finds an eloquent expression through this slightly bizarre act. Symbolically speaking, in her rejecting the pregnancy she finally rejects Amit. This is the first major symptom of her neurotic problem. The psychic drive finds psychological representation in destructive forces. The aim of the death urge looming large on Dimple is manifested in hate, aggression, and thoughts of suicide and murder. The crumbling of the self is complete and overpowered by her neurotic impulses we find Dimple talking to herself, we witness an uncalled irritation and hatred for her husband Amit, her regular bouts of insomnia. Despair sets in her life thinks that marriage had betrayed her and not provided all the glittering things she had imagined.

In the second part the scene shifts to New York. Materialistic, unreal and violence-ridden the city shocks her. Glued to T.V. and stunned by the incredible violence she is trapped in a diabolical trap, a forwent without hope of either release or relief. The violence, ridden city of New York does her no good either. The neurosis arises from the clash between a requirement for adaptation and the individual inability to meet the challenge. To Dimple death appears in myriad forms. Her frenzied imagination conjuring nine different ways to die.

> 'Set fire to sari made of synthetic fibre' head in oven nick wrist with open glass, in a sink full of scalding dish water; starve; fall on bread knives while thinking of Japanese Samurai revivals. (154)

The stages in her mental derangement are developed meticulously. Before committing murder of her husband, she starts getting afraid of the things around her.

> Everything scared her; the sputtering radiators, the brown corduroy sofa with depressions the needless in the rug, the ironing board—the leggier prints, the cactus that had not flowered the way it was supposed to, the smudgy white windows behind the dining table. (156)

Instead of becoming self-destructive we see her gradually shifting the blame upon her husband. Finally she behaves like a 'psychotic' sharply differentiated from the normal individual by the bizarreness of her actions, the incoherency of speech the absurdity of her hallucinations and delusions, the inappropriateness of her emotional responses and her general confusion. Thus we find Dimple's behaviour unaffected by rules of logic, cultural mores or outside happenings.

In her desire to die she kills Amit. Again, her reaction to Amit's innocent act of love is violent and her stabbing him with a knife reveals her sado-masochistic pleasure, which she derives from violence. Her act of killing Amit and the thoughts that occur are elaborately presented.

> She had a sudden desire to examine the body, touch the curves of cheek and chin, trace all dents, depressions, scars, probe the weakened spots until she knew just where to strike or pierce and make him bleed in the dark. Her intensity shocked her she had not considered herself susceptible to violence so she tried to explain it as unnatural sexual desire. 'Love is dread' she whispered loudly to the sleeper. (116)

And then almost like the murderess she had watched in T.V. a number of times she stabs Amit to death. Dimple's a neurotic who is pitted against the will to live and love is the will to die and destroy. There are several inter-related conditions responsible for this condition of hers which are normlessness, powerlessness, isolation and self-estrangement.

Thus, Dimple's frustration arises out of psychological barriers in the form of reality and ethical breakdown. She suffers from loneliness. Her consciousness is coulded and her mind is confused and restless. Her convictions in life are unsettled and the problems of life touch her with pain. Thus, she seeks refuge in non-involvement and inaction, which she misconstrues for freedom. But her detachment becomes a delusion, as she cannot free herself from self-engrossment and selfish desires. Here is the alienation of the soul, not of geography. It lay within her and propelled her from crisis to crisis. Her life could be summed up from the lines of *Bhagvad Gita*:

> Krodhad bhavati sammohan,
> Sammohat simriti vibhramah,
> Smriti bhramsad budhinaso,
> Bhudinasat pranasyati.[2]

From anger arise bewilderment, from bewilderment loss of memory and from loss of memory the destruction of intelligence and from the destruction of intelligence he perishes.

REFERENCES

1. Bharati Mukherjee, *Wife* (New Delhi, Sterling Publication, 1976). Subsequent page numbers in parentheses are from this edition.
2. Jaya Daya Goyanka, *Shrimad Bhagvad Gita As It Is* (With English Translation) (Gorakhpur, Geeta Press, 1984), Ch. 2, verse 63.

Communicative Chaos in Anita Desai's *In Custody*

8

BINOD MISHRA

Human existence in this world faces various onslaughts with changing times and shifting situations. The outside world, which is full of hype and hoopla, affects our inner lives insidiously. Many of us become the unwanted victims and start leading a peripheral existence, taking it as a twist of fate. Living in such a state becomes an ordeal and fans the furnace, the flames burn the bodies and give the souls numerous bruises time cannot heal. The root cause of such catastrophes is the failure of communication, which could bring cohesion and cordiality between individuals distanced by wings of time and pings of overwhelming desire.

The present paper is an attempt to understand the intricacies emanating from the lack of communication in various characters in Anita Desai's novel, *In Custody*. The paper also endeavours to unravel the miasma of society's expectations from individuals, sandwiched between desires and denials on one hand and reticence and rhapsody on the other. The need to come out of this trap, in the words of Matthew Arnold, is to ensure love for each other. Arnold says:

> Ah, love, let us be true
> To one another! for the world, which seems
> To lie before us like a land of dreams,
> So various, so beautiful, so new,
> Hath really neither joy, nor love, nor light,
> Nor certitude, nor peace, nor help for pain;
> And we are here as on a darkling plain
> Swept with confused alarms of struggle and flight,
> Where ignorant armies clash by night.[1]

The realization of such a beautiful thread that can unite can really go a long way in our subsistence.

Anita Desai is an excellent novelist in revealing the intricacies that mar human relationships. Her greatness as a fiction writer emerges in touching the dark unfathomed aspects crippling the existence of people in a fast changing electronic age. Desai's pen spills not common and day-to-day stories but it portrays the panorama of our lives, the ignorance of which can hamper the once so cordial bond of love. In a world where human beings, queued like ants, want to supersede each other, the so-called small and considered insignificant issue gets so congealed that its outlet becomes anguish. The demon of big things deforms everything and individuals pray for the god of small things, who could reform. Desai ideates such small aspects to awaken human sensitivity gone dud amid the noises of technical gadgets. Desai excels in her novels not because of her neatly woven stories but also because they are like the psychological case studies of a psychiatrist.

Desai is a writer with a purpose. The web of her stories seems complicated at times to the readers but Desai, despite her dexterous use of words, is conscious of her responsibility. She delineates the psyche of her characters no doubt, yet she's wary of the complexities pervading in society. The problem of mankind in a shifting and flexible world, the duties and responsibilities of man to man and the ability to understand the subtle shades of the complex human personality also come under Desai's discipline. Much like Virginia Woolf, Anita Desai marvelously plays with changing time and consciousness. The novel *In Custody* besides telling the story of a young couple Deven and Sarla raises an important issue, namely of the importance of communication in a technologically advanced world. The author is alive to the fact that in a scientific world of today, human relations flourish or famish because of the effectiveness or ineptitude of communication. Anita Desai's superb novel *In Custody*, apart from a commonplace story discusses at large many issues involving man and society. Dealing with the story of Deven, a college lecturer whose infatuation towards the world of imagination, of poetry, of a new world, offers peace and harmony away from the madding world of gains and losses, joys and sorrows. The novel presents a kaleidoscopic picture of the world where love, fondness, friendship and loyalty can change with a gust of wind. In a fast changing world even a bond of friendship is based upon selfishness.

The present paper also makes an attempt to show the helplessness that the characters of the novel suffer from. To begin with, Deven, the hero of the novel is an apostle of simplicity and has the depth of boundless sea whose tides are realized by him and no one else. He is a conscious being who realizes his household responsibility yet is incapable of doing anything. His fondness for poetry and his craze for popularity blind him to such an extent where wife and children are the subjects of less importance. But that does not mean his neglect of Sarla is not intentional. He feels guilty and is grateful to her parents who satisfy Sarla and Manu's world. Despite his frequent trips to Delhi, he craves for his son and wants to play with him. He oscillates between Mirpore and Delhi, between his college and Nur's Alma Mater of poetry. In his blind search of tracing Nur's poetic sparks, he fails to understand the rhythm that Sarla can offer to his poetry. It is an irony that the great poet, Nur found his inspiration in his two begums and his verses are born of his two mistresses. No doubt, Deven, too, like Nur, has his two mistresses but he prefers poetry to be his first mistress. The portrayal of women in a lighter vein in the novel is based on Desai's real experience of women's condition in Urdu poetry. In one of her interviews, Anita has admitted:

> I could hear them always screaming in the background, banging on the doors, being very hysterical. I asked myself "Why have I made all these women so awful?," and I thought "Well, if that was the house they were made to live they would probably be awful."[2]

Deven is a victim of his ambition. He places his ambition high over other diurnals. He goes an extra mile and of course, is cheated by all. His one time classmate and his only friend, Murad has an overwhelming effect on him. The editor of an

Urdu magazine uses Deven for his self vested interest. He is more business like than Deven and milches him literally. The purchase of a second-hand tape-recorder and the appointment of a boy for operation are the tricks played by Murad. Behind the mask of friendship, Murad exploits Deven's weakness for Urdu poetry. It is only at the last moment that Deven realizes the ugly face of Murad who denies him an advance for his article. Deven loses more than he could really get. But then the pecuniary loss is not a debatable question as compared to Deven's urge for poetry. The proposal for going abroad and making money as one of his colleagues cuts no ice for him. He suffers all because the poet in him is alive. The bills sent by Nur's begum and the demand for the room rent trouble him. Nur's increasing demands and Deven's sense of gratitude criss-cross. Poverty-stricken yet love-lorn Deven sympathizes with Nur. His words, though in the form of letter affect Deven with their poetic tinge. Nur's verses have a magical impact on Deven. It is a moment of delight when after much brainstorming and hectic sessions; one of Nur's begum agrees to arrange for the interview. The remuneration for such an arrangement is not a barrier at all.

Deven and Sarla's marital life suffers disharmony because of the lack of communication in it. They are familiar with each other but cordiality seems to corrode out of their union. They live like ghostly, ghastly appearances crawling reluctantly, perhaps having lost the purpose of being united or brought close to each other. Their company frightens each other and a sizzling silence stupefies where both of them want to come out to get an emotional release in the free firmament. The couple seem miles distant from the coercion, which can bring consummation in their lives. The reasons of this untimely breakdown in their coalescence are caused by their inability to make a proper rapport with each other. They fail to understand the fact that impaired communication can create chaos only. Since they communicate less, they find it difficult to face each other. Their brief chats comprise taunts and undesirable queries put under duress. Desai describes the chaos succinctly:

> The door opening on to the courtyard creaked as he released the bold, making him fear he would wake up the child as well and anger Sarla, but there was silence from both of them and once he was out, he felt relieved after all. In place of some emotional release from all that choked him, this simple physical one from the small, stifling room into the open night air would have to do.[3]

Deven's wife, Sarla, a housewife though is conscious of her position in the society. Delineated as a minor character in the novel, Sarla is alive to what's happening around. Choked inside at times and not happy with Deven's dissipating Delhi trips, she sometimes wants to burst but maintains self-restraint. Her confinement to her own world provides a camouflage to her argumentative ability. Despite the arrival of summer, Sarla is opposed to moving out cots in the courtyard since she had nightmares about 'robbers climbing over the wall and attacking them in their sleep.' The nightmare is symbolical of her insecure position in this world. Their dreams of a progressive life have had a premature death and they seem to accept what fate had in store for them. Initially a choice of Deven's family members, Sarla later feels her neglect because of her unattractive features resulted by the ravages of time. Deven, too like the members of his family, had not suspected Sarla's aspirations. Sarla's great expectations are thwarted and she resigns to her fate. But both the husband and wife share a secret. Desai sympathizes deeply with the couple:

> Although each understood the secret truth about the other, it did not bring about any closeness of spirit, any comradeship, because they also sensed that two victims ought to avoid each other, not yoke together their joint disappointments. A victim does not look to help from another victim; he looks for a redeemer.[4]

Deven's inability to understand the non-verbal feature of communication often results in his angry outbursts. Tearing his unwashed shirt and turning Manu out of the room because he was crying are signs of his emotional eruption.

A charge commonly labeled on the women characters of Desai is that they are confined to their inner selves. A number of scholars and critics attribute it to the impact of independence which provided education and gave room to a rethinking of various social stigmas. The elimination of these stigmas in later years provided women with a free environment and earmarked more space. But with some good things came some disadvantages too. And that affected not only the women but mankind as a whole. The disappearance of joint family system and the emergence of nuclear family, in a way affected the adults as well as the children. Anita Desai herself realizes the catastrophic impact of this change.

> Only the last two generations can be said to be educated, and only one has experienced the luxury of privacy. Having broken away—often amidst tears, tempers and threats—from the accepted system of daughters not receiving a regular education and from the large noisy, busting joint family, she has now acquired an education and set up her own home. This had its disadvantages—no grandmother to lull the squalling infant to sleep, no sister-in-law to help with the cooking and washing and no one, for the most of the day, to gossip with it does afford woman who craves it, with a degree of silence and privacy in which to work.[5]

Much to the realization of the readers, we find the lines of communication severed because of the absence of an elderly person (father or mother) who could facilitate the couple to break the silence and encourage the growing kids to bubble and jostle by their bedtime stories.

Deven proves himself a poor communicator throughout the novel. The reasons of his failure can be traced in his vulnerability. His ambition of being popular through his passion for Urdu poetry blindfolds him. He has ambition but he lacks the tact to fulfil his ambition. The lack of practical wisdom and cleverness of purpose have always eluded him. It is his simplicity and meekness that tempt him to be bamboozled even by his friend, Murad. Deven's message gets a wrong channel and the intermediary cause a severe barrier in his way.

Neither a glib talker like Murad and nor a charmer like Nur, Deven is exposed to the outside world and becomes a laughing stock. He is unable to effectuate the timing of his message and as a consequence, his entreaty falls on deaf ears. His impatience and his excessive avidity to interview Nur are the ample proofs of his immaturity as a communicator. Ignoring the somber mood in Nur's house when Imtiaz Begum's illness takes her to hospital, Deven asks the poet for the interview. His inability to understand the gravity of the situation at times enrages the poet. He not only ignores the role of time and place in communication but also the psychophysical condition of Nur, the poet. Desai decries and pities in the following lines:

> But he had little gift for speech, for conversation, so little practice in it, and knew only how to stumble awkwardly to the point. Gracelessly. Nur Sahib, you remember I spoke to you of this special issue of Urdu poetry in *Awaaz*? I had hoped that today—since I have come so early—we might be able to discuss it a little.[6]

The lack of proper communication dogs Deven not only at his home front but also at his workplace. Blinded by his passion for Urdu poetry, he ignores his responsibility as a teacher. His dereliction of duty had made him a boring teacher and students looked at him with utter disregard. It is quite ironical that Deven, the poet is unable to command the attention of his students. He is unable to satisfy students' curiosity not because he lacks knowledge but because he lacks the ability to understand them. He feels bored with them and tries to avoid eye contact with them. One can find Deven's reluctance and his nervousness in the following lines: 'The expression he saw—of boredom, amusement, insolence and defiance—made him look away quickly and focus his eyes upon the door at the far end of the room, the door that opened on to the passage, freedom and release.'[7] One of his senior colleagues of Hindi department, Mr. Trivedi is furious to understand Deven's frequent absence. Deven's request for a week's leave angers him and poor Deven bears Trivedi's ire. Deven is threatened to be demoted and transferred. He controls himself and leaves Trivedi's room without giving any convincing explanation.

Deven ignores his position and shows no interest in College Board's meetings. He lacks self-confidence and depends on his colleagues even for petty matters. Worried most of the time because of his job, he remains docile and maintains a low profile.

Technology, a major part of communication today plays an equal role in creating commotion in Deven's mission of recording Nur's poetry. Advised by his trusted friend and sponsored by Deven's college, the tape-recorder brings with it all sorts of complexities. Murad technically handles the show, lures Deven to buy a second hand tape recorder and also bear an appendage in the form of Chiku who'll assist in recording Nur's renditions. Desai, through the use of this mechanical device shows how our inclination to technology results in chaos. Chiku, in his effort to record Nur's verses, records all that is dross and leaves all that is to be recorded. Unable to understand the subtleties of poetry and the ever-changing moods and whims of the poet, Chiku often feigns, forgets and fails, causing much to the ire of Deven. The machine, too at times whirs, jerks and on some occasions roars. The inexperienced Chiku fails to realize the acoustics and contributes to the chaos. The benediction of proper intonation in the recitation of poetry is lost amid the hue and cry of the outside world, 'A pause would follow, not exactly of silence because outside the traffic blared and bleated and in the room the electric fans clicked wildly and a restful of sparrows in the skylight flapped and twittered but certainly of silence from the poet.'[8]

Time plays an important part in creating communicative chaos in the novel. It takes long to organize an interview with Nur who in his crapulent mood decides to recite everything without caring about the mood and backgrounds of the audience. The listeners in Nur's poetic soiree comprise street urchins and yokels having nothing to do with poetry. Their presence is because of their temptations for sumptuous food and drink. Nur, too considers himself a know it all and times without number responds to Deven's queries crazily. In reply to Deven's curiosity about his youth time poetic leanings the poet bursts:

> Poetry of the period? Do you think a poet can be ground between stones, and bled, in order to produce poetry—for you? You think you can switch on that mincing machine and I will instantly produce for you a length of raw, red minced meat that you can carry off to your professors to eat?[9]

Ironically enough we find the poet reciting his verse soberly sometimes early in the mornings before the agents of Bachchus overpowered him. Even Chiku is upset with the odd hours of Nur singing in his full-throated ease with doses of meat and biryani. Chiku, the so-called technician grumbles quite often of the singing spree twelve hours a day. He often feels drowsy and induced to sleep, forgets to turn the tape in time to record the gems sprouting forth from Nur's lips. This not only adds to the chaos but also makes Deven angry and repentant on having lost the remarkable renditions he and the world of poetry vouched for. The basic purpose of recording Nur's poetry receives a severe jolt when Nur's crowd pullers, all idle men ask him foolish questions and the poet answers them with aplomb.

Not only Nur and his followers but Deven's students, too consider him vulnerable and want to exploit from him as much as possible. The tapes, which contained less of poetry and more of noises, exchange one hand after another in order to be edited and freed from redundancies. This process brings Deven across many multi-dimensional mechanics that are good for nothing. To name a few Chiku Pintu and some of Deven's students with their self-vested interests of getting extra marks for fixing tapes make the communicative process more chaotic. Deven feels himself trapped since the tapes give much cry and little wool. His failure to provide something memorable to Urdu lovers tears him beyond repairs. The money procured from his college hangs like a Damocles' sword on him. Nur, the pernickety poet also makes Deven's life prosaic by sending his orgiastic demands. Deven's blind fascination for poetry makes him a plaything in the hands of Murad, Nur, Chiku,

Pintu and others. Deven is exploited mentally and monetarily. The poet considers even his cataract operation as Deven's responsibility and wants him to arrange for it. The mediums of Deven's communication with the poet lead him to such a chaotic stage where he smoulders and yet does not shriek having squandered much of what he had. He feels isolated and the exorcists of the charges of misappropriation of funds haunt him. He longs for a backward journey:

> He hoped his former life of non-events, non-happenings, would be resumed, empty and hopeless, safe and endurable. That was the only life he was made for, although life was not perhaps the right term. He needed one that was more grey, more neutral, more shadowy. He sifted through alternatives like torn pieces of grey paper, letting them fall to the floor of his mind with a whisper and bury him in sleep.[10]

What sprinkles salt to Deven's injury is Nur's last letter, which is an entreaty for the arrangement of his pilgrimage to Mecca when the last of his pigeons is gone. The poet puts Deven in a panicky situation considering him an all time serendipity. The failure of communication in the novel is also born of some circumstantial lapses. To call Deven a total failure would be a lop-sided view. He communicates intra personally when he finds himself unsuccessful at interpersonal communication. It is penchant for poetry enables him to ignore the practical needs and necessities of everyday life. Sarla tries her best to mend the walls but feels snubbed realizing her position. She believes in renewing the bond and goes to her parents' house. Sandwiched between Nur and Murad, Deven keeps himself plying from Mirpore to Delhi. Engrossed wholly in him pursuit he forgets to open Sarla's letter and later feels guilty when she comes back on her own. Deven undergoes an inner journey and feels the emptiness lying in his room. The atmosphere of the house too becomes chaotic when Sarla goes to her parents house. The novelist sympathizes with the dissatisfaction of the couple in the following lines: 'It was not like Sarla to leave behind largesse in any shape. The state of dereliction here was only a reflection of the dereliction of their marriage, perhaps even of themselves.'[11] This vacuity gives Deven time to realize his lapses. Nur's dilly-dally and Murad's mish-mash shatter Deven. He feels the pangs of his guilty conscience on having ignored his home and hearth. His communication with his inner self leads him to self-discovery. The readers, too, are touched to the core when Desai says, 'There was after all nothing left to do. Oddly enough, the certainty that he could expect no more help from Murad had a calming effect upon him. Perhaps when everyone had cut him off and he was absolutely alone, he would begin to find himself and his own strength.'[12]

Deven is benumbed with sensations and feels himself ill at ease. Painfully aware of damage done to Sarla, he longs to bridge the gaps, though lately. The wild cravings for fame and recognition come to flames when the noble emprise becomes nothing but a fiduciary one failing because of the frenetic fervours of queer Nur. Distraction with the outside world because of its falsities, Deven longs for relief in the sweet and sober soothings of Sarla, who appears soigné and sophisticated despite her worn clothes. Desai shows her compassion with Deven in the following lines: 'He considered touching her, putting an arm around her stooped shoulders and drawing her to him. How else could he tell her he shared all her disappointment and woe?'[13] Despite his longings, he is unable to do so since his position of power over her will be challenged. This shows his frozen evaluation and his resistance to change. He asks for Manu and snaps the tie.

Desai also is keen to say that too much of communication can mislead mankind and create chaos. Starting from Murad and then the pack of letters, reminders, requests and bills blur the basic purpose of communication. Nur's nefarious nuances of extracting much from Deven keep pouring in. His first wife's letters also adds to Deven's despair. Finally when Deven decides to come out of the ludic project, Safiya Begum's couth communication comes as a phantasmagoria to tempt Deven. But he feels disillusioned and finds himself in dander:

> How many more bills, more requests from Nur could he place before them after all? Nur would never stop

> writing, demanding. The letters would keep pouring in the way the tapes had kept on grinding. He had launched himself, and them, upon a course it now seemed impossible to stop.[14]

Deven wonders if these bills would ever come to an end or he'll have to arrange for Nur's funeral too. The wish with which he had undertaken this dream project leaves him nowhere and Deven's miserable condition reminds us of Shakespeare's Macbeth, who, too, is ruined because of his over ambition. One can find an echo of Macbeth in Deven's character:

> I have no spur
> To prick the sides of my intent, but only
> Vaulting ambition, which o'erlaps itself
> And falls on the other.[15]

Surely Deven needed a Lady Macbeth who could expedite his ambition by obviating the milk of human kindness from him in order to catch the nearest way. Macbeth, too, accepts his defeat in the end when he finds the great Birnam woods moving to Dunsinane as predicted by the witches. Deven realizes his lapses at last while explaining everything to Siddiqui. What he tells him is not only a realization but also remorse:

> I worked hard—I prepared for it and I worked—but I was fooled and cheated by everyone—the man who sold me the secondhand equipment, the technician who said he could do the recording but was completely inexperienced, by Murad who said he would pay and did not, by Nur who had never told me he wanted to be paid, and by his wife, wives, all of them.[16]

Thus an overall view of the novel tells us how communication is at stake though there's too much of it. Deven, who initiates communication comes across many who communicate and confuse him. Deven's interview with Nur undergoes serious threats because of restrictive environments, which include several distractions. The interview arranged in a busy marketplace, a room with poor acoustics, and a second-hand tape recorder with an inexperienced operator records the sounds and furies only. The audience in the room, all tipsy cheer the panicky poet and distort the message. The poet unscrupulously seeks personal gains and worsens the aim of the interview. The various agents, too, with their biased notions and self-vested interests add to the commotion. Nur's wives endeavour their best to claim their dues from the poet and their rivalry tears the poet apart. The poet's poor health, too, is behind his garbled voice. He is unable to make a balance between his personal story and poetry. This results in information overload and worries Deven. He tries his best to edit and compile and this process has many transfer stations, which cause distortion to the real message.

Likewise, Deven's communication with Murad suffers breakdown because of their differing background and lack of existence of co-operation despite a common frame of reference. Murad is every inch a professional and Deven a poet to the core. Deven's communication with Sarla suffers because they fail to sustain interest in each other and both of them hesitate to initiate meaningful conversation. Sarla's parental background and her pride over possessions given by them are impediments for Deven. Sarla and Deven also differ in their perceptions. Sarla fears Deven and Deven finds hard to face her because of his inability to fulfil his responsibilities. At times, we also come across Deven's negative emotional behaviour. Deven is of a rigid category and fails to understand the emotional currents undergoing in Sarla's mind. Deven's students and his colleagues also underrate him. He receives thrashes from his seniors and threats from his students. The atmosphere in his home also stifles him. His only consolation is his son Manu, with whom he feels relaxed and rejuvenated.

There are other symbolical agents in the novel too. The *neem* tree in his courtyard symbolizes sourness. Nur's pigeons also are sources of communication to the poet and he decides to go on a pilgrimage after the death of the last pigeon. As we all knew that for a successful communication, the importance of internal as well as external atmosphere is essential. The novel fails to establish a balance between the two. As a result, an academic endeavour of preserving a culturally rich Urdu poetry's representative voice of Nur Shahjehanbadi for the succeeding generations is defeated. At the close of the novel, the protagonist finds himself worried by the phantoms of future and forsees his son 'consider his father a failure.' The fiction *In Custody*, thus, as a whole, appears to be suffering from a communicative chaos.

NOTES AND REFERENCES

1. Matthew Arnold, *Dover Beach*.
2. Anita Desai in an Interview to Magda Costa, Published originally in Spanish Magazine *Lateral*, March 2001.
3. Anita Desai, *In Custody*. Great Britain: Penguin Books, 1984, 130.
4. *Ibid*., 68.
5. Anita Desai, "Women Writers," *Quest*, No. 65 (April-June 1970): 40.
6. Anita Desai, *In Custody*. Great Britain: Penguin Books, 1984, 113.
7. *Ibid*., 12.
8. *Ibid*., 155.
9. *Ibid*., 156.
10. *Ibid*., 183-84.
11. *Ibid*., 177.
12. *Ibid*., 190.
13. *Ibid*., 94.
14. *Ibid*., 197.
15. William Shakespeare, *Macbeth*, Act I, Scene VII, lines 25-28.
16. Anita Desai, *In Custody*. Great Britain: Penguin Books, 199.

Continual Journey to Search in *Journey to Ithaca*

9

SADHANA AGRAWAL

Human being is on an uninterrupted search. The search either for Self or for Truth or for Wisdom or for Enlightenment has been continuous since the time immemorial. The search as differently called is present everywhere not only for worldly gains but for something indefinable. The search is a truth. The truth is that man being a sojourner in this world wants to get at last united with the Lord. Hence, man's eternal journey to salvation starts and it never ends.

Anita Desai, who "occupies a distinct and distinctive place in the realm of contemporary Indian English fiction" (Bachchan 61), is undoubtedly "one of the most powerful" Indian novelists in English (Pathak 11). She is the usherer of psychological fiction in the Indian literary arena. She is an artist of a high order for "laying bare the inner recesses and the existential trauma of human beings" (Budholia 20). The exploration of human psyche, the problem of human relationships, the protagonist's quest for identity, the racial problems, the question of feminism are her main concerns made almost in all her novels from *Cry, the Peacock* to *Fasting, Feasting* but all such issues have been kept outside the purview of her novel *Journey to Ithaca* (1996). She shifts to a new subject, the persistent journey in this novel. What keeps Anita Desai preoccupied here is the idea of a continuing journey something like that of a well-known Upnishadic term 'Charaybeti' (go ahead; don't stop).

However, in this paper, the main focus will be placed on the journey undertaken by the protagonists with a fixed or unfixed intention to the search of the root of spirituality. With this intention it is better to go to search the root from where the mystery of the truth, the eternal journey of the existence starts than live as slaves without making efforts to gain something new. Suman Jana rightly quotes from 'Aitreya Brahman' (Rig Veda):

> There is no happiness for him who does not travel...
> Living in the society of man, the best man becomes a sinner...
> Therefore, wander! The feet of the wanderer's are like flowers,
> his soul is growing and reaping the fruit...
> Therefore, wander! (Jana 353)

This is the leitmotif of the novel *Journey to Ithaca.* This novel is about the soul's journey to enlightenment and awakening. Unlike E.M. Forester's *A Passage to India* which largely seems to grasp the 'mystery' and where the borderline between the 'muddle' and the 'mystery' is never clearly drawn, this novel is Anita Desai's "assertive statement that the truth, the enlightenment and the totality of an all-encompassing spirituality is in the heart of India" (Jana 353). The materialist Eurocentric vision is thus directly negated to acknowledge the existence of the mystery, the secret mystic truth of life. Journey is a recurrent theme in the literary classics of both the East and the West. Rama Kundu has given an exhaustive detail of the journey that haunted the literary mind from the days of early civilization (Kundu: Note 1, 283-84). *Journey to Ithaca* is another such journey where Ithaca ceases to be a specific place. Ithaca is the symbol of that certain light-house which eternally summons man to wander, to be in quest of spiritual truth, heart's truth, a quest for reaching one's homeland. And man's inner self is his true homeland.

In a way, *Journey to Ithaca* is about one's journey within oneself, a journey towards India—the land of the destination, the thought, the vision, and the philosophy. This novel is a saga of multiple journeys undertaken by three different characters at many different planes of existence. Three journeys form the core of the novel. While the journey of the first two Matteo and the Mother culminates in India, that of Sophie commences from India. Each of these journeys is interlinked to the others and it never ends. Suman Jana rightly says, "The value is not what you find at the journey's end, but the significance lies in one's undertaking the journey, the journey being more important than the destination, the search more meaningful than the object of the search" (Jana 354). As Desai quotes in the epigraph to *Journey to Ithaca*:

> Always keep Ithaca fixed in your mind.
> To arrive there is our ultimate goal.
> But do not hurry the voyage at all.
> It is better to let it last for long years. (3)

Anita Desai's inclusion of *Prologue* in the novel helps her disclose the inner human motives for higher values of life. In *Prologue,* the protagonist, Matteo's early life is exposed us. To Matteo, the school was like a "theorem set within a larger theorem" (17). We are informed that the school life "baffled him like the geometry and algebra" (17). He fails in school, as his answers to questions appear sullen and monosyllabic. In *Epilogue,* information about Matteo's journey to India, his marriage with Sophie and the role of his parents in nurturing their children is given. Matteo's reading of *Journey to the East* acquainted by Fabian moulds his mind towards the philosophy of *Vedanta.* Later he admits to his wife, "It was the book that opened my eyes" (8). It was "my destiny to join in a great experience...a unique journey..." (22).

Matteo's journey to Ithaca forms the centre-stage for the first part of the novel. Born in a luxuriant Italian family Matteo makes his journey in search of brightness in the heart of his Ithaca—the mystery that is in India, the India which alone is aware of that mystery. It is the India '*a punya bhumi*' where man comes across the blessed people and quenches his insatiable thirst and which has continued to influence and fascinate the Western mind in respect of "the extravaganza of natural scenes and the occult spell of a very ancient religion—oriented philosophy which seemed to mystify them beyond comprehension, and therefore, never ceased to charm" (Kundu 275).

Matteo right from his childhood had been a peculiar child defying the decency and decorum of his home. "He found the villa with its velvet hanging and tapestries and brocades stifling" (19). He considers money, more money, business, cars and hundreds of luxury items only material things (5). He feels that he does not belong to this world of his land but somewhere else lies his real life. He looks over the lake "with the eyes of a man who is planning a long voyage" (28). And finally, Matteo's journey to the East, the seed of which was sown by Hesse, began "in the summer of 1975, Sophie and Matteo, having first married to pacify their tearful and lamenting parents, left for India, dressed in identical blue jeans and T-shirts and sports shoes.... Sophie still wore her hair very short and Matteo growing his long. They left on foot" (30).

Thus Matteo and Sophie move towards India in search of peace, tranquility, the divinity, the meaning of existence and the ultimate Truth. All this is a well thought of and fully planned objective of Matteo. He wants "to find India, to understand India, and the mystery that is at the heart of India" (54). But Sophie comes to India only to provide company to her life-partner, Matteo. She asks Matteo—"I want to know why we are here" (54). He replies that it is only in India that it is possible to understand the mystery—"over there people don't even know there is a mystery.... There are people—great sages—to guide you. I need such a person" (55). Sophie, on the other hand feels suffocated and wants to leave the unsavoury atmosphere of the ashram. For Matteo,

> There is the path of joy and the path of pleasure.... Pondering on them the wise one chooses the path of joy, the fool takes the path of pleasure. (32)

But Sophie considers the path of joy and the path of pleasure the same. Anita Desai comments:

> It was true, though from the beginning it had been as though there were a design, a pattern, a pattern, to their wanderings. At every turn they seemed to be shown signs, given directions, drawn further, taken deeper, of that Matteo was convinced, and he never ceased to try and convince the scoffing Sophie. (32)

Thus from Hotel Monaco begins his designed journey. In India Matteo dressed up in wide pajamas and a cotton vest. He feels disgusted whenever Sophie reminds him of his own country. "The past is over, Sophie, ...over, over, over—not to be repeated. Don't repeat it, and he pressed his finger on her lip, hard" (41). There was an added drug of self-delusion for Matteo. The path chosen by Matteo since his early boyhood was to be a difficult task. Lack of proper guidance and knowledge about India Matteo was distracted and deceived by a series of "fake yogies" (65) and other absurd fallacies (66-70). Matteo tells Sophie that "we'll never come to know India" and Sophie asks "Why not? ...Go to Goa...to Kashmir...lie in the Sun...; but Matteo shouts back "that is not India! We must search for what it is...." Even when he fell ill he "does not need a doctor—he needs a Guru" (147). So the doctor advised him to acquire knowledge through the book—he can find the way for a flash of light. But Sophie always cursed "that damned book, the *Journey to the East*" for following "this guru of yours to your death." At this Matteo responds, "the book has opened my eyes—it does not lead to my death, but to my awakening I go." The body does not matter, not even the earthly life. My destiny seems to be "never cease seeking..." (88).

Shuttling from one ashram to another in search of a guru he steps on the first step of the ladder leading to spirituality in an ashram on the mountains in the North and at last he finds peace, joy, deep contentment under the guidance of the Mother, the head of the ashram. It seems that he is very close to his goal. He is transported to a unique experience "an experience of unity, the unity of the spiritual with the physical, the dark with the light, the human with the natural.... The Divine force is everywhere.... Everywhere we turn...we come upon the divine power. Turn, Turn—where you turn.... Be open to the divine" (99). Having found his guru, Matteo as a seeker after truth says: "What matters is—is the search. She takes me with her on her search" (84). Sophie tries to coax and asks, "What do you hope to find Matteo?" "I have found it, I have; what I never had before, what my life had been empty of—and now it is not" (88). In this way his journey comes to an end in total surrender to the mother with the firm belief that she is the "one who can reveal the unknown to me" (141).

Matteo was very much impressed by the enlightening lecture of the 'Mother' and her personality: "You must know I mean honey made from spiritual nectar, to nourish your souls. All organizations are useless and dry and empty, if they do not contain the nectar of the spirit. I want it to be rich, rich, rich with this nectar" (118). Matteo as *sadhaka* considers this "nectar" as the essence of life. Without any question and grumbling he willingly did, whatever he was asked to do with all patience. He even scrubbed dirty pans and pots day in and day out without any single frown and hesitation. He confessed the higher and nobler vision of "niskama karma." So he followed blindly the teachings of the Mother before his wife, Sophie: "She teaches us to work without desiring the fruit from that work. Isn't that a higher way of life" (120). He realized love as the central part of the thing for God realization. Matteo admitted his sacred love towards the mother:

> Sophie, my love for her isn't the love one feels for a beautiful or glamorous or intriguing woman, a legend, as you say. You must see that! There is a difference between sacred and profane love. Listen, in her presence I feel I am more alive than I am in the presence of any other living creature.... When I leave her, I feel I am falling, down, down into darkness. No, not darkness but greyness, flatness, emptiness. (136)

More and more words from the mother made Matteo spell-bound. She also told, "Always remember the master.... I am there to drive away Darkness and remove screens so that.... See the master and his light.... Awake, O man, from thy deep sleep, Awake...." Matteo remained in the air in the void, hardly breathing, hardly existing, only that particular moment mattered. He felt, "Why even the paradisaical surroundings of his home on the lakes had been for him empty and desperate—because no one had been there to show him that they were an expression of an eternal and essential truth" (107). The untiring devotion of Matteo made the Mother please and she expressed, "...yes, yes, Mat-t-eo is planning to join us. Mat-t-eo is going to stay" (123).

Matteo realizes that truth comes to him in the form of an experience of bliss—"*anandam kevalam*" as expressed in the *Upanishads*: A 'bliss' that comes with a sense of being 'loved' (93). Following the secular image of India about the presence of God in the heart of man, creating the character like Mother, Desai, who is working on the universal norms of life, puts the words in the mouth of Mother about the futility of all religions—the truth, the mystery thus:

> It is not like going to the church.... Not like going to the temple...we do not bring any offering with us.... We have no religion. Religion? Like the black crown up in the tree caw-caw-caw.... We do not listen to the black scolding voices of religion here. Religion makes one ashamed, makes one guilty, makes one fearful. The master has told you not to feel guilty, not to feel ashamed, not to be afraid...open your hearts to love and light and the joy of loving. (93)

Matteo finds in the ashram *Kripa*, *Diya*, *Prema,* a community of bliss, selfless love and joy. But Sophie's Eurocentric points of view prevent her from comprehending the essential nature of bliss. In this connection Suman Jana writes, "Matteo seems to have plunged into the genuine interests in life, an obliteration of personal goals, goals which ever prevent one on embarking a glorious journey to Ithaca. Sophie cannot drown her rational analytical Europeanised mindset into the ever-flowing deluge of love. She wants a palpable tangible comprehension of the Truth through rational scanning.... Matteo...gradually learns to stop struggling, to allow the master to pick him up and carry him" (Jana 362-63).

Helpless, unhappy, exhausted and constrained Sophie feels like "a beast in cage" (79) following Matteo. She never wants to move from ashram to ashram scratching mosquito bites; she only wants to lead a decent, comfortable life of a normal western couple, no-nonsenselife of hard work what she finds at last living with Matteo in the ashram—nothing but hostility and unacceptance. She urges Matteo to return to his land to work for his father's business, not to work here for the Mother. But Matteo shouts back, "Mother does not make me work for anything—she teaches us, work without desire, work without fruit...the higher way of life." Thus the distance between them widens to complete break down and she finds "Matteo had vanished in the heart of the world that remained shut to her" (121). Sophie considers the Mother only a woman: "Call her what you like—the cosmic, the absolute but she's a woman" (141). She feels jealous of the Mother and regards her "a monster spider who had spun this web to catch these silly flies" (121).

The constant jealousy of a woman in Sophie makes her enquire all about the past of the Mother and so she leaves the company of her husband. Her curiousness paves the way her to find out her arrival in India as a dancer, "looking for a rich somebody to pick her up" (131). Thus Sophie undertakes a more interesting and complex journey to peep into the past of the Mother "to travel back, back in time, although not her own time but the Mother's" (155), and also to explore into the past of the "paradoxical, contradictory" woman who "looks Indian, sounds Indian, but not Indian" (125).

Finally Sophie leaves India with her children first to her parents' home in Frankfurt and then to the villa on the lakeside which was larger, warmer in Italy. Out of the ashram she feels alienated herself from the mundan world outside. She finds herself misfit with the so-called normal people which she had longed for. The thought of Matteo living in the ashram in India torments Sophie's soul. Unconsciously she too was pursuing the ways of Matteo. She thought of not talking about India, but when a telegram informed that Matteo was taken to the hospital, she at once packed her bag, bought the ticket with such speed that it seemed nothing mattered to her now, she just wanted to be with her Matteo. She realized that though physically away, her mind had been with Matteo all this time. Feeling relieved regarding her children's safety with their grandparents, she realizes that in her determination to discover the truth about the mother she had actually abandoned her children as much as Matteo had abandoned her in his search and that "in following her she is entering an area of the chill, bleak, bitterness of renunciation" (238). "The Mother's life, her past, the reality behind legend, is rediscovered in pieces and plots, through which ultimately the whole emerges. It is not merely Sophie's journey through Alexandria, Caire, Paris, Venice, and New York to India, that Sophie reaches her Ithaca, her truth, her enlightenment, it is ultimately a journey within, a real pilgrimage into the heart of the beckon, a meaningful journey, a sojourn into the awakened awareness of the real face of India where all masks dissolve into insignificance" (Jana 366).

Sophie is now very eager to see Matteo, to share the truth about the Mother that she has discovered. When Sophie arrives the hospital, they inform her that Matteo has left the hospital and gone. No one is able to tell her where could he go. Sophie is confused. She realizes the futility of her quest, for the Mother is already dead and Matteo has left the place to pursue his search. As she herself admits, the journey provides her "nothing much" about the mother (296) it has revealed to her "why the Mother went on that pilgrimage, why everyone goes on a pilgrimage and why she must go too" (298). Sophie is of the view that one quest ends only to begin another, a totally different one. Sophie comes to know through the senses the higher position of Matteo as a seeker after truth in the guidance of the mother: "The urgency to see Matteo, to tell and reveal, had so overtaken her, she had not thought that for Matteo too, the wheel had turned" (303). The word "wheel" stands for the transformation of Matteo as a regenerated man. Sophie was informed that Matteo would travel north to the mountains where the Mother had received enlightenment and light—and might find peace. Sophie also feels burning with the fire of spiritual thoughts. Ultimately she decides to follow the path and ideas of Matteo as a seeker. When it was asked, "Will you follow him," she says to Diya "I'll have to.... What else?" (297). As Budholia writes, "She now intends for completing an inner journey of consciousness like Matteo for esoteric experiences. Thus, Desai through her visionary perspectives achieves a great success in this novel by outlining the higher values of human love, humanism, realism, mysticism and unified code for the universal vision of brotherhood" (Budholia 25).

It is Sophie's hindered examination to set free Matteo from the enchanting woman that takes her to Egypt, Venice, Paris and New York to reconstruct the Mother's past. Her search reveals another peculiar journey of a young, different and determined girl Laila, the daughter of Hamid and Alma. Laila like other heroines of Anita Desai seems to become rebellious for her spiritual quest and finally comes to India for her spiritual emancipation. Like Matteo, Laila is misfits, uniquely dislocated from their ambience. She is an odd, headstrong and independent child-causing headache to her parents and teachers. She too considers the home an inadequate shelter, it is like a prison trapping her freedom. Longing for something different she cannot conform to the conventions of her society. Her insuperable desire for some sublime experience led her astray, even to a revolutionary camp. But nothing could sustain her for long: "What drew her would have been hard for anyone to tell at that stage for the truth was that she was drawn in one direction, then another, wherever she saw passion taken to its extreme, whether celebratory or ascetic" (167).

So Laila is sent to Paris to her French aunt, Francoise. From here her odyssey begins. From college she does not return home but roams around the city. Once she joins Madame Beaunier's dancing class but very soon she starts defying Madame Beaunier and explains that for her dance is a divine expression, something which can never be learnt in mechanical routine. Her momentous encounter with the hagdeh who professed her future "eastwards to find a temple...the temple of the Mother Goddess of the World (170) propelled her disturbed soul to a new direction. But it was a poster announcing "Krishna Lila" pinned to the door of curio shop that transfigured her life. The two words Krishna and Lila, together and in separate forms caught her like a snare and precisely at that moment "she was confronted by her true self" (192).

Suman Jana remarks: "Thus she desperately pleads to the dancer/Krishna to adopt her, train her and make her an Indian dancer, hoping to dance the Krishna Lila and in her dance offer herself to the real Krishna. It is through this dance that she hopes to find her enlightenment, her Ithaca" (Jana 370). Her eagerness and devotion to "meet the great sun, the great light" shut her to the reality that he was only wearing the costume of Krishna. The reality that this "Krishna had shown her only devotion to world success" when finally dawned on her she had already travelled far into the East. Laila as a Muslim girl revolts against her parental religion, asserting "I am a seeker after truth and have given up all orthodox religions...I find them the repositories of ignorance and suppression" (199).

Her strong conviction that there must be a master somewhere to show her "luminous wisdom, ... the answer to her queries" (283) finally enabled her to find him in the North of India. For Laila, the truth lies in India and it is in India, through the means of dance, would she arrive at her Ithaca, her enlightenment. On her journey to the Himalayas, with the desire to be free of this world, to escape into a better and brighter one, she had the vision of Eternal light setting her on fire: "I was on fire, the tree was on fire, light blazed and the whole sky was illuminated" (286). At the mountains her "soul too set out in quest" and her dance in prayer and joy brought the Master to her pronouncing her 'Shakti' and the 'Supreme Power.' Her earlier attempts to seek through dance the harmony between the body and the mind, thought and action, the world and the spirit had brought her only disharmony. But now her soul got satiated. Henceforth the Master and the devotee became one and she became the Supreme of the ashram after him. There ended the most turbulent phase of her search providing her bliss, wisdom, enlightenment and her great transformation from Laila to the Mother which paved the way for many a search. As a dancer she fails, but as a seeker after truth, she succeeds in fulfilling the final goal of her life.

There are two women who revolt in this novel against their surroundings: Sophie and Laila. Sophie longs for worldly freedom while Laila aspires for spiritual freedom. As Suman Jana writes, "Sophie's actual journey to Ithaca begins from India (after her second visit) and ends in India with the revelations from the Mother's diary.... The Mother's journey to Ithaca had ended in Prem-Krishnaji, Sophie's journey to Ithaca ends with her discovery of the Mother's past, but it is Matteo's journey to Ithaca that actually is on. Matteo's final journey begins from the Mother's ashram. He becomes a pilgrim of eternity" (Jana 372).

Journey to Ithaca is undoubtedly a fresh creation of Desai where she, as Budholia suggests, "united varied groups of people from different parts of the world in order to present cosmic vision of human life. The novel transcends the barriers of caste and creed. The incomplete journey of Hugo in *Baumgartner's Bombay* for his spiritual quest comes to its completion in *Journey to Ithaca.* The chief protagonist of this novel, Laila, defies social code and comes above the narrow round of caste, creed and a particular religion for attaining the higher vision of human life" (Budholia 29). Desai seems to confess about carrying a European core in her, which protested against certain Indian things, which always maintained its independence and separateness. It seems also that Desai writes about India as an Indian, her root, her origin, her destination lies here but thinks about it as an outsider. In *Journey to Ithaca* Desai maintains to achieve something unmatched. Desai foresees in afterlife that all religions of the world would mingle into a single stream, representing the religion of humanity depicting the character, Laila. She also concentrates on how to bring spiritual change in man and "attains a harmonious, clear vision of India, a sense of delighted, joyous, serene fulfilment" (Kundu 283). Thus *Journey to Ithaca* is totally a different novel from the other novels of Anita Desai, a novel of persevering journey to the root of spiritual origin (*Gyan*) like the Indian concept of *anantyatra* the seed of which lies deep down only in India.

WORKS CITED

Bachchan, A.K. "Anita Desai's *Journey to Ithaca:* A Novel of Spiritual Quest." *The Indian Journal of English Studies.* Vol. XLI. 2003-04, 161-69.

Budholia, O.P. "Journey Beyond the Senses: An Analysis of Anita Desai's Journey to Ithaca" in *Critical Responses to Anita Desai.* Ed. Shubha Tiwari. Vol. 1. New Delhi: Atlantic Publishers and Distributors, 2004.

Desai, Anita. *Journey to Ithaca.* New Delhi: Ravi Dayal Publishers, 1996.

Jana, Suman. "*Journey to Ithaca:* a quest Novel" in *Critical Responses to Anita Desai.* Ed. Shubha Tiwari. Vol. 2. New Delhi: Atlantic Publishers and Distributors, 2004.

Kundu, Rama. "'Journey to the East' Once Again: Anita Desai's *Journey to Ithaca,*" in *Critical Responses to Anita Desai.* Ed. Shubha Tiwari. Vol. 2. New Delhi: Atlantic Publishers and Distributors, 2004.

Pathak, R.S. "The Alienated Self in the Novels of Anita Desai," in *Indian Women Novelists.* Ed. R.K. Dhawan. Set 1, Vol. 2. New Delhi: Prestige Book, 1991.

Jasmine: A Rebel Against Traditional Conservatism

10

G.A. GHANSHYAM

> What did this journey mean, this new world mean: discovery? or a return to terrors he had sailed from, known before?
>
> —Edward Brainwhite

Women have, to their credit, a whole series of literary achievements over the last decade, and the fact that creative writing has spread to a great extent to the urban middle class and is a hopeful sign of increased literary output. Current women authors have taken up the issue of alienation in most of their novels. Alienation from self, from family and from society are the themes dealt with by many authors like Anita Desai and Shashi Deshpande. Closely related to this issue is the cultural alienation by men and women migrating to other countries leaving their motherland due to different reasons. This issue of cultural alienation by South Asians specially Indians migrating to abroad has been vividly taken up by Bharati Mukherjee, a contemporary women writer from India settled in America.

Jasmine[1] (1990) another novel of Bharati Mukherjee is primarily a novel of cultural transplantation. Different from *Wife* it presents a diametrically opposite picture of the women who can be termed as the 'New Woman.' This woman has come to signify the awakening of woman into a new realization of her place and position in family and society. Conscious of her individuality, the new woman has been trying to assert her right as a human being and is determined to fight for her survival.

Jasmine is a bold story of a young widow and her successful attempt to reshape her destiny and achieve happiness. It does not appeal to her imagination to be a suffering and sacrificial individual. As she feels the need for self-expression and individual fulfilment, she begins to question the conventions and defies the tradition which tends to undermine her importance and individuality. Thus, *Jasmine* is the story of a rebel, who revolts against the existing moral codes and social norms, which either in theory or in practice relegate woman to a secondary place.

Born in a poor family and doomed to widowhood by an astrologer Jyoti is married to a young ambitious professional Prakash who is determined to change her.

> He wanted to break down the Jyoti I'd been in Hasnapur and make me a new kind of city woman. To break off the past he gave me a new name Jasmine. (77)

But Jyoti the stern woman proves herself to be unlike the village girls and after her husband is shot down by the Khalsa Lions she decides to go to America on her own to fulfil the unfinished dreams of her husband.

Her journey from India to America is an attempt to reshape her own destiny. It also signifies the rejection of her old traditional Indian shelf in favour of a more liberated, free and sensuous American life. But behind this bold step of going to America, one can visualize Jasmine's attempt to escape from the tradition bound, conservative society of Hasnapur where "bad luck dogged-dowryless wives, rebellious wives, barren wives. They fell into wells, they got run over by trains, they burned to death heating milk on kerosene stoves" (85). America comes across as the land of freedom and promise and self-fulfilment, where there is a premium on individual effort and where man-woman relationships are based on mutual and equal partnerships. It is in America she is introduced to the transitoriness of human life and realizes:

> In America, nothing lasts I can say that now and see it doesn't shock me but I think it was the hardest lesson of all for me to learn. We arrive so eager to learn to adjust

> to participate, only to find the monuments are plastic.... Nothing is forever.... (181)

Good looking and attractive her arrival to America is followed by a series of adventures first these in the 'half-face' who in the guise of helping her out from a difficult situation outrages her modesty. But here we get a very different reaction from a naïve village girl and 'Kali' like she wrecks her own revenge and slits the throat of her rapist. Thus, we are introduced to the 'New Woman' who refuses to suffer and whose survival instinct is strong enough to help her through moments of crisis. The ruthlessness suggested by the word 'murder' is part of her evolving consciousness as she comes to terms with America *vis-à-vis* her past. Jasmine is a fighter, survivor and achiever.

With the help of Mrs. Gordon she ultimately reaches the 'Professor' who could have helped her I realizing Prakash's dreams. But stifled by the claustrophobic atmosphere she makes the Professor promise to acquire her a green card and in return promises to keep his secret.

Each incident of her life lends her strength and after every mishap she emerges out even more determined to survive. With the help of her Lutheran benefactress she becomes 'Caregiver' to Wylie and Taylor and their little girl Duff. Now here we witness a strong emotional relationship between Taylor and herself when his wife Wylie decides to leave him for her lover Stuart. But the relationship does not last long and after seeing Prakash's assassin around she takes no time in deciding to leave Taylor and her love for her survival. The transformation is quick and she is in terms with the transitory American life. Thus the contrast between the old Indian world and America is a contrast between annihilation of personality or self-negation on the one hand and triumph and fulfilment on the other hand. Jyoti emerges as a strong character who pushes everything within her aside to succeed in the 'mission' she has undertaken. It is the saga or story of a woman who refuses to commit suicide under adverse circumstances and propels herself on a journey of self-discovery and self-satisfaction.

While with Bud is crippled and whose child she is carrying when it comes to choosing between him and Taylor, she sheds another of her Indian aspect that of dutifulness and without even a pang of guilt chooses Taylor. Jasmine comments:

> I have had a husband for each of the woman I have been, Prakash for Jasmine, Taylor for Jase, Bud for Jane, Half-face for Kali. (197)

The absence of any feeling of guilt over leaving Bud reveals the undominatable spirit of Jasmine. Instead of marrying Bud and being tied down to a conventional life she chooses the vast expanse of freedom and liberty by remaining single and moving out with Taylor. By the end of the novel she emerges to be in total control of her life steering it according to her wishes. In the novel, nowhere is the question of sexual morality raised, suggesting that it is of no importance to her.

Jasmine is a more positive and optimistic character than Tara and Dimple, who seems to assimilate into American culture much easily. In the case of Jasmine, who has been a rebel of a sort from her childhood, social ceremony may have little relevance for her. In any case, the social or legal processes of getting married have no meaning for Jasmine, as she never married anyone of her so-called "husbands" except Prakash. But here she equates even rape with marriage! In her feminist zeal, she seems to subvert even the very fundamental feminist position for sexual freedom. Clark Blaise's writes about Calcutta and Indian mores: "Family, family, family. In India all is finally family. If we in the West suffer the nausea of disconnectedness, alienation, anomy, the Indian suffers the oppression of kinship" (1977). Jasmine's journey of self-actualization leads her not just to a comfortable life and fluid identities but to forging new alliances to form what she, as an Indian, is obsessed with—that is, family.

Thus, Bharati Mukherjee through her novel *Jasmine* has attempted to project woman as the central figure and has succeeded in presenting the predicament of woman most effectively. Through her intuitive perception and insight she has tried to present her problems and perplexities and the complex working of their inner-selves and their emotional involvement and disturbances. Though the much-honoured

'Sita' image still holds the sceptre, the pulsating heartbeat of the humane woman is felt in general and is occasionally even sympathized with. Thus, she presents a life-size picture of the contemporary woman with all her longings and aspirations hopes and frustrations.

WORKS CITED

Mukherjee, Bharati. *Jasmine*, 1989. New Delhi: Penguin, 1990.

Blaise, Clark and Bharati Mukherjee. *Days and Nights in Calcutta.* New York: Doubleday, 1977.

Woman: Her-Self and the Other, Conflict and Resolution in *The Dark Holds No Terrors*

11

S. AMBIKA

Down the ages, the place of women in the tradition-bound, male-dominated Indian society has been quite unenviable. Under colonial rule, the image of nation or culture as a woman worked to evoke both female power and female helplessness, as they were granted limited agency. Despite the unstinting efforts of social reformers like Ram Mohan Roy, Bal Gangadhar Tilak, Mahatma Gandhi and many others and despite the steady growth of women's organizations and movements, and the advent of declarations and constitutional rights in favour of women, the position of women in economic, social, political and cultural strata of Indian society continues to remain far from reassuring. For the post-independence Indian women, society was not completely free from the material realities and the modes of representation common to colonialism and patriarchy. As a result Indian women found themselves doubly colonized.

Feminism and post-colonialism share the mutual goal of challenging the various forms of oppression and gender difference. Both are fundamentally concerned with the politics of othering, marginalisation and the construction of a subaltern or subordinated subjectivity by colonialism and/or patriarchy. Gayatri Chakravorty Spivak, Trinh T. Minh-ha and Chandra Talpade Mohanty are some of the popular post-colonial theorists. Spivak's "Can the Subaltern Speak?" is a bold attempt to empower the third world women by speaking to and not for them.

Shashi Deshpande is one among the prominent women writers writing in post-independence India who has nine novels and five short story collections to her credit. Deshpande was born and brought up in Dharwad, Karnataka, and is the daughter of the renowned Kannada dramatist and Sanskrit Scholar, Sriranga, who is described as the Bernard Shaw of Kannada theatre. A close study of Deshpande's novels and short stories reveals an author who is intelligent, articulate and relatively free from prejudices regarding gender, but at the same time, highly sensitive to the issues concerning women. The relentless probing of man-woman relationship by the author intrigues the reader enough to question her stand on feminism. Despite her vehement denial of being a feminist, Deshpande's novels contain a great number of issues that can be regarded as the staple material of feminist thought, like women's sexuality, gender roles, and a ceaseless attempt at self-discovery. But she accepts that she is a feminist if at all, only in a certain specific sense as she says in one of her collection of essays "Why I am a feminist," "I believe that the female of the species has the same right to be born and survive, to fulfil herself and shape her life according to her needs and the potential that lies within her as the male has. And how can feminism be anti-men when it is really working for a better, a more meaningful and companionable relationship between man and woman" (83).

Since the crux of the problem of man-woman relationship is closely concerned with the change of human mind and heart, and the crusade is against centuries of established and traditionally sanctified system, the change is not likely to be as fast and easy as is expected. In order to make this process of change smooth and meaningful, it is necessary to study, understand and expose those human factors that affect this process of change.

The title becomes significant, loaded with words like "Self" and "Other" represented by the women protagonists of Deshpande, the "Self" being the alienated female subjectivity, the 'I' that craves for recognition and strives to assert its individuality. The "Other" revolves around notion of difference, generally a way of defining oneself by designating a person as Other by placing him/her outside or in opposition to a norm. The study deals with protagonists passionate quest for Self and to identify the priorities of Deshpande's revealed through the psyche of her characters, one coinciding with the other. Deshpande, who portrays an inside view of a woman's world, writes of the suffering of these women who try to strike a balance between the roles the society expects them to play and the role that they wish to play.

Deshpande's protagonists are caught up in a conflict between wifehood and motherhood on the one hand, and their careers and fulfilment of the desires of their soul on the other. The tension arising out of this conflict is further accentuated by the confusion that prevails within the heroines themselves, who struggle for answers to questions of identity and for solutions to their psychological dilemmas. "Knowledge" says Deshpande in her essay, *Writing from the Margin*, "after all, 'always starts from within, it comes out of the fight with oneself' as I heard the noted writer Prof. U.R. Ananthmurthy once say, it originates in the questions one asks of oneself" (151). In their desire to be more of themselves they struggle to find their own voice and struggle continuously in an effort to define themselves by means of an inner search.

The identity question she deals with is as old as human nature. Ever since man became aware of his self, he took rapid and insightful strides towards realizing it; there has been an ongoing search for the unattainably attainable. Of the two aspects of this question, the crisis of identity implies the overbearing inflated ego covering up the self. The quest for the self means moving in the direction of diluting the ego or the 'I' in realizing the self. It is reflected in various shades and modes. For the first, it is an individual question, but sometimes it acquires the extent and significance of being social or natural, wherein the individual just recedes into the background. Obviously, the identity question has been the basic paradox of life and so will it ever be.

On the physical plane, when it is an individual question, it presents a queer, confused, illusion-layered, tension-ridden, fragmented, alienated, and distorted personality—a nearly perfect model of the crisis of identity, which is, perhaps, the major problem an individual of the present times experiences psychologically. When individuals come into contact and confrontation with others, there arises in them a need for the quest, and the inevitable striving begins. The chief concern in Deshpande's novels is, evidently, self-assessment, which she presents through realistic techniques. First, there is the fear to face oneself. Then, there is the reason to fear oneself. The reason is, in fact, the want of moral courage and the anxiety of possible loss of happiness, which is more often than not illusory. Even though illusory, this fear drives them on and finally, they discover a way to evade it and regain their own selves. This strange phenomenon reveals that fear does not exist at all. Deshpande, through her women protagonists, is in constant search of meaning and the purpose of life in relation to her existence as an individual. But self-psychosis is a forbidding condition to reckon with, as it creates hurdles in the way of gaining one's own identity, although it is only a one-moment-realization and the person knows what he/she is. Unfortunately, the malaise is that individuals do not know what they want to know, or know only that they do not have the courage to know what they are. And, in this 'catch 22' situation, they can be happy only when they rise to the occasion, and do what is expected of them.

As Deshpande's objective is to probe into the deeper layers of human sensibility, she shows that an individual's basic desire is to be himself/herself, but the pressure of external factors is so overpowering that this basic desire is lost in wilderness. What Paul West remarks about Faulkner's characters is, perhaps, applicable to Deshpande's characters, too: "Before a man can be valuably involved with others, he has to be himself—have a clear sense of himself. But identity is a process, not a fixity and the result is that, as Gide complained of Henry James's characters, 'men never seem to exist except in relation to each other'" (256).

Man innately knows what he should seek; still he wants to secure and possess what his ambition and self do not require.

Later, he repents, but this repentance is without remorse for the illusion that has been the basis of his life till then. The garb of hypocrisy that covers his personality leaves him ultimately a helpless creature fit only for self-pity in some rare moments of objective analysis. He drifts afar from his 'ME' and then revolves around the life-machine, impatient, artificial, confused, and scared. As self-psychosis is her prime concern, death, loneliness, and the alienated self become Deshpande's murky realms through which Deshpande wades towards her yet-to-be attained goal of securing a satisfying glimpse of the meaning of life, identity, and her own individuality.

Deshpande's protagonists want to be free and individualistic, but not at the cost of losing domestic harmony. They are intensely aware of the need for harmony in the family, and are very cautious that they do not disrupt their family life. It is these conflicting feelings that force the typical Deshpande protagonist to be more of *her-self*, and act according to what her self-awareness dictates, a process that inevitably results in various encounters and misunderstandings. The female protagonists of Deshpande's novels seem to be more of themselves when they are away from their routine life, that is, *back home* or *return home* where they spent their childhood—the place where they can freely indulge in introspection turning wholly inward. In *The Dark Holds No Terrors*, Saru comes back to her father's place to find comfort and solace after her nightly nightmarish experience with her husband. The instinctual sense that they should act according to their inner calls and wishes, and not live as slaves listening forever to what their *others* dictate, is evident in the way Saru goes against her mother by choosing Medicine as her career. Curiously enough, here, the *other* is Saru's mother, a woman! The reason may be that Saru's mother, who has all along been treated as the *other* in an essentially patriarchal society, imposes this *otherness* on her daughter. Saru's defiance can also be analysed as an inherent quality. As Premila Paul observes, "Saru is highly self-willed and her problems ensue because of her outsized ego and innate love for power over others" (61). It is evident also in her choice of husband, who is a non-Brahmin. She considers her marriage as instrumental in creating in her the typical middle-class inhibition. Marriage seems to be the open sesame of all enjoyment for her. But that happiness is always so "unreal," "full of illusions" (40). And how "there was no 'I' then, not as yet, craving for recognition, satisfaction" (53). But even at times when the 'I' craves for recognition and satisfaction, it is accompanied by a sense of guilt that the 'I' should not dominate a male, "as if I was doing something that took away shreds of my feminity" (53).

Saru's frustration develops to such an extent that she is ready even to leave him. "Can I divorce my husband?" (97), she thinks at one stage. And she is ready to sacrifice anything, and in her own words, "Even my work? Yes, even that" (78), "To sleep alone in a room, to be myself on a bed, to be untouched, unhandled" (80). "A picture of grace, harmony and happiness. Could I not achieve that?" (80). When reminded of her mother's domination in her family, Saru decides that she should never take after her. But she experiences incidents in her own married life when, at times, she goes against her husband's wishes. And, to her, strangely, it is not a rebellious or assertive act. On the other hand, she feels that "there was something outside herself driving her on", and "that her own will counted for nothing." "Can one never control one's life? Do we walk on chalked lines drawn by others?" (86). Self-interrogations as these are suggestive of the fact that she leads a hypocritical life, hiding her real feelings and emotions. Or, hers is a rather split personality. But she shows that she has an inner strength in her that drives her to have "a conception of the kind of life I wanted" (92). In order to achieve her goal she even goes in search of the "fairy God father to make things easier, miraculously, wonderfully, easier for me...if only I could please him" (92). Saru finds how difficult it is for her to change the course of her life. To quote from the text, "She remembered having read somewhere in a magazine may be, Betty Friedan, saying that it was easier for her to start the women's lib movement than to change her own personal life" (107).

The Dark Holds No Terrors is about the quest of an anxious, eager, ambitious, self-assertive and self-righteous woman, Sarita (Saru) who regains her *self* fairly successfully. Her quest leads to uncover that strength in human beings which makes living a pleasurable possibility. The untitled observation made by Deshpande, the novelist, so autobiographical in tone, just before the beginning of the novel reveals the traumatic experience of a woman who is conscious of her individuality. She writes:

> It was a monstrous invasion of my body. I tried to move, twisting my body, wriggling under the weight that pinned it down. It was impossible. I was pinioned to a position of an abject surrender of myself. I began, in sheer helplessness, to make small whimpering sounds, piteous cries...I could not, I would not bear it. I began to fight back, hopelessly, savagely. (10)

Obviously enough, it is Saru who is referred to here. Nevertheless, the terrible experience portrayed here is every helpless woman's experience.

Saru does not want to regard her sufferings and depressions as the common problems of women. Her hesitancy in revealing her difficulties to her friend Nalu is clear evidence. To quote from the text, "But to her, I would be a woman, my problems a part of women's problems. But this is mine, Saru's and has as much to do with I am, apart from my being a woman" (121). The feeling that she is an individual is clearly evident in her words: "My life is my own.... Somehow, she felt as if she had found it now, the connecting link. It means you are not just a strutting, grimacing puppet, standing futilely on the stage for a brief while between areas of darkness" (220). Saru's frankness and openness come out to the open when she confesses, "But the thought...I am a woman...had come to her when she had first felt a male look at her" (123). Another instance of her candidness occurs when she mourns her losses in her life, "the thing she knew she had lost forever...the eternal female dream of finding happiness through a man. It would never come alive for her again. Too soon, I lost it too soon, she thought" (124). Saru identifies herself with cloistered, bridled women. She is reminded of Virginia Woolf's "room of her own" (135). "But neither she nor I have that thing 'a room of our own'" (136). The amount of depression and frustration she herself experiences, and the injustices meted out to womenfolk, on the whole, by the patriarchal society that makes her feel, "No partnership can ever be equal will always be unequal, but take care that it's unequal in favour of your husband" (137). "You can nag, complain, henpeck, whine, moan, but you can never be strong" (137). Marriage life, according to her, should open new vistas of life—preserving her inner happiness. But, "To get married, and end up doing just what your mother did, seemed to me not only terrible but damnable" (140).

Saru is also reminded of Shakespeare's plays and says how "woman recedes into the background" "Cordelia recedes into the background." "Cordelia, Ophelia, Desdemona. Poor, feeble shadows" (156). She is reminded of a typical man's view of life "the man at the centre, the woman always on the periphery" (156). In the context of the domestic disharmony that erupts between husband and wife, she wonders, "who is the victim and who is the predator? Are the roles so distinct, so separate? Or are we, each of us, both?" (159). Her bitter experiences in life and her frustrations, seem to be a hurdle for her in performing her duties perfectly as a mother. She wonders at herself, as "Was she an unnatural, unloving mother? She had sworn that she would never fail her children in love and understanding as her own mother had done" (161). When she thinks of Renu, she says, "Would she not fail her as her own mother had failed her?" (162). Her dejection makes her feel, "Every thing in a girl's life, it seemed, was shaped to that single purpose of pleasing a male. But what did you do when you failed to please?" (163).

Saru's inner urge to talk openly and frankly and her interest to have somebody to talk with have been completely suppressed as she, in her introspective mood, says, "Part of it was, perhaps, the usual adolescent turmoil, the restrained, suppressed sexuality of a growing girl; part must have been my growing dislike of the atmosphere at home. And there was no one, absolutely no one with whom I could really talk" (169). Saru's strong sense asserting herself to show her individuality is seen when she is reminded of her daughter Renu's birthday when she runs after her father. She thinks, "clinging, pleading, the eternal female, the thing I detest above all" (173). Saru's grievances are brought out in her words, "She was not a wife, not a mother, not a professional woman whom others looked up to. She was the wronged child again, the unloved daughter, the scapegoat" (182). Saru's sense of expiation and her condescension and her sense of remorse at what she has done to her mother and Dhruva show her eventual realization. "It's because I wronged her that I'm suffering now. And the more I suffer, the greater the chance, perhaps of my expiating that wrong" (204). Her remorse and her inability to bypass the present situation or the present patriarchal society is reflected in her words, "Telling all women for all time...your duty to ME comes first" (207). Saru becomes more philosophical towards the end after undergoing many psychic ordeals when she says, "It's my life. It's my life." "We come into this world alone and go out of it alone. The period in between is short. And all those ties we cherish as eternal and long-lasting are more ephemeral than a dewdrop" (208) and when she says, "I'm a realist. We are realists. We deal with the ultimate reality ...the human body" (208). Saru has both, "the suffering as well as the guilt" (219). Her determination to sustain the family values, and conviction that she is not interested in the disruption of family life are very clear in her realisation which makes her philosophical towards the end, when she concludes and consoles herself that arranged marriages would eventually end up in good in the sense that the parents would be there to support the girl in case of a breakdown in the marriage. And when she thinks, "therefore the only thing is to go on as if it is real, knowing all the while it is only an illusion" (220). She boldly claims, "My life is my own" (220). She feels that since she failed to assert herself in each and every situation, as sister, daughter and wife, she has been forced to cling to the tenuous shadow of marriage that has long since disintegrated. Knowing very well that she has been a coward, unable to voice her protest against the injustices done to her, she feels, "I have been my own enemy" (221).

Towards the end of the novel, however, Saru receives a telegram from Manu that he is coming to take her back to the city. She prepares herself to confront Manu. No definite or inclusive meanings can be unearthed from such an open ending. It is clear that she will no longer remain an object for Manu to expend his frustration on. Though the novel has an open ending, the reader is left in no doubt as to the intentions of the novelist. One may here have a look at what R. Mala has to say on the novel's ending:

> The novelist's credo is to 'take refuge in the self which means that the self is not metaphysical but psychological.' In other words, Deshpande means that the heroines will in future assert themselves; they will no longer allow their 'she' to get deceased. By this assertion of the self, Deshpande certainly takes her heroines to the pole of feminism though she may not have aimed at propounding such an 'ism.' (56-57)

From this insightful comment, one may infer that Saru is fully determined to take control of her life by shedding her passivity.

Man's relationship with woman is akin to the bond that exists between a master and a slave. Woman is an object and she is essential to man because, as Deshpande herself observes in *The Dilemma of a Woman Writer*, "it is in seeking to be made whole through her that man hopes to attain self-realisation" (33). It is in such a culture, in recent times, that voices of dissent are heard. Taking into account her remarks, admissions, anxieties, and confessions, as recorded in her metafiction, *Writing from the Margin*, one may say that Deshpande feels embarrassed to be called a woman writer, and that she is not very enthusiastic about the label 'feminist'. However much she may deny the influence of feminism in her novels, it, indeed, is the core of her novels. Her heroines speak of Virginia Woolf's *A Room of One's Own*, and Betty Friedan, and it becomes quite obvious that the women she has created are feminists, if she is not one.

One of the primal and seminal concerns of feminism is to declare that a woman is a being. She is not an appendage of men. A woman is not the *other*. She is an autonomous being, capable of, through trial and error, finding her own way to salvation. But it is a truth universally acknowledged that women, who are physically and mentally equipped to perform on par with men, have not only been denied existence as complete human beings, but also deprived of the opportunity to give expression to their feelings, their thoughts and their anguish. As Sushila Singh puts it, "Human experience for centuries has been synonymous with the masculine experience, with the result that the collective image of humanity has been one-sided and incomplete. Woman has not been defined as a subject either in her own right but merely has an entity that concerns man either in his real life or his fantasy life" (7).

The Dark Holds No Terrors reveals the life of Sarita/Saru, who is always neglected and ignored in favour of her brother. To quote Sarabjit Sandhu:

> The mother is very attached to her son. Her attitude is a typical one—after all, he is male child and therefore one who will propagate the family lineage. In another sense also, the male child is considered more important than a girl, because he is qualified to give "agni" to his dead parents. The soul of the dead person would otherwise wander in torment. (83)

The first thought, when Saru hears the news of her mother's death, is "Who lit the pyre? She had no son to do that for her. Dhruva had been seven when he died" (17).

When Dhruva was alive, her mother's discrimination between the two had been very apparent to Saru. In one of her recapitulations, she records her conversation with her mother thus:

> "Don't go out in the sun. You'll get darker."
> "Who cares?"
> "We have to care if you don't. We have to get you married."
> "I don't want to get married."
> "Will you live with us all your life?"
> "Why not?"

"You can't."

"And Dhruva?"

"He is different. He's a boy." (40)

Saru is not given the importance that Dhruva gets. No parental love is showered upon her even on her birthdays. Her brother's birthdays, however, are celebrated with great enthusiasm including the performance of religious rituals, whereas her birthdays are hardly acknowledged. Saru often wonders if her birth was a cause of displeasure to her mother. In one of her nostalgic recounts, she muses:

> Birthdays were not then the tremendous occasions they are made out to be now; but the excitement of having one, of being the centre of attraction never palled. It was always a fascinating thought—'I was born.' But of my birth, my mother had said to me once.... It rained heavily the day you were born. It was terrible. And somehow, it seemed to me that it was my birth that was terrible for her, not the rains. (169)

The aforementioned passage has its affirmation in the research conducted by Anandalakshmi who records thus:

> The supremacy of the male is so well established that the average Indian is surprised to even be queried about it. Whatever the ecology of the social group, even in communities where the women may be the breadwinners, the male is considered superior. Within the family the sense of inferiority of the female is pervasive. The sex ratio is unfavourable for girls and forces us to conclude that the survival of the girl is a matter of indifference in a considerable number of families. The birth of a son gives a woman status and she invests herself in her son's fixture, creating a deep symbiotic bond. (31)

She remembers how her brother was named. "They had named him Dhruva. I can remember, even now vaguely, faintly, a state of joyous excitement that had been his naming day. The smell of flowers, the black grinding stone" (152). When her brother is drowned, she is blamed for the tragedy. Her mother, in particular, always scolds her for being responsible for her son's death. "You killed him. Why didn't you die? Why are you alive, when he's dead?" (173). Her mother's oft-repeated accusation, in effect, makes Saru wonder if, in reality, she has killed him. It is much later, after rethinking and pondering over the event, after her mother's death, that she realises the accidental nature of her brother's death.

Saru rebels against her mother by going to Bombay to study medicine. The hostel life is a kind of "rebirth" into a totally different world where she does not have to stay outside for "those three days, you are no longer an 'untouchable'; you can even talk about it; "Oh, damn. I must change again. It's like a tap, that's what it is" (87). Saru falls in love with Manohar (Manu), and, it is a token of her defiance of the authority of the mother. Her mother, being an old, traditional, orthodox woman, does not want her daughter to get married to a person who is from a lower caste:

> "What caste is he?"
> "I don't know."
> "A Brahmin?"
> "Of course, not."
> Then, cruelly "...his father keeps a cycle shop."
> "Oh, so they are low caste people, are they?" (96)

It is her mother's neglect and father's complacent attitude that drive her to desire male love which, she hopes, would give her confidence in herself as "my being loved, my being wanted" (35). She hardly believes it when Manu tells her with such ardour that he loves her. How could she "the redundant, the unwanted, an appendage one could do without evoke so strong an emotion in anyone? How could anyone love her and need her? And that too a boy like Manu with his confidence and attractions, all the college girls had a crush on?" (66). Her mother's angry query about his caste only strengthens her determination. It is Saru who proposes to Manu—one more way of rejecting the fact of her being a woman.

She succeeds and emerges as a successful, well-known and reputed doctor. At the same time, her marriage begins to crumble under the burden of success in her profession. Till now, "he had been the young man and I his bride. Now I was the lady doctor and he was my husband" (37). Manu, her husband, cannot tolerate people greeting her and ignoring him. Saru realises it: "now I know that it was there it began ...this terrible thing that has destroyed our marriage" (37). This is the awkward situation in which she is placed. The disparity of achievement between Saru and Manu leaves the latter thoroughly insecure and the former is happily aware of the fact:

> (W)hen we walked out of our room, there were nods and smiles, murmured greetings and namastes. But they were all for me, only for me. There was nothing for him. He was almost totally ignored. a+b they told us in mathematics is equal to b+a. But here a+b was not, definitely not equal to b+a. It became a monstrously unbalanced equation, lopsided, unequal, impossible. (42)

At a personal level, she experiences a gradual disappearance of love and attachment that she once had for Manu.

The financial ascendance of Saru comes to have a terribly negative impact on Manu. It renders Manu impotent. The only way he can regain that potency and masculinity is through sexual assault upon Saru, which for him becomes an assertion of his manhood, and which becomes in him a sort of perverse nocturnal abnormality. Strangely enough, he is a cheerful normal human being, a loving husband during day, who turns into a rapist at night. It terrifies and humiliates Saru so much that she cannot even speak about them, even to him. To quote her, "(A)nd each time it happened and I don't speak. I put another brick on the wall of silence between us. May be one day I will be walled alive within it and die a slow painful death" (88).

Saru ironically refers to her family as 'a most happy family' of four, each of them being a type, that too uninspiring: "A happy family. With the skeleton locked firmly in the cupboard" (21). She is reduced to a mere heap of chaos of personality, a symbol of complexity and confusion, and as a result, she miserably fails to observe the reality. To quote:

> Busy, engrossed, as if I'm writing notes on the patient who has just left. But I'm only doodling. And always the same thing. One circle entwined in another, one circle entwined in another. Ending up sometimes with a complex intricate pattern of a strange mystifying beauty. (22)

Saru herself has undergone the traumatic experience, and is able to successfully present a picture of her fragmented personality in the anguish-ridden words: "There is this new fear of disintegration. A terrified consciousness of not existing. No, worse of being just a ventriloquist's dummy that smiles, laughs and talks only because of the ventriloquist" (22). Naturally enough, she is apprehensive of her own "emptiness" (22) and in constant fear of losing something. She reveals the extent of the ingrained crisis and explains the cause of the crisis thus: "And behind this fear the uneasiness that comes from losing something. No, not losing it, but being unable to find it because I've hidden it to keep it safe. Hidden so well that I can't find it myself now" (23). Further, "I struggled to find the right thing to say. And the child began to cry...I relaxed. It was easy now. I was in charge. No, not I, really, but the dummy in white coat" (23).

As a girl, Saru was depressed. The reason is that she was an ugly-looking girl. And her mother constantly and insensitively reminded her, "You will never be good looking. You are too dark for that" (61). If she found Saru looking at herself in the mirror, as all growing children do, she would taunt the girl and say "Looking at yourself in the mirror? I will give you a certificate to say that you are beautiful. Will that satisfy you?" (61). And, "you should be careful now about how you behave. Don't come out in your petticoat like that. Not even when it's only your father who's around" (62). And, "you're growing up, she would say. And there was something unpleasant in the way she looked at me.... And it became something shameful, this growing up so that you had to be ashamed of yourself" (62). And ultimately she starts hating her own womanhood: "I can remember closing my eyes and praying.... Oh god, let it not happen to me. Let there be a miracle and let me be the one female to whom it doesn't happen" (62). Many things are forbidden to her, and to quote Premila Paul who rightly remarks, "The archetypal Terrible Mother sees Saru only as a burden to be eased, a problem to be solved, a responsibility to be dispensed with, a person who has no right to any choice in life" (66). The agonising feelings, bred by such growth, are monstrous. The hurdles and limitations of the society try to strangle her. Not surprisingly, Saru feels helpless: "A kind of shame that engulfed me, making me want to rage, to scream against the fact that put me in the same class as my mother" (62).

As far as Saru's mother is concerned, she herself had been brought up by her maternal grandparents. Her father had left home a few years after marriage to become a *sanyasi* (a saint) leaving behind his wife and two little daughters. For Saru's mother it must have been a traumatic childhood—to be treated like an unwanted burden. Saru tells her husband, "we always had to remember we did not really belong. We were only to be tolerated" (194). Naturally, she was quite depressed and frustrated due to her parents' callous as well as indifferent attitude. The very grooming for becoming a successful female was denied to her. Referring to her father, she says, "He never took any interest in my school or college. He left it all to her. And she never really cared. Not after Dhruva's death. I just didn't exist for her. I died long before I left home" (32). Even now, the smile that Baba/Saru's father offered to Madhav—a college student whom he accommodates in his house, and enjoys being with—carried pure affection with it, but to her, he had "always been a negative man.... But if he could smile that way, it was like being a child again" (30).

Since the pain of fragmentation has sickened her, the sense of loneliness and rootlessness is dominant in Saru's mind. She notices such an intense sense of alienation in her child, too, as she sees, "cold, shrewd, objective, observer behind those little girl's eyes of hers" (33). Saru is reminded of a room whose doors are closed whenever she looks at her daughter, Renu. Even when she comes back home, she "felt herself enclosed" (19). It is relevant here to quote Ramamoorthy, who makes the following observation:

> The image of the enclosed walls suggests the suffocation these women undergo not only in their parental homes but the homes they have chosen as refuge. The "room" and the enclosed feeling also relate them quite often to mere objects and cattle where they have no light of their own. They do not belong to the room; they are merely an addition to it. (41)

Although she hates her mother, there is one thing that Saru finds she shares with her—"neither she nor I have a thing 'a room of our own'" (136). She sees the 'hollowness, emptiness, nothingness' (22) in their lives, when she applies this phrase and relates it to their lives. Saru's plight is such that she does not even have a home. She cannot call her husband's home in Bombay, her home because it was not a home. And, neither was her father's home a home to her. She stands at the crossroads, feeling "How odd to live for so long and discover that you have no home at all" (215).

Women themselves are quite responsible in certain contexts in treating the other women as the *other*. Saru remembers that when she wanted to study in medical college, her mother was against her studies. Though unsuccessful, her mother tried her best to persuade her husband not to send Saru to medical college. To quote from the text:

> You don't belong to that [moneyed] class. And don't forget, medicine or no medicine, doctor or no doctor, you still have to get her married, spend money on her wedding.... Let her go for a B.Sc....you can get her married in two years and our responsibility will be over. (144)

Here is a clear instance of the fact that girls are seen as belonging to a different family altogether and their socialisation stresses their future roles as wives. Veena Das quotes an informant saying thus:

> Daughters are comparable to something kept in trust for another (*amanat*). You have to care for them, love

> them, and you will be held responsible for them but you are destined to lose them. Once a daughter is properly married and goes to her own house it is like a debt that has been paid. (93)

There are references in the novel to a woman, who, ill-treated by her in-laws, drowns herself in a well. There is a reference to yet another woman victim who is tied to a peg by the in-laws and fed in the cattle shed. Saru detests the merciless judgment of her mother who dismisses the topic saying, "She perhaps deserved it" (87). In this context, Premila Paul makes the shrewd remark: "The thrust here is not on man's cruelty to woman but woman's cruelty to woman, the internalisation of the patriarchal cruelty by woman" (37). Women at times shudder inwardly due to their own desperation and frustration when they see such events and are scared and wish that the same thing should not happen to them. In fact, they lead a wishful life, a life of willing suspension of disbelief. For instance, one day Saru, in her hometown, sees a woman who is, a widow. She remembers that during her childhood she had seen the same woman in happier days. In those days, she lovingly sent her husband off to office. But now the same woman is a widow.

The sight of this widow makes Saru desperate. She sadly ruminates, "But her eyes, lost and empty, were the ghastliest signs of her widowhood.... To put all of yourself into another and then be left alone.... But I'm not that either" (135). And when she sees Mavshi, when she attends to her in her home, to her, "The woman looked completely unfamiliar without her kumkum and black beads. They had been such an integral part of her that without those symbols of her wifehood, she seemed a colourless ghost" (76). And Mavshi herself considers Saru's mother to be a lucky woman because she died a 'Suhagan.' She asks Saru: "Why am I, a fat, old, unwanted woman left alive when he is dead?" (77). This shows that widowhood is the worst calamity a woman has to face. As Madan observes, "the death of a child may be seen as a calamity but the death of a husband is seen as altering the social identity of a woman" (55).

Saru remembers the suffering of her grandmother who had been deserted by her husband but "had never, so she had heard, complained. It's my luck, she said. My fate. It was written on my forehead" (70). Baba, that is, Saru's father, tells her while referring to his relationship with his wife "Silence had become a habit for us" (181). This silence, which symbolises the distance between Saru's parents, is praised by Maikaki who called Kamalatai a brave woman of courage who never complained. "She never told anyone about what was happening to her. The amount she ate...I tell you, a sparrow would have eaten more. Your father never noticed because she never ate with him" (99). According to Elaine Showalter, this suggests "that women constitute a 'muted group,' the boundaries of whose culture and reality overlap, but are not wholly contained by, the 'dominant [male] group'" (346). Saru's classmate Padmakar tells her that he hates his wife because "she cannot talk about anything but servants and children. And prices.... She never has her food until I go and have mine, she cooks just what I like and she never calls me by my name" (120). But though Saru tells him that he has a woman who is a good wife and he should be satisfied with her, in her heart of hearts she knows what would happen to a wife if she calls her husband by his name, and assumes the so-called sophisticated 'high status' role. It is a commonplace observation even today that many a man expects his wife to be educated and modern, and yet, to have the traditional qualities of devotion and submissiveness.

According to Manu, the law-maker of the Indian orthodox culture, a woman can never be a decision-maker. Doniger Wendy interprets Manu's observation thus: "A girl, a young woman, or even an old woman should not do anything independently, even in [her] house" (115). Saru is reminded of her friend Smita, who after her marriage changed her name to become first Geetanjali and later Anju because, to quote Smita, "He (her husband) chose it himself when we got married" (106). He did so because he had been reading Tagore those days. Smita further tells her that her husband "hates anyone calling me Smita now" (106). Smita has to face in her married life, not only anonymity but also financial problems. She has to borrow one hundred rupees from Saru because "he had given her just enough to buy a small gift for the baby" (107). She tells Saru, "You don't know how lucky you are not to have to ask anyone for money" (107). The readers are reminded here of Deshpande's words in her essay, *Why I am a Feminist*: "Many women do enjoy housework and find fulfilment within the home. They have every right to do so. But there are hazards of not being able to support yourself when it may be necessary to do so, ... To be dependent means to be a burden on another, at times to be forced to endure violence because there is no choice" (84).

The paragraph above shows that marriage brings different kinds of constraints to a woman that go on erasing her personality into nothingness. In yet another context, Saru is reminded of the wife of one of Manu's friends who ungrudgingly accepts total effacement of her very presence and position by remaining as a silent, unobtrusive "nameless waiter in a hotel" (159) till the end of the dinner, unintroduced, to the friends of her husband. And, Saru rightly assumes that the lady obviously remains a shadow and nothing more than that, for to men, a woman does not exist at all. When asked by her friend Nalu to talk on *Medicine as a Profession for Woman* to some college students, Saru cobbles up an imaginary speech in which she sarcastically sums up the conditions necessary for a successful marriage:

> A wife must always be a few feet behind her husband. If he's an MA, you should be a BA. If he's 5' 4" tall, you shouldn't be more than 5' 3" tall. If he's earning five hundred rupees, you should never earn more than four hundred and ninety-nine rupees. That's the only rule to follow if you want a happy marriage. Don't ever try to reverse the doctor-nurse, executive-secretary, principal-teacher role. It can be traumatic, disastrous. And, I assure you, it does not work. He'll suffer, you'll suffer and so will the children. Women's magazines will tell you that a marriage should be an equal partnership. That's nonsense. Rubbish. No partnership can ever be

> equal. It will always be unequal, but take care that it's unequal in favour of your husband. If the scales tilt in your favour, god help you, both of you. (137)

Saru's bitter realisation is that a woman must necessarily remain a step behind her husband. Surprisingly enough, no less a person than John Ruskin holds a similar view that is cited in Suman's article *Women in the Novels of Shashi Deshpande*, thus: "A man ought to know any language or science he learns, thoroughly; while a woman ought to know the same language or science only so far as may enable her to sympathise in her husband's pleasures, and in those of his best friends" (71).

To speak from within a woman's world is not a destructive or disintegrating attitude. Deshpande uses this point of view to present social reality as women experience it. To present the world of mothers, daughters and wives is also to present indirectly fathers, sons and husbands. The relationships between men and women themselves, thus, become important from the perspective of social interaction.

At present, we have a new breed of women, who are educated and modern in outlook. But centuries-old tradition is so deep-rooted in them that they are torn between two opposing forces—tradition and modernity. It has to be noted here that it is only the class of educated Indian women that has begun to show signs of change. There are still generations of women who follow the patriarchal tradition quite complacently. In the absence of a complete annihilation of the unilaterally male-oriented traditional values, the modern Indian woman finds herself in conflict with the age-old traditional values and customs that are outdated and meaningless compared to the modernity that infuses her sensibility.

This external conflict with the society results in an internal conflict within the women themselves. Writing of Indian women, their conflicts and their predicaments in contemporary India, Deshpande stands out from the rest of her kind in her refusal to sell India abroad by exaggerating the Indianness of her stories. As Premila Paul observes, "Shashi Deshpande does not betray any inclination or ulterior motive to sell India abroad by liberal doses of oriental mysticism or sociological data. For her the psychological milieu of the individual is quite an empirical canvas to work on" (61).

Deshpande's journey through the psyche of her characters coincides with the journey undertaken by her protagonists who make an earnest attempt to resolve their internal conflict by means of establishing a harmonious relationship between their turbulent selves and the society. According to Sarabjit Sandhu, Deshpande's heroine, like the modern Indian woman, is now a "changed person who is aware of the stirrings of her conscience, her quest for identity, her individuality, her place and role in the family and society" (178). The modern women, needless to say, suffer from both an external and an internal conflict. The major reason for the external conflict is the inability of the modern Indian woman to cut herself totally off all her ties with the tradition she belongs to. To Adele King this conflict arises out of the Indian woman "being both (herself) and fitting a traditional role as a 'good daughter,' 'good wife' or 'good mother'" (161).

Deshpande presents the women's point of view, mainly to highlight the suffering her protagonists undergo while trying to strike a balance between the roles they are expected to play and the role they wish to play. The conflict is, in fact, one between their wifehood and motherhood on the one hand, and their careers and desire to fulfil their latent desires, on the other. The tension arising out of this conflict is only accentuated by the confusion that prevails within the heroines themselves, who struggle simultaneously for answers to questions of identity, and for solutions to their psychological dilemmas. Resolving to put an end to the conflicts within themselves, the protagonists make a sincere attempt at re-discovering their own selves. This search for the self first takes them to a far-off place quite a distance from where they live now. This journey symbolises a Shakespearean distancing from the problems at hand—a distancing that is not just physical but also psychological. Free from the routine chores of life, the vision of the protagonists now gets clear and, consequently, they find themselves in a position to see their whole life in proper perspective.

In India, a woman is always seen in the context of her relationship to the external world, that is, her husband, her children and the society that she is in immediate contact with. As a result, there arises the confrontation of the protagonists with their husbands. Given the closeness of the husband and wife in the modern Indian milieu, the conflict is the most intense between these two. Constantly thrown together by the changing Indian socio-economic scene that demands that the wife share an equal amount of the husband's burden, this changing cultural milieu is the elementary reason for the conflict.

Moreover, as the novel deals with the modern Indian women, yet another conflict arises within them and they cause it by their own awareness of the fact that they are career women. As Sandhu suggests, it is true that Deshpande's women "after attaining all types of rights, are now struggling to adjust rather than to get free from the traditional world" (16). The women reconsider the values held aloft by the traditional world. They, at the same time, attempt earnestly to create a space for their own feminist stance in this tradition-ridden world. Women's struggle for a fuller self-development, greater self-reliance and a clearer articulation is constantly accentuated by their awareness that the world still owes them something. Deshpande's portrayal of women's relations is a process of balancing the modern with the traditional, an intrepid individualism with a mellowed selflessness.

Saru in *The Dark Holds No Terrors* carries her own private devils within herself. Her brother Dhruva's death, and the guilt of having been indirectly responsible for the tragedy stay as a weight in her conscience. The accidental incident that results in engendering the sense of guilt in Saru happened only because of the sort of atmosphere in which Saru spends her childhood. Saru is born and brought up in a patriarchal society where the female child always has to play second fiddle to her male brother who, one day, will grow up to be the man of the house. Moreover, Saru is also forced to be aware by her mother that Dhruva is always the preferred child. This attitude that Saru is forced to face and live with kindles the fire of sibling jealousy in the young Saru and colours her judgment so much that she herself is unable to clearly define her part in Dhruva's tragic death. "If" becomes a two-lettered word for futility that torments and tortures Saru.

> If only I hadn't gone there that day...
> If only he hadn't come with me....
> If only I hadn't left him alone. (184)

And Saru is haunted by the words of her mother, especially after the death of her beloved son. Her mother repeatedly tells her, "You killed him. Why didn't you die? Why are you alive, when he's dead?" (19). Saru was only ten when this happened. Still, in her womanhood, also, she carries the scar. In this context, one may agree with Premila Paul who remarks, "Saru never boldly refutes or denies the charge of murder except in the confession to her father. This is because she had in a way passively watched him die and therefore has passively contributed to his death" (67). If once she was just a young girl not strong enough to tackle the problem and not turn her back on it. Now Saru realises that the doubts would always be there. She confesses, as though to seek salvation, "(T)here can never be any forgiveness. Never any atonement. My brother died because I heedlessly turned my back on him" (217). Yet, she realises that she has to let the dead go. She seeks to escape from her agony by being an elder sister again, this time to Madhav. Nursing Madhav through a bout of fever, she tries to seek retribution for turning her back on her kid brother. But the truth strikes her suddenly, "It's not Dhruva. It was never Dhruva. I can never bring him back" (212). She realises that she has to carry her burden as long as she lives. She does not sidestep the problem of her guilt concerning Dhruva. She faces it bravely and realises that it is a futile exercise to try to get rid of her guilt. Saru decides to do just what Jaya tells herself in *That Long Silence*, "Take your pain between your teeth, bite on it, don't let it escape" (135). Saru gradually realises that her life has been chalked out to be one of suffering. There is no point in deceiving herself and the others that it is not so. There will be no more pointless pursuits of happiness. She will live her life as it is. If pain and suffering is her lot, so be it. She decides not to run from it any more. This ultimate understanding and acceptance by Saru signals a renewal of herself.

The other guilt that Saru carries in her heart is with regard to her mother. The natural antagonism between the mother and the girl child develops an intense bitterness in Saru. She experiences an oppressed childhood because of the fact that she is a girl. Many things are forbidden to her. As a consequence of all this, Saru's entire life becomes a gesture of defiance against her mother. Years later, Saru accuses her mother of being the reason for all her problems. She feels that if only her mother had not so violently opposed Manu, she would never have married him. If only her mother had not initiated in Saru so early in life the fight for power, she would not have sought for domination over her husband for, it is her domination that undermines the masculinity of Manu and results in the crumbling of their marriage.

At the same time, Saru also carries within her a sense of guilt at having deserted her mother. She attributes this desertion to her mother who used to curse her as the root cause of all her sufferings. As Premila Paul observes, "Saru's obsessive remembrance of the mother is indicative of both her sense of guilt and her sense of defeat. Death seals off all possibilities of straightening things" (66). Even after her death, Saru is not free from the adverse impact of her mother's curse. She tells Baba that it is because of her mother's curse that she is unhappy and destroyed. In reeling under the pangs of the guilt that she carries within her, and in her attempts to seek atonement, Saru only succeeds in turning her back on her real problems. Her tendency to cling too much to the past renders her incapable of savouring the present and of looking forward to her future. This prevents her from accepting the fact that her mother is dead and that she has to let the dead go. Instead, she lets the sense of guilt grow in her, and hence, strongly feels that there is no forgiveness for her and that her mother died 'alone,' because she, her only child after Dhruva's death, deserted her. But Saru refuses to accept the futility of persecuting herself and blaming herself. It is only much later that she realises that her life is her own and that she has to live it on her own. "We are alone. We have to be alone" (194). Loneliness, one of the major concerns of modern society, is not a disease, but a symptom of man's condition and this awareness is the first milestone in one's journey into oneself. Edmund Fuller remarks that, "man suffers not only from war, persecution, famine and ruin, but from inner problems—a conviction of isolation, randomness, (and) meaninglessness in his way of existence" (3). However, the awareness of being left alone does not leave Saru in despair for long. On the other hand, she lets herself initiated into an understanding of the meaning of human life. To quote her, "All right, so I'm alone. But so's everyone else. Human beings...they're going to fail you. But because there's just us, because there's no one else. We have to go on trying. If we can't believe in ourselves we're sunk" (220).

What Deshpande brings in her fiction is, in fact, a note of positive affirmation by offering her protagonist the realisation that if life is an illusion it is the only reality that we know, "Therefore the only thing is to go on as if it is real knowing all the while it is only an illusion" (220). What is the point in Saru's blaming herself for her mother dying alone or her brother drowning? Once she realises these things, it becomes easier for her to face her problems. She stops looking for escape routes and begins for the first time to look forward to what life has in store for her.

The major conflict that rages within each and every middle-class Indian woman is the conflict that develops in their married lives. The major reason for the conflict in the husband-wife relationship is the break-up in the cultural modes of modern India. The new socio-economic forces have shaken the tradition-bound society of India to its very roots. This change has immensely affected the family that is the nucleus of the Indian society. The husband-wife relationship has undergone drastic changes like all other changes in the Indian milieu of today. Bhatnagar records Deshpande who remarks that in the old family pattern, "the two (husband

and wife) met only briefly in the darkness of the night" (128). So there was hardly any conflict. "But with husband and wife constantly thrown together in the present pattern,...there have arisen the problems of incompatibility and maladjustment" (128).

The problems faced by Saru in *The Dark Holds No Terrors* are of a cosmic kind, of what female domination can do to a man and how it can destroy him. Constantly run down by her mother, Saru develops at a very early age a drive to succeed. Thus far "the redundant, the unwanted, an appendage one could do without" (66). Saru is completely swept off her feet by Manu, the man of her dreams. To quote Premila Paul, "As she always feels insecure in her parent's home, her marriage to Manu is a means of that love and security which she had always lacked in life" (69). In spite of living in a single room in a chawl, Saru lives a happy married life. But the rot in her marriage sets in when the situation changes from that of a young man and his bride to that of a 'lady doctor' and her husband. Saru's love for power and recognition makes her dissatisfied with being just a wife. The relationship between Saru and Manu now becomes a monstrously unbalanced equation. Saru realises "(T)he same thing that made me inches taller made him inches shorter" (42). To quote Premila Paul again, "When the society confers so much importance on the doctor in her, she proudly wears it on her sleeves, whereas it leaves Manu thoroughly insecure" (62).

Manu's sexual sadism begins the day, the interviewer for a women's magazine asks him, "How does it feel when your wife earns not only the butter but the bread as well" (35). Saru is cruelly unmindful of what she is doing to her husband—undermining his masculinity—as she drinks up the glory her profession brings her. She sees herself as a successful woman who has combined so well a career and a family and says, "It's all a question of adjustment, really. If you want to make it work, you can always do it" (118). Though she thinks that she has struck upon the perfect formula for compromise, what really happens is that while she grows day by day in her stature as a successful doctor, she neglects her role as a wife more and more. In this context Sandhu observes, "While there is a decline in her conjugal relationship, her status in society rises day by day. It may imply at one level that her rise in importance is inversely proportionate to the fall in the importance of her husband, creating a conflict between her achieved position and the ascribed position of Manu" (85).

There is a vast change in Manu also. Saru has reduced him from a man, supremely confident of himself and on the brink of brushing on to the literary sky, into becoming "just another man clinging on to a job" (65) and he is now "a wreck, a ruin, a sadist" (91). There is a lot of change in the relationship between Manu and Saru. A kind of emotional fencing now goes on between them. Both Saru and Manu hate themselves for what they are doing to the other. "What he does to me, he does it not because he hates me, but because he hates himself. And I...I hate myself more for letting him do it to me than I hate him for doing it to me" (98). The total annihilation of herself once seemed to Saru, perfectly natural, as she sought to become what Manohar wanted her to be, "a blindly adoring female" (53). From a humbly adoring, worshipping lover, who dreams of "the age old dream of a superior, conquering male" (53), with no independent identity craving for recognition, Saru slowly strives to become her real self. "The dream of total submission to 'a superior superhuman male,'" as Sandhu observes, "is only a transient stage in the emotional growth of her personality" (109). In the early days of her marriage, Saru shows herself to be a woman capable of a passionate response, eager to be absorbed by the man she loves. Now, Manu's perversion makes sex a dirty act, relief from which she earns for. The most despairing thing about her whole life is that she has, too early in life, lost, "the eternal female dreams of finding happiness through a man" (124).

Boozie is another reason for the relationship between Manu and Saru turning sour. Saru turns to Boozie, her fairy Godfather, for the money Manu is not able to provide. Instead of trying, in the true male tradition, to put things in the proper perspective, Manu who is quite happy with what Saru's money buys, chooses to ignore the implications of the relationship between Saru and Boozie. A grave mistake is done by Saru who waves away the connection and refuses to volunteer the information that behind Boozie's facade of virile masculinity, there is absolutely nothing for he is only a homosexual.

It is only later that Saru realises that she is the reason for what Manu has become. She confesses, "My husband is a failure because I destroyed his manhood" (217). When she left home to marry Manu she had sworn never to dominate and never to follow the footsteps of her mother who had reduced her father into nothing. In spite of that Saru feels that, "there is something outside her own self, driving her on" (86) that makes her take the upper hand. The main reason for the problem assuming enormous proportions is what Saru discerns to be the split in Manu's personality. Shocked by what happens the first time, Saru panics at even the thought of looking at Manu again. But, Manu seems to be perfectly normal with her and is quite oblivious of the events of the previous nights. Used to the life of ease that Saru's money has made possible, Manu shows himself to be not strong enough to make the sacrifices that will turn the tables in his favour.

Saru, who sees her bed as an intensely private place, refuses to expose the happenings there to the outside world. What has happened is to her is "A disease like syphilis or leprosy. Something that could not be admitted to others" (69). In spite of her later urge to confide in someone and in spite of the fact that she has come to Baba looking for comfort, Saru is unable to open her heart even to Baba, afraid of the judgment that will of necessity fall on her. The fear that she will be accused of having caused Manu's degeneration prevents her from unburdening her heart. To quote:

> The fear that by speaking she would be unlocking the door of a dark room in which someone has been murdered.... Her greatest fear was that they would all know the dead body to be his, her husband's. They would know too what she herself did...that it was she who was the murderer. (44)

Saru, who marries Manohar defying her mother, swears to her that she would never come seeking the comfort of her mother's bosom, if her marriage fails. This determination and fear of proving her mother true prevents Saru from accepting the fact that her marriage is indeed a failure, and to realise that to go on with the fiasco that her marriage has become would only amount to flogging a dead horse.

Faced with failure in marriage, Saru's profession, which is the reason for the deterioration of her marriage, becomes the prop that holds her up. She realises that there is nothing in her except her profession and this realisation is her only consolation. It keeps her sane. To quote her, "It had evaporated long since, my pride in my professional status. There was only the work left. And that was now sheer necessity the only thing that held me together (78). Saru becomes aware that now she is only a puppet, a lifeless one that has a smirk pasted on to its face. She is overcome by the fear that she cannot go on. Her profession now becomes the ventriloquist that gives her an identity and a pattern in which to behave. As she says, "My ventriloquist is my profession. For, as long as there is a patient before me, I feel real" (22).

With this understanding comes the fear that once she lets her profession go, she may disintegrate. She becomes unable to relate to the world in any capacity except as a doctor. She is afraid that one day there will be: "Just a white coat, containing nothing" (22). Her existence becomes that of a two-in-one woman—a doctor by daylight exuding an air of professional confidence and a terrified woman at night, struggling in vain to keep off the sadism of her husband. She understands that whatever be it, she can never do away with her profession. Even when hysteria threatens to overpower her on hearing about Manu's arrival, the call that comes to her in her professional capacity as a doctor is what restores her sanity. As Premila Paul rightly observes, "The novel's ending with Saru setting out to attend a patient indicates the assertion of her career. There can be no compromise about it" (75).

Coming back to her father's place results in the break of the established routine of her life, forcing her to take stock of the situation. This is when she realises the extent of the damage her ego has caused to her marital life. Her love and attachment, in Sandhu's opinion, is "Now replaced by a psychological conflict which is uncalled for, but inevitable" (87). As a result of the various conflicts, realisation dawns on her, she is finally liberated and is no longer afraid of the dark. Kamini Dinesh's observation aptly sums up Saru's development as an individual in her own right, "To be true to herself, the woman has to excoriate the film of super-imposed attitudes and roles. Her emancipation is not in repudiating the claims of her family, but in drawing upon the untapped inner reserves of strength. The wife in the end is, therefore not a rebel but a redeemed wife—one who is no longer afraid of the dark" (204). Happily enough, realisation descends on her in the end. She becomes fully aware that she and her mother did not have "a room of their own" (135). She has desperately been searching for this room in her parents, in Dhruva, in her husband Manohar and her children, always outside herself but in vain. The preamble of the novel, taken from the Dhammapada, authentically reflects her self-realisation:

> You are you own refuge;
> There is no other refuge.
> This refuge is hard to achieve.

All biological dread and psychological difference subside in her. Now she must step forward and open the door of all human relationships as an enduring persona. Yet her final words to her father, "And, oh yes, Baba, if Manu comes, tell him to wait, I'll be back as soon as I can" (221), only suggest that she has overcome her earlier hesitation and is now capable of facing her husband and asserting her own rights and individuality.

Whatever her faults had been, whatever her life had been, Saru does ultimately reach the depths of self-actualisation. At last she reaches a stage, which in the words of Elton, McNeil and Zick Rubin, when she is "not beaten by other people's rejection—by low self regard, by anxiety, or by conflict" (445). Their theory goes that "the self develops in an open, flexible, expansive manner, the individual will continue on the road to self-actualisation" (445). Saru introspects philosophically and arrives at the conclusion that escape is a ridiculous idea. There is no escape. Suddenly it was "as if she was vouchsafed a vision" (200), the kind of vision her mother had just before her death—the vision of mythical Duryodhan awaiting his enemies and ready to face them boldly. Saru remembers Madhav's words, too: "I cannot spoil my life.... It's my life after all" (189). She realises that she is powerful enough to fix into a whole the fragments of her splintered personality. To quote:

> They came to her then, all those selves she had rejected so resolutely at first, and so passionately embraced later. The guilty sister, the undutiful daughter, the unloving wife...all persons spiked with guilts. Yes, she was all of them, she could not deny that now. She had to accept these selves to become whole again. But if she was all of them, they were not all of her. She was all these and so much more. (201)

Saru also realises that women are charged with greater responsibility, as they are required to play more challenging roles. It is her resolving and reconsolidating tendency that makes her come out with questions like, "Who is the victim and who is the predator? Are the roles so distinct, so separate? Or are we, each of us both" (144). This shows that a woman has to take more responsibility to make the base of the family, which stands on the emotional support, particularly based on the bringing up of the children, with greater understanding and strong friendship, deep and solid. She has applied the same towards her relationship with her husband, a relationship of mutual trust and confidence, maintaining a delicate balance between her own and her husband's selfhood. Thus relationships within the family need to be built on human values of understanding and trust rather than on the prescribed rules of discipline.

David Kerr rightly observes, "It is not history, nor fate that enslaves us, it is our own fears, our own willingness to be slaves, our own failures in the courage to be" (138). This is what really causes the hardships women face. Introspection and the acceptance of what they are given them the courage to face the challenge of an identity crisis. The characters created by Deshpande choose to be neither slaves nor revolutionaries. Their desire is to strike a compromise and the realisation of this desire is made possible only by the searching introspection that the protagonists subject themselves to. This reconciliation that they arrive at is accepted by the protagonists and the readers only because of the Indian reality for women that the introspection gives the heroines. As Bhatnagar opines:

> Shashi Deshpande makes her heroines choose security through reconciliation. The ethos in the novels is neither of victory nor of defeat, but of harmony and understanding between two opposing ideals and conflicting selves. This is quite representative of the basic Indian attitude. (128)

WORKS CITED

Ahuja, Suman. Review in *The Times of India*, 8 October, 1989.

Anandalakshmi, S. "The female child in a family setting." *The Indian Journal of Social Work*. Vol. II, No. 1, Jan. 1991.

Bhatnagar, P. "Indian Womanhood: Fight for Freedom." In *Roots and Shadows Indian Women Novelists*. Ed. R.K. Dhawan. New Delhi: Prestige Books, 1991, 120-28.

Das, Veena. "Reflections on the Social Constructions of Adulthood" in Sudhir Kakkar, ed. *Identity and Adulthood*. Delhi: OUP, 1992.

Deshpande, Shashi. *The Dark Holds No Terrors*. New Delhi: Penguin, 1990.

Deshpande, Shashi. *Writing from the Margin and Other Essays*. India: Penguin Books, 2003.

Elton, B., Me Neil and Lick Rubin. *The Psychology of Being Human*. 2nd ed. Cansfield Press.

Fuller, Edmund. *Man in Modern Fiction*. New York: Random House, 1958.

Kerr, David. "History and the Possibilities of Choice. Upamanyer Chatterjee's *English August* and Shashi Deshpande's *That Long Silence*." Ed. R.K. Dhawan. New Delhi: Prestige Books, 1991.

King, Adele. "Shashi Deshpande: Portraits of an Indian Woman." *The New Indian Novel in English: A Study of 1980s*. Ed. Viney Kripal. New Delhi: Allied Publishers Limited, 1990.

Mala R., "Sexual Predicament and Shashi Deshpande's Woman," *Indian Women Novelists*. Ed. R.K. Dhawan. New Delhi: Prestige, 1991.

Paul, Premila, "*The Dark Holds No Terrors*: A Woman's Search for Refuge." *Indian Women Novelist*. Ed. R.K. Dhawan. New Delhi: Prestige, 1991.

Paul, West. *The Modern Novel II*. London: Hurt Chrisom, 1963.

Ramamoorthy, P. "My Life in My Own: A Study of Shashi Deshpande's Women." *Feminism and Recent Fiction in English*. Ed. Sushila Singh. New Delhi: Prestige, 1991.

Sandhu, Sarabjit. *The Image of Woman in the Novels of Shashi Deshpande*. New Delhi: Prestige Books, 1991.

Showalter, Elaine. "Feminist Criticism in the Wilderness" in David Lodge ed. *Modern Criticism and Theory: A Reader*. London: Longman, 1988.

Singh, Sushila. *Preface, Feminism and Recent Fiction in English*. New Delhi: Prestige, 1991.

Writing from the Margins: A Study of Shashi Deshpande's *That Long Silence*

12

RAM SHARMA

In the way the bulk of post-colonial New English literature has been generally preoccupied for the last few decades with the marginalised and the under dog. In India the focus naturally falls on women and backward classes.

Edward Said suggests that the canons of the center should be read contrapuntally with the work coming from the margin. Thus the binary exists even though Said's vision for the future is more Utopian in nature. Shashi Deshpande's novels reveal the inability of the woman to speak and the positive movement is always the movement towards speech, towards the breaking of 'That Long Silence.'

That Long Silence which won Shashi Deshpande the Sahitya Akademi Award for 1990. tells the story of an Indian housewife who maintains silence throughout her life. The novel ends with her resolve to speak, to break her long silence. The novel depicts the life of Jaya at the level of the silent and the unconscious. A sensitive and realistic dramatisation of the married life of Jaya and her husband Mohan. It centers inner perception of a protagonist of women who is subtly drawn from inside, a woman who finds her normal routine so disrupted that for the first time she can look at her life and attempt to decide who she really is (King, Debonair, 97). But could she?

The question "Who am I?" (24) haunts her so obsessively that she fails to find herself. She is "an utter stranger a person so alien that even the faintest understanding of the motives of her actions seemed impossible" (69). Hence her agonised cries "I can't hope, I can't manage. I can't go on." In such a stifling and suffocating domestic ambience and patriarchal set-up, she finds her female identity effaced.

Gayatri Chakravorty Spivak writes in her article "Can, the subaltern speak?":

> Between patriarchy and imperialism subject—constitution and object formation the figure of the woman disappears, not into a pristine nothingness, but into a violent shuttling which is the displaced figuration of the 'Third-World Woman' caught between tradition and modernization.

Jaya is Suhasini and also "Seeta" the pseudonym she assumes to write columns about the plight of the middle class housewife. Both "Suhasini' and "Seeta" are as Jaya says "the many selves waiting to be discovered each self attached like a Siamese twin to a self of another person, neither able to exist without the other" (69). Hence if life is "to be made possible (193), she is to live neither as 'Suhasini' or 'Jaya' nor as 'Seeta' or 'Anti-Kusum.'" She is to live but not in fragments. Deshpande, reveals the consciousness of Jaya through an exposition of her mind in the process of thinking, feeling and reacting to the stimuli of the moment and situation. In doing so, who goes on to assert the feminine psyche of the protagonist, all ago, to break away from the stranglehold of a quagmired social fabric rooted in patriarchy which repels as it attracts:

> And I was Jaya. But I had been Suhasini as well. I can see her now, the Suhasini who was distinct from Jaya, a soft smiling, placid motherly woman. A woman who lovingly nurtured her family. A woman who coped. (16)

Jaya is not totally a silent and mute sufferer. She is an actor participant as well as an observer in the novel. She steps out of the narrative action as a witness as it were a critic to perceive the tenor of the story filtered a female consciousness.

> Sensual memories are the coldest. They stir up nothing in you.... These emotions and responses seemed to belong to two other people, not to the two of us lying

> here together...whatever my feeling has been then, I had never spoken of them to him. In fact, we had never spoken of sex at all. (95)

Jaya is a modern predicament and the flood of consciousness that ensures out of it is a silent stream of thoughts and feelings. "Jaya succumbs and surrenders to Mohan without revolting. Silently she wills to his will. She never says 'Yes' when her husband asks her whether he has hurt her. She endures everything, tolerates all kinds of masculine oppression silently in the emotion that governed my behaviour to him, there was still the habit of being a wife of sustaining and supporting him."

Simone de Beauvoir expresses his own views on man-woman nexus—"man represents both the positive and the neutral, as is indicated by the common use of man to designate human beings in general, whereas woman represents only the negative, defined by limiting criteria, without reciprocity" (*Seldom*, 1988: 534).

A woman is never regarded as an autonomous being since she has always been assigned a subordinate and relative position.

> Man can think of himself without woman. She cannot think of herself without man. And she is simply what man decrees...she appears essentially to the male as a sexual being. For him she is sex...absolute sex, no less. She is defined and differentiated with reference to man and not he with reference to man and not he with reference to her, she is the incidental, the inessential as opposed to the essential. (*Seldom* 1988: 534)

Shashi Deshpande uses a beautiful image to describe Jaya's married life. "A pair of bullocks yoked together...a clever phrase, but can it substitute for the reality? A man and a woman married for seventeen years. A couple with two children. A family somewhat like the one caught and preserved for posterity by the advertising visuals I so loved. But the reality was only this. We were two persons. A man and a woman (8).

Jaya does not immediately react to the situation but the reader is insinuated through the flash back technique used by the author.

Jaya being renamed as Suhasini after her marriage is not a case of the loss of identity since Jaya and Suhasini are the two facets of the same coin and these two collateral names of the Deshpande protagonist are symbolical in their sociofamilial import. Jaya, her premarital name means 'Victory' and Suhasini the post marital name given to her by her husband means a soft smiling placid motherly woman. A woman who lovingly nurtured her family A woman who coped" (15).

> Jaya is a woman who adjusts and accommodates unlike the modern women who find themselves forced into the background by the claims of culture and hence they adopt "an inimical attitude towards it." (Freud, 1939: 73)

She is not the structurally patterned woman of the traditional Indian society where woman was the follower and man the leader, where woman was the sufferer and man the ordainer. Jaya flounders to break out of the yoke.

> Stay at home, look after your babies, keep out the rest of the world, you are safe. That poor idiotic woman Suhasini believed in this. I know better, now I know that safety is always unattainable, you are never safe. (17)

Jaya's drift of thought and her evanescent mood captured through the broken and fragmentary stream of consciousness. "A husband is like a sheltering tree." "Take on it, don't let it escape."

Jaya's self-questioning attitude comes as a split in the narrative. She broods over the metaphor of the 'Sheltering tree."

> A sheltering tree, without the tree, you are dangerously unprotected...equally logically and vulnerable. This followed logically. (32)

Jaya desperately needs to protect herself from dissipating and sinking in the crumbling world around her. Deshpande thus presents the subterranean and subliminal impressions of human life through digressions in the narrative.

In their stream of thoughts both Jaya and Mohan look at their marital relationship where there is nothing but suppressed silence Jaya wants to flee from the cribbed confines of an incarcerated domestic life in order to find a new identity for herself, a new mooring for her fugitive self-communication at the domestic and personal level is a failure.

> Nothing between us...nothing between me and Mohan. We live together but there had been only emptiness between us. (185)

Jaya had never confessed her frenetic feelings to Mohan as it has seemed "like a disease a disability" (97).

Which he had to hide from everyone Jaya, pines for social communication but the society is impervious to her spiritual need.

There is hardly any communication between Jaya and Mohan, neither verbal nor emotional. Mohan wanted a well-educated and cultured wife not a reciprocating and loving one. There develops disheartening silence between the husband and the wife. Mohan queries remain unanswered by Jaya for she is unable to find a word of response. She is unable to speak her trouble out for she is a woman who faces the suffering of her life and the opposition of the milieu in the true spirit of ideal Hindu womanhood where obedience and loyalty has degenerated to the state of dogged subservience could a modern woman nestled in tradition like Jaya understand a traditionalist like Mohan who is rooted out and out in customs and whose repressive use of silence pressures Jaya into conformity with his expectations? Deshpande presents here not a woman who has a desire to revolt but the one who ultimately reconciles to her hapless lot. Having failed to discover the truth, she remains silent and reticent revealing her most personal and private thoughts in her writings. Mohan wonders as to how could women be so rebellious and esoteric, so angry and recalcitrant. To him, it is unwomanly to be angry for it is against the ideals of feminism.

> A woman can never be angry she can only be neurotic, hysterical frustrated. There is no room for despair, either. There is only order and routine, today. I have to change the sheets tomorrow scrub the bathrooms the day after clean the fridge.... (147-48)

Marriage subjugates and enslaves women and it leads her to "aimless days indefinitely repeated, life that slips away gently towards death without questioning its purpose" (De Beauvoir 1974: 500).

Woman pay for their happiness at the cost of their freedom and De Beauvoir emphasised that such a sacrifice on the part of a woman is too high for anyone because the kind of self-contentment, serenity and security that marriage offers woman drains her soul of its capacity for greatness.

> She shuts behind her the doors of her new home. When she was a girl, the whole countryside was her homeland, the forests were hers. Now she is confined to a restricted space.... (*The Second Sex* 502)

It is against this encoded and pre-ordained role of a woman that Jaya revolts. For her "in this life itself there are so many cross-roads so many choices" (192).

But a married woman has a few or practically no choice left to her save what her husband wills and desires. Unlike other married woman slavishly tagged to tradition, she has her own say. She unfurls and unburdens herself to activate the creative impulses smothered within her artistic self. Deshpande has laid bare the psyche of Jaya which is reluctantly responsive and passively secluded. The author's unrelieved stress on obliterating herself from the novel as a storyteller, giving full freedom to the protagonist to unveil herself using her resilient mind to decumbent her vision to life has imparted an unquestionable credibility of the realism of the stream of Jaya's consciousness.

The metaphor of silence under which the novel is organized helps to impose a quietude and discipline the inner dynamics of a self cut off from human communication. *That Long Silence* is not an intrusion into the world of silence but a silent communion with the oppressed self straining for articulation, for a voice. Jaya and Mohan hardly spoke to each other of love and sex. Love-making for them was silent and in articulate affair.

> God, how terrible it was to know a man so well. I could time it almost to the second, from the first devices wooing to the moment he turned away from me, offering me his hunched back. (85)

In the process of self-revelation through writing Jaya comes to recognise herself as a failed writer because when she had continued writing, her stories had been rejected for lack of genuine feelings which she had laid aside. In other words, she is self-alienated Jaya's creative urge and artistic zeal frees her from her cramped and dubbed domestic and societal roles. At length she resolves to break that silence by putting down on paper all that she has suppressed in her seventeen years silence—that long silence which had reduced herself to fragments.

> I am not afraid...any more. The panic has gone. I am Mohan's wife. I had thought, and cut off the bits of me that had refused to be Mohan's wife. Now I know that kind of fragmentation is not possible. The child hands in pocket, has been with me through the years. She is with me still. (191)

Through the image of a woman crawling into a hole, Deshpande describes the woeful plight of Jaya, unprotected and unshelled Jaya says:

> Distance from real life scared of writing, scared of failing oh God I had thought, I cannot take any more. Even a worm has hole it can crawl into. I had mine as Mohan's wife as Rahul's and Rati's mother. (148)

Towards the end of the novel Jaya consciously acknowledges her writing as a kind of fiction and quotes Defoe's description of fiction as a kind of 'lying' which may make 'a great hope in the heart.' Hence she decides to 'plug that hole' as said earlier by speaking and listening and erasing the silence between her and Mohan. It is this erasing of the silence that symbolises the assertion of her feminine voice, a voice with hope and promise, a voice that articulate her thoughts. The novel doesn't depict Jaya's life as a totally dismal and hopeless struggle. It suggests "hope" and "change" for the better.

> We don't change overnight. It's possible that we may not change even over long periods of time. But we can always hope without that life would be impossible. (193)

Such an ending, suggests a new beginning for Jaya and Mohan. Thus Shashi Deshpande tends to depict the oppression of women with greater self-oppression of women with greater self-consciousness, a deeper sense of involvement and often with a sense of outrage.

REFERENCES

Beauvoir, Simone de. *The Second Sex* Trans. and Edit H.M. Parshley (New York: Vintage Books, 1974).

Deshpande, Shashi. *That Long Silence* (1988, New Delhi: Penguin Books, 1989). All textual citations in the article kept in parentheses are from this edition of the novel).

Spivak, Gayatri Chakravorty. "Can the Subaltern Speak" from *Colonial Discourse and Post Colonial Theory* (Harvest Wheatsheaf, 1994).

Shobha De: To Read or Not to Read

13

NARINDER KUMAR NEB

Shobha De is one of the most popular and the most prolific writers among the contemporary Indo-English novelists. De's treatment of a particular fictional world that has not been explored so far by any other Indo-English novelist secures an enviable place for her among the contemporary fiction writers De's ironical narrative stance and her critical understanding of the feminist concerns make her fiction unique, interesting and artistic.

Shobha De has often been considered not worthy of academic research and study, because of the doubt raised by certain critics about the literary merit of her fiction. She has been deliberately neglected and criticized for the treatment and presentation of sex and sexual relationships in her novels. She has often been criticized as, "high priestess of gossip and innuendo."[1] Her writings have been regarded "equivalent of Hindi films with their peephole voyeurism."[2] Some critics have been so harsh against her that they are not ready to acknowledge the obvious fact of her being amongst one of the best-selling writers in India. Such critics attribute all of Shobha De's success to her treatment of sex only. "One discovery De has obviously made is that the route to readers' hearts and pockets, and of late university curricula, is through orgasms."[3] But a close study of Shobha De's fiction reveals the biased and unjustified nature of these comments.

It is uncharitable to think that Shobha De's novels have been recognized by the Bombay University without giving any consideration to literary merit. Moreover the School of Oriental and African Studies, London has also acknowledged the literary worth of De's fiction. Even if her novels had not received recognition in the literary and academic institutions mentioned above we could not have denied her the rightful literary examination simply because she has treated sex in her fiction. Hers is not the only example of this type. Even earlier writers like Sasthi Brata and Khushwant Singh have been criticized for the same reason. The use of vulgar language and obscenity has been a charge against Mulk Raj Anand's fiction also. Even in British and American literature several writers like D.H. Lawrence and Philip Roth though patently recognized as indecent, have not been discarded for literary studies. Therefore a study of Shobha De's fiction is not only justified from a literary point of view but also necessary for a critical evaluation.

Another objection against De's writings has been that she writes popular fiction for the market concerning mass culture. Her fiction, like much other popular fiction, is said to have only temporary mass appeal. "The writing is inelegant, trite, workaday, a journalist's quotation copy, a popular seller's easy-to-digest mix."[4] Her fiction, according to this point of view, has only specific group of people as the expected readers and concerns a specific history of a particular period related to low culture. The critics who reject De's fiction for being popular fiction fail to understand the fact that popular fiction has its own value. It doesn't remain limited to specific history of a particular period but forms a dynamic part of the history of that period. Popular fiction articulates the tensions and contradictions within the society giving them popular expression. The literary value of popular fiction cannot be undermined for "popular fictions are not some trivial exhibits, waiting to be discovered and mined by historians whose respect for great literature persuades them that they should leave the task of re-reading the traditional texts to their literary colleagues: they too have specific formal structures which need careful analysis."[5]

The distinction between popular fiction and high literature seems anyway arbitrary when we find that a text is read by different generations differently to make meanings according to their understanding and circumstances. Sometimes popular writings maintain their popularity among different generations. The difference between high and low, serious and popular literature seems ironical and amusing when we find conscious efforts made to make a serious work of literature popular. The film based on Shakespeare's *Henry V* and the television serials based on *Mahabharata* and *Ramayana* can be called such attempts. Similarly the works of Charles Dickens and William Thackeray highlight the arbitrary division between high and popular literature and expose the myth that popular literature is written by a lesser known person and high literature is the work of a creative genius. Dickens consciously remained involved in writing popular fiction for the masses, yet he is equally known for writing serious fiction. Therefore the objections against De's fiction do not have any serious basis. They seem to be the result of narrow and partial understanding of De's writings and her critical stance.

The available critical response to De's fiction is not only limited in volume but also seems to be based on only traditional perspective of the critics. There are critics like A.G. Khan who do not find De's fiction worth any critical evaluation simply because the life spectacle presented in her novels does not seem to them compatible with traditional Indian cultural ethos.[6] Such critical remarks about De's fiction, as a whole, have generally been formed, after reading one or two of her novels; Another recent book on Shobha De's novels *The Fiction of Shobha De*[7] though seems a full length study, yet falls short of becoming a comprehensive study due to the critics' rigid notions of literature and art. What these critics fail to notice in De's fiction is her specific narrative stance and the irony in her style and attitude towards not only her characters but also readers. Almost all the critics have been very harsh on De's fiction for the treatment of sex in it. Some have also been critical of the elements that approximate her novels to popular films. These critics have not taken into account the fact that the author's purposive stance makes her work more complex. Moreover the traditional concepts of the reader-writer relations based on the 'suspension of disbelief' and/or 'the illusion of reality' have been replaced by a certain disintegration of the concord between the reader and the writer.

Literature in the present context "assumes the form of a quintessentially personal, idiosyncratic, even weird vision of life, provoking, teasing, confusing, amusing or bewildering the reader in a playful, informal, knowing manner."[8] The striking features of the contemporary fiction include the unprecedented use of the fantastic and the author's deployment of various strategies to remind the readers that the work is indeed fiction. The conscious subversion of established social and literary norms also forms part of the contemporary design. So, an understanding of these elements prevalent in current critical circles and their application could also help examine De's fiction from a different perspective. De's treatment of the subject matter traditionally understood to be outrageous, deviated from the mainstream and placed on the margin of the social or moral propriety places her fiction in the postmodern category. The whole of De's fiction, thus demands a new perspective for its proper understanding.

A casual reading of De's fiction may give the impression that De doesn't have any serious concerns in her fiction and she simply depicts uninhibited life. Her fiction seems to be limited to the depiction of a particular segment of society having no sense of values or moral considerations. De's treatment of female sexuality gives the impression that she propagates free sex and macho female behaviour as a means of women's emancipation. But the reality is different and De's real concerns are rather otherwise. Her prime concern is to expose the futility and meaninglessness of such kind of pseudo feminist behaviour. Due to the irony involved in the narrative stance and De's clever handling of the subject matter the readers often fail to understand the hidden meaning and take the images created by De as reality. In this context those ideas expressing De's real concern related to the so-called modern women's behaviour in her fiction are worth quoting. "We are dying of cardiac arrest because we are foolishly cloning male behaviour. And paying a heavy price for our cheap mimicry. Look around you. See all those macho women? See how desperate they are to out-macho the men? To prove themselves? To establish their killer instincts? To win? Nothing wrong with any of this. Provided that women watch out for themselves. Protect themselves."[9] All these arguments establish that De is not only a popular writer but also a writer having social opinion that demands careful analysis and evaluation.

The formal and thematic aspects of contemporary Indo-English fiction, as briefed above, are the result of different theoretical developments that have influenced our understanding of life and literature in the recent past. These developments include post-colonialism, postmodernism and more particularly feminism. As Jasbir Jain writes, "postmodernism in its multiplicity, in its fragmented sense of reality, in its fractured sense of character and inconclusive and ambiguous endings is essentially the "ism" of the refugees, the post-colonials, the oppressed and the marginalised. It questions the concept of a centre and of singularity."[10] The understanding of reality governed by these views has exhibited a definite change in the nature of fictional narratives. As a challenge to the monolithic structure of culture and meaning, the contemporary novels exhibit multivalent voices and fusion of genres. In the changed scenario, "It is difficult to talk of a plot while discussing contemporary novels. There is no way one can recalculate a story. They are about experiences, situations, moods or happenings. Narrative strategies are equally nebulous, there are interrupted and disrupted narratives, there are multiple voices, multiple points of views and perspectives."[11] The impact of these theoretical developments on contemporary ways and narrative styles is quite evident in De's novels. Her text turns out to be slippery, deceptive, unstable and multivalent in nature. The indeterminacy of meaning prevents the critics from completely rejecting De's fiction as depiction of sexual orgies only. De, no doubt, writes popular fiction and has been bitterly criticized for this, but her writings reflect postmodern insistence on momentary pleasure and rejection of canonized literature and culture. De's creative use of multilingualism and her sceptical attitude towards her fictional world also speak of her unorthodox narrative stance.

De's fiction is largely built around the upper strata of modern Indian society and the world of showbiz. It forms the dream of the middle class people but it is, at the same time, a reality for the socialite people of Indian cosmopolitan cities. As the editor of popular journals like *Society*, *Stardust* and *Celebrity* and a fashion model, De herself had an opportunity to observe closely the life depicted in her novels. Therefore, she seems to knowingly concentrate on the life and the lifestyle of a section of society that she is familiar with, "I write about the section of Bombay society of which I have had a ring side view ...I'd be a poseur if I wrote about anything else."[12] The world created by De presents a glamorous and attractive picture of the affluent people and the people related to the showbiz. She cleverly and artistically exploits the romantic image of such people in the minds of the ordinary people. A careful study of De's fiction reveals that she herself doesn't believe in the world she depicts. The world of cut-throat competition high individualism and economic affluence does exist of course, but De doesn't propagate it. This makes her relation with her fiction as well as her readers quite ironical. Her creation of such a world becomes a lucrative co-incidence only. And she turns out to be a manufacturer of fiction like a commodity. The treatment of sex and the description of sexual relationships forms a major promotional backdrop of her fictional world. But a careful scrutiny reveals that these sexual activities are not meant to be a source of spiritual satisfaction or self gratification rather lead to frustrating and painful experience. Thus De's presentation is not only concerned with its outward glamour and attraction of the celluloid world but also brings out its trauma, sufferings and unhappiness underlying such a charmful world. De's aim in depicting such a world is not merely to exploit the taste of the common readers for popular images but also to expose the hollowness and inherent misery of this otherwise attractive world.

De's ironical narrative stance makes her fiction complex and artistic. De's narrative texts reveal their significance through the narrator and her own narrative stance. Be it the first person character-narrator or the third person omniscient narrator, neither of them can be identified with the author. De has been successful in maintaining that authorial distance. De's understanding of the public mind helps her make her fiction popular among the masses as she creates the romantic world of their dreams. She successfully exploits the popular image of the affluent, socialite people in the minds of the ordinary people. She uses stereotypical incidents, characters and situations to produce her work according to the public taste. She herself seems to be fully aware of the tactics she uses to create such a type of fiction. She, therefore, treats the fictional stereotypes ironically and satirizes their propagation. De's attitude and her narrative stance can be clearly seen from the endings of her novels. All the characters who lead uninhibited, promiscuous life of the richie-rich industrialists, starlets and the social prowlers, either finally disappear from the scene or repent and regret such a life.

The women characters, in particular, may seem aggressive and uncontrollable yet ultimately become domesticated and exhausted turning to ordinary settled family life. The recurring theme of search for inner happiness and the presentation of unhappy family life of the people populating De's world also makes her position clear. Not even a single couple, who indulges in the explicit pursuit of leisure and pleasure has been shown leading a happy, peaceful life. De has mocked at the society ladies, their behaviour and thoughts. She knows the frailties and frivolous concerns of this world. Her narrative strategies exploit these weaknesses in a highly effective and subtle way.

Shobha De's novels largely explore the physical and mental agonies of women characters. So the intrusion of feminine concerns is almost an imperative. De's thoughts about women's problems as presented in her fiction demand a special attention as they are expressed equally well in her prose writings. For example, in *Shooting From the Hip*, a collection of articles, she says, "Women the world over are given a raw deal. A rotten one. For this second sex, second class citizen status has always been the system."[13] De's concern with the women's problems, especially emotional and social, finds a central place in her fiction. Women characters in De's novels have been presented as autonomous beings free from all restrictions imposed by society, culture and their own sense of guilt. These women, in order to free themselves from male domination, assert their right and control not only on the social and economic aspects of life but also on their life and body as well. They suffer due to their misunderstanding of women's liberation. De's genuine feminist concerns can be understood from the unhappy relationships, sufferings and frustration of women who indulge in an imitation of the male behaviour. Her apparently deliciously depicted human relationships can be understood only if we match them with her ideas expressed in her prose works. For example, take her views as expressed in *Surviving Men,*[14] where she seems to be offering some useful lips to the modern women to avoid misery and heartaches at the hands of men. Her wit and warnings hide her contempt for the incompetence and idiocy of the so-called forward looking women. De's feminist stance, therefore, can be comprehended only if we watch the difference between what she seems to present and what she actually tries to say. De's advice to the so-called modern liberated women is implied clearly when she says. "Isn't it time we unlearn few guy things and started being women again."[15]

In her effort to exhibit different aspects of women's world, De tries to portray them from one extreme of highly conservative women who accept the traditional Indian cultural ethos to the radically modern, uninhibited and assertive women who challenge the patriarchal view of male hegemony and attempt to establish their own supremacy. There are women like Malini, Maltiben and Nisha's mother who have to bear the marital infidelity of their husbands and Maya who has to lead a secluded, lonely and charmless life, in spite of her being a qualified textile designer, due to the uncaring and selfish behaviour of her husband. These women suffer their subjugated and marginalised position yet they do not rebel openly. They try to adjust in spite of their restlessness and small protestations revealed only at the times of extreme oppression. On the other hand there are modern women like Aasha Rani, Anjali,

Karuna, Ritu, Meenakshi Iyenger and others who try to beat men at their game. These women indulge in uninhibited, promiscuous and unconventional sexual behaviour to challenge and reject male domination. This type of behaviour forms their efforts to gain independence and real joy. As a critical reader one can discover that De shows a lot of scepticism about the relative merits of either of these feminist positions. She seems to be eternally in a dilemma to give her final opinion on the issue of liberation of women. One noticeable view that keeps recurring in her different fictional and prose works is that man-woman relationships need to be redefined.

However, from a number of dialogues and direct statements found in De's fiction one can conclude that she is not very comfortable with the typical feminist stance of her characters (especially of the sexually liberated or promiscuous type). The challenge these women seem to put against the patriarchal male behaviour comes out in the form of their indulgence in uninhibited sex. This also brings out the ultimate disgust and revulsion that these women experience even during the sex act that apparently seems charming and joyful: "He'd come into her in thick, smelly, hot spurts, grunting at the release, sweating profusely, his eyes squeezed shut, his ugly mouth hanging open, dribbling saliva between her moist breasts. Reema had gone home and rushed to the bathroom to wash herself that night" (*Snapshots* 98). Another thing that makes this kind of conclusion a more plausible proposition is the typical fate, a failure that her liberated characters meet in the end. Their quest for real love, lasting happiness and viable human relationships turns futile. In *Socialite Evenings* Anjali turns to religion and Ritu goes back to her husband after leading an uninhibited life. Similarly Malika and Alisha in *Sisters*, Aasha Rani in *Starry Nights* express their dislike for the type of promiscuous life they had been leading and Meenakshi Iyenger in *Strange Obsession* meets a tragic end. De is the master of the art of trivialisation. Her mocking of these society women marks her ironical attitude towards serious issues. Her narrative can be absolutely cool and morally non-committing about the insidious ways of her characters. Talking about a man, for example Rashmi, in *Snapshots*, says, "His name was Anupam and he was one of many. I mean he wasn't my boyfriend or anything. Just one of the guys I was sleeping with" (134).

In spite of the revulsion, cool indifference and morally neutral stance in De's fiction, the dilemma about the right and the wrong persists. De does not give clear cut and final views on the issue related to women's liberation or identity. Her not giving any alternative in eternal, ultimate and totalitarian terms brings her close to the postmodernist position where everything is provisional and relative. De's clever handling of the issue gives the readers an opportunity not only to assess the novelist's views but also to judge the relative merits of the different feminist positions presented there.

An analysis and evaluation of De's language will also reveal her serious concern with human communication and interpersonal relationships. Throwing away the conventional use of pure and standard language, De has changed, moulded and added of her own to the existing forms and uses of English language. She is the pioneer in the use of mixed code. Since her 'Startdust' days, she has popularised a form of English that is the natural outcome of extensive contact between English and the Indian vernaculars. The language used by De, despite its lexical and grammatical aberrations, suits her characters. Different characters use the language according to their social status and professional requirements. An interesting example of De's use of language can be observed in 'English laced with Hindi;' as used by a professional in the film world. "Myself Kishenbhai, producer, actually speaking assistant producer. Madamji, I am on look out for new talent. I am knowing everybody...all big-big producers, hero log, heroines, everybody...South Indian girls are good. No khit-pit, no faltu nakhras" (*Starry Nights* 7). Whereas De's creative use of Hindi words into written English makes her a vanguard of literati, the use of some typical regional expressions like 'sadela' lagaoing, 'Innu voru dam addi' and complete sentences in Hindi "Lubna begum ab budhi ho gayi hai" (*Starry Nights* 57) create problems in understanding her fiction.

De's use of language exhibits the actual tendency in contemporary social life towards the fragmentation of linguistic norms. Nowadays each group favours a curious use of a private language and every profession has developed its own code or dialect that ultimately marks its members as distinct individuals, at the same time a part of a highly solidified group. De's clever use of a typical language also becomes a highly suitable medium for showing the true colours of her characters. On too many occasions, she has used language to mirror the hypocrisy, vanity and such other dubious social acts of her phoney characters. Linguistic code switching thus suits her ironical stance and reveals her deeper concern about internal conflicts, individual aspirations, cultural fusion and pragmatic obligations.

Although De is a popular fiction writer, yet her writings cannot be understood in crass commercial terms only. Her artistic, creative and literary concerns deserve serious and close look. Her fiction does not attempt to reform the society but present it amusingly in naturalistic terms along with its idiosyncracies. As a disinterested observer she tries to portray the life of a section of society that no doubt exists in the modern Indian metropolitans and the world of showbiz. She presents what she has observed leaving the job of reforming or improving it to the social organisations, politicians and moral preachers. Her success has, however, ensured that the literary boundaries are arbitrary and no fiction is worth its salt if it is not readable and contemporary in its appeal. A study of De's fiction is therefore likely to yield us new perspectives on the expanding literary horizon of the contemporary Indo-English fiction. It will also ascertain the impact that emerging formats of fiction have caused on the global literary trends.

REFERENCES

1. "Raj Reversal," *Sunday* 8-13 Dec. 1990, 32.
2. Sunanda Swarup, *Feature in Femina*, 8 May 1993, 9.
3. Ravi Shankar, "Sleaze-Shots, De's Magnificent Obsession," *India Today* March 31, 1995, 207.

4. Tarun Tejpal, "The Beastly Beautitudes of Shobha De," *India Today* September 30, 1993, 97.
5. Peter Humm, Paul Stigant et al., "Introduction," *Popular Fictions: Essays in Literature and History* (London and New York: Methuen, 1986), 6.
6. A.G. Khan, Shobha De *Vatsyayani*, Veena Noble Dass, R.K. Dhawan (ed.), *The Fiction of the Nineties*, 47.
7. Jaydip Singh Dodiya (ed.), *The Fiction of Shobha De: Critical Studies* (Delhi: Prestige Books, 2000).
8. M.K. Bhatnagar, "Post-modernism—An Introduction," M.K. Bhatnagar, M. Rajeshwar (ed.) *Post-Modernism and English Literature* (Delhi: Atlantic Publishers and Distributors, 1999), 2.
9. Shobha De, "Time to be Women Again." *The Week* January 17, 1999, 10.
10. Jasbir Jain, "The Plural Tradition" *Spectrum History of Indian Literature in English*, 87.
11. *Ibid.*, 84-85.
12. Shobha De, quoted by Ranjit Hoskote in "The Dawning of a new De," *Times of India* 2 April, 1995.
13. Shobha De, *Shooting From the Hip: Selected Writings* (New Delhi: UBS Publishers and Distributors, 1994), 116.
14. Shobha De, *Surviving Men: The Smart Woman's Guide to Staying on Top* (New Delhi: Penguin Books, 1997).
15. Shobha De, *The Week* January 17, 1999, 10.

The Holder of the World: A Saga of Alienation and Assimilation

14

G.A. GHANSHYAM

"She did not believe him, but she too longed for escape."[1] The question is "why would a self-possessed, intelligent, desirable woman like Hannah Easton suddenly marry a man she recognised as inappropriate and untrustworthy? (69). The answer is obvious 'escape.' An escape from isolation, alienation and detachment from her own existing claustrophobic Puritan society.

Hannah Easton, the main protagonist of Bharati Mukherjee's fourth novel, *The Holder of the World* is an orphan adopted by Robert and Susannah Fitch at an early age of fifteen. As the first part of the novel reveals, she is a misfit in the rule-bound, conservative, Puritan society, surrounded by gray and gloom, for, she is a girl desirous of riches and colourful life. Her suppressed desires are unveiled through her colourful, bright embroidery she weaves. Unable to belong, she is alienated from her society and family, making her a typical heroine of Bharati Mukherjee.

Bharati Mukherjee, a world-acclaimed novelist of post-modern era, has taken up the theme of alienation and assimilation as one of the major themes in all her five novels and two collections of short stories, depicting the psychological, cultural and spiritual stress and strain faced by expatriates migrating to other countries in search of fortune. She, like Anita Desai, Arun Joshi, Shashi Deshpande and many other postmodern writers, probes into the inner dimension of her protagonists, critically analysing and artistically delineating the mental trauma and tension of modern men and women. Twentieth century being described by many, as the age of anxiety and age of alienation novelists have drifted from external to internal and social to individual mental odyssey of their protagonists. With modernisation expanding its tentacles, squeezing the traditional social and family system, breaking them apart, man is engulfed by an identity crisis and man's greed for material possession has made him migrate to different lands, uprooting himself from his culture and society to re-root in an alien land. But striking one's own root is a painful process, involving mental, spiritual and emotional trauma leading to cultural and self-alienation, because to feel uprooted is against man's nature, for, as a physical being, man needs to be located in space. As Ashley Montague points out in *Man in Progress*:

> No living organism is either solitary in its origin or solitary in its life. Every organism from the lowest to the highest is normally engaged in some sort of social life. The solitary animal in any species, is an abnormal creature.[2]

Born in India and married to Canadian writer, Clark Blaise, Mukherjee lived in Canada for fourteen years as an expatriate and later came to the United States to settle down as an immigrant. Her various life's experience is a saga of alienation and assimilation. She has woven her own life experience and her immense literary knowledge, blending with her imagination, into beautiful, interesting mind-capturing fictional work. All her novels depict the theme of alienation and displacement of the protagonists at the beginning and finally ending with reconciliation leading to assimilation.

In Bharati Mukherjee's first novel, *The Tiger's Daughter*[3] (1971) Tara Banerjee Cartright displays an expatriate sensibility and a sense of exile. She returns to India after seven years in America, to find nothing to her liking in her own land. She fails to link herself to either of the two cultures, East or West. This 'Trishanku' situation frustrates and bewilders her, alienating her from herself as well as her own culture. Dimple Dasgupta of Mukherjee's second novel, *Wife*[4] (1976) appears as victim of conflicting cultures. She fails to be at peace with herself as well as with her surroundings. Both Tara as well as Dimple suffers from cultural alienation by rejecting and repelling from reality. Eventually escaping into illusion, they drift farther and farther away from reality, leading to nowhere. But Mukherjee's third novel *Jasmine*[5] (1990) represents assimilation of alien cultural more. Jasmine the title character is under transformation to adopt to the new land, she enters by her fate.

Like *Jasmine* Mukherjee's fourth novel, *The Holder of the World* too, is a story of alienation and assimilation, but with a difference. In this story the protagonist is not an Indian but a white Puritan woman of 17th century who comes from West to East in search of love and life. Mukherjee artistically unveils the hidden mute motives and impulses of Hannah Easton, which bring her to exotic India of Mughal period from Puritan 17th century New England, finally going back to America as Christian-Hindu-Muslim lady. Mukherjee, a great artist of psychological insight delves deep into protagonist's psyche to reveal her thoughts and experiences. The journey of Hannah to 'the physically conscious self-indulgent and fastidious passionate world of east' is not an accident; rather it is a long, cherished dream come true. Hannah's early life clearly reveals her passion for love and emotions, a life essentially denied to her in Puritan World of 17th Century. This denial suppresses her latent urge, leading to alienation. Though she keeps mum, there is an inner volcanic lava ready to burst open at the very first opportunity, which comes in the form of her marriage to swashbuckling, sea-farer, Gabriel Legge, who joins East India Company but later, is killed in an encounter in India while pirating.

At this point, the novel is, like Bharati Mukherjee's other novels, a fiction of expatriation, a quest and a journey, not only to culturally variant societies, which help to question and abandon conventional moral and social values but it is a search for identity. Hannah's life succeeds in questioning and discovering new ways of defining reality, in a world, which is essentially orthodox.

Mukherjee develops the theme in a totally new and unique way in this novel. She knits the three hundred-year-old history with the help of most modern computech. The story is constructed through two narrators, belonging to two different ages. One being, modern American assets researcher, Beigh Masters, who is married to Venn Iyer, a computech engineer from Madras. Both together develop the latest computer programme to reach the most precious diamond 'The Emperor Tear' and in the process find the white Puritan woman, Hannah as Salem Bibi with the diamond in her hand standing in Aurangzeb's court. The second is Hannah Easton, born in wilds of Massachusetts Bay colony in 1670, whose father dies of bee sting and mother elopes with her Nipmuc lover when Hannah is only five years old, which leaves unerasable impression on the young child's mind.

> The ultimate unnatural crime of Puritan life.... She witnessed the fall, not Adam's Fall Rebecca's Fall.... She is the witness not merely of the occasion of the sin, birth of the sin itself...in the scorched sceptic month of August. (30)

This ineradicable imprint of her mother's crime and perhaps her birth (genetic) does not permit her to belong, making her live in exile in her own family and country, devoid of any sustaining sense of connection to her environment, for, 'Hannah is a person undreamed of in Puritan Society' (59).

Mukherjee depicts Hannah's character as 'bold, independent and ready to act' kind which is unthought of in an orthodox, conservative society, which is the reason for her alienation. Thus, for Hannah, like Bharati Mukherjee herself, the exile from her old culture and immigration to new land becomes an exciting and exhilarating process.

Hannah could overcome the cultural barriers and hold the colliding worlds into which she steps in. A time when people hardly had the concept of cross-cultural interaction and a sense of tension and pain, when people only traveled for material gains, purpose of Hannah's journey was entirely different. For Hannah, the voyage was not a physical journey but an internal or mental one. "She was alert to novelty, but her voyage was mental, interior. Getting there was important, but savoring the comparisons with London or Salem, and watching life being transformed, that was pleasure. She did not hold India up to inspection by lamp of England or of Christianity (or Salem) upon the completion of Gabriel's tour" (62).

Hannah did not feel bereft of her roots and traditions while in India, like other white women, though; her life was exposed to a range of adventures and misadventures. She could totally embrace Hindu world, understanding Hindu philosophy of human existence as "Moksha is achieved when the I-self overcomes the binary view of the world as self and others."[6]

This view of Indian philosophy enables the immigrant to lessen the pain of alienation and displacement. Bharati Mukherjee, through this novel has strongly believed in the Hindu philosophy of 'Vasudhaiva Kutumbakam.'

The exalted self of Hannah enables her to be at peace, embracing the diversities of culture and identities. Her new identity as Bibi (mistress) of Jadav Singh of Devgad (whom she loves deeply) and her intimate companion Bhagmati fulfils her craving for love. She is depicted as embodiment of peace and love. Even when Aurangzeb kills her lover and arrests her, she remains calm, advising to shun the path of violence and war which only brings misery.

Hannah is different from other white women in the novel because she is still connected to the emotional realities of human life at all levels and places. For her an Indian or any other person, was above all a human being, with whom she could readily seek link. It was this openness of experience and connectedness to human beings that enables Hannah to merge with the ultimate, enjoying the true bliss of assimilation, even with different identities and in an alien land.

The meticulousness of Bharati Mukherjee is manifested in developing the complexity and depth of the story. The exuberance of the New World is emphasised by juxtaposing Hannah's claustrophobic life in Puritan society with life in India. The novel moves in three-time span simultaneously past, present and future, making the reader feel like a 'time traveler.'

The novel is an account of adaptation, not rejection. Mukherjee demonstrates how one can adopt and assimilate and also have moral centre and focus in spite of the physical disaster and psychological injuries. Detachment doesn't mean withdrawal from life and action but renunciation of selfish desires. To quote *The Bhagvad Gita*:

> Yas tv indriyani manasa
> Niyamyarabhate'rjuna
> Karmendriyaih karma-yogam
> Asaktah sa visisyate[7]
>
> (But he who controls the senses by the mind, O Arjuna, and without attachment engages the organs of action in the path of work, is superior.)

REFERENCES

1. Bharati Mukherjee, *The Holder of the World* (Toronto: Harper Collins Publishers Ltd., 1993) 67. (Rest of the extracts is from the same edition of the novel).
2. *The Foreigner: Chaos of Cultural Confusion*, Ailing Alien. 81.
3. Bharati Mukherjee, *Tiger's Daughter* (New Delhi: Penguin Books India Ltd., 1990).
4. Bharati Mukherjee, *Wife* (New Delhi: Sterling Publishers, 1976).
5. Bharati Mukherjee, *Jasmine* (New Delhi: Viking, 1990).
6. Sudhir Kakar, *The Inner World: The Psycho-Analytic Study of Childhood and Society in India* (New Delhi: Oxford University Press, 1978).
7. S. Radhakrishnan, *The Bhagvad Gita* (London: George Allen and Unwin, 1948) Ch. 3 verse 7.

Arundhati Roy's Shock Treatment: Comments on *The God of Small Things*

15

SHUBHA TIWARI

We do not have a Shakespeare in our midst. A Shakespeare might have known how to create out of pure imagination. He might have known how to make his readers weep and laugh through the pages without himself doing so—a master craftsman, a detached creator almost like God! Well, we do not have any such one in our midst who could create sheer, unpolluted and impossible joy of an *As You Like It* or thick, weighty, overwhelming pain of a *Hamlet*. What we have instead are some talented and some not so talented people prone to writing who live out their own life stories in the pages, sometimes mixing a mild dose of imagination just as an expert cook uses spices. But the backbone of the narrative remains the life of the author. The intensity in the words comes only when the author describes something s/he has gone through. There is a spate of such fiction these days. The difference comes only with the caliber of the writer. But there cannot be any doubt about the fact that this novel of the present wave is born out of narcisstic compulsions of the author. Some succeed in enlarging the frame and bringing in some universality; others make it a morbid tale of self-love and self-justification. Arundhati uses the material from her life in a very unsettling, unique way. The subtle mixes with the grotesque, the delicate with the worldly. She crosses limits. She sets her own rules. The novel, *The God of Small Things* is the biggest success story of recent Indian fiction simply because of Arundhati's ability to shock in style, to describe sex without looking vulgar, to portray child abuse with compassion, to suggest sibling sex as an urgency, police atrocities as suggestive of a larger sickness, and to show our society as one big cell pool without stench. The stuff is the same, just the same—inter-caste love and sex, child abuse, social ills etc. Her life is uncommon in its utmost commonness. But its presentation gives it the tinge of sublimity. Just as a seventy mm screen transforms ordinary acts into symbols and comments, Arundhati's power of uncompromising portrayal alters the ordinary into extraordinary. She creates her own language. Sentences need not necessarily be grammatically correct. Spellings are played upon. New words, new meanings, and new images are created.

The positioning of the author in the scheme of things is important to understand the novel. *The God of Small Things* is a story of Estha, a boy and Rahel, a girl. They are twins. Arundhati is more or less Rahel. Estha is her wronged brother. He is wronged in various ways. Their mother Ammu is also wronged. Ammu, Estha and Rahel are on one side, the rest of the world on the other. It is a tale of self-love and self-defense. Whatever Rahel does is compassionately described. Whatever the world does to her is described with extreme hostility. Words transform everything. Words are so deceptive, really. Use words in one manner and the situation arouses sorrow, use words in another manner and the same situation arouses repulsion. But then, this is fiction, an art of using words. And we can hardly expect an author to write her own tale with someone else's perspective.

Before going into analysis, our own loyalties as readers need to be fixed. Naturally we are with the author's team. But I must warn that fixing loyalties as readers is a tricky business. Usually you sympathize with a character who looks and feels like you. But what to do with a novel where no one comes near you. To go for a reader's necessary process of identification and catharsis, you have to imagine and then sympathize with a character and her group. But for this book, we as readers will exercise our right to go back on our *loyalty* sometimes and offer one or two terse comments on *our* side as well. This to me seems to be a suitable way of criticizing this book simply because I cannot commit myself completely to one side here. The activities, actions, reactions, problems and their solutions used and found by *our* side become too much for my sensibilities. This is where I say that Arundhati goes beyond limits.

Let us begin with Estha and Rahel's relationship. It is true that they are a butchered lot. They suffer humiliation, abuse, unjust accusation, separation and what not. But to suggest sex between the siblings as a kind of urgent and only solution seems absurd and perverse to me. Arundhati is against love laws. Throughout the novel she satirically repeats the words, '...Love Laws lay down who should be loved. And how. And how much' (177). She tears apart traditions, caste consciousness, and any rule which even remotely dictates 'who should be loved. And how. And how much.' But what she finally suggests between brother and sister is in no way acceptable in the name of rebellion against love laws,' Estha, sitting very straight, waiting to be arrested, takes his finger to it (Rahel's mouth).... His hand is held and kissed.... Then she sat and put her arms around him. Drew him down beside her.... There is very little that anyone could say to clarify what happened next. Nothing that...would separate sex from love. Or needs from feelings.... Only that there was a snuffing in the hollows at the base of a lovely throat. Only that a hard honey-coloured shoulder had a semi circle of teethmarks on it. Only that they held each other close, long after it was over.... Only that once again they broke the Love Laws. That lay down who should be loved. And how. And how much' (327-28).

What Arundhati suggests here is not only disgusting but also against her own view. At more than one point in the novel, she criticizes inbreeding among Syrian Christians. She says that inbreeding in a community increase genetic disease as well as cases of insanity. Chako said that the high incidence of insanity among Syrian Christians was the price they paid for Inbreeding (223). At one point she is against inbreeding and yet at another she suggests the worst form of possible inbreeding. A very simple answer that comes to my mind is what film critics used to say about Raj Kapoor's films. He was always ahead of his times in portraying sex on screen. When other heroes only dared to look in the heroine's eyes, he would kiss her. When others started kissing, he began striptease calculatingly unfolding the heroine in *Bobby, Satyam Shivam Sundaram,* then *Prem Rog,* and finally *Ram Teri Ganga Maili.* And he did it in style-fetish vulgarity. The same is true here. Arundhati has words, wonderful words. She has tremendous style. In the novel also breaking of love laws proceeds step by step. In Ammu's times no one dared to love a low caste man, so Ammu did that. In Rahel's times, no one would bother if an America returned divorcee goes with a Paravan, or Dhobi, so she goes for her own twin brother. Certainly it startles and shocks the reader. I am told that Raj Kamal Jha's novel, *The Blue Bedspread* is all about sibling sex and incestuous relationships. But then he might be lacking in panache. Amitabh Bachchan presented *Kaun Banega Crorepati,* where the prize money could go up to a maximum of one crore. The show was an all time record-breaking success. The TRP ratings soared up and up. Anupam Kher and Govinda also presented their respective shows, where the prize money could go up to ten crores or so and yet the shows were flops. So that is the power of chic and élan. That is how the market works, be it a tele serial, film, modish novel or any commercial product. That is how I view *The God of Small Things*. The book is the single biggest hit of Indian fiction. I do not think that it will make a mark hundred years hence. But for the most powerful *now,* it has succeeded in raising a storm, turning our Arundhati into an international star. She knows how to use her celebrity status. It is a different matter altogether that awards, prizes, and sale statistics are no measure for a book's real worth. Gandhi never got a Nobel, and Premchand never a Booker. And Saddam Hussain would have got Nobel Peace Prize, had he surrendered before the Americans prior to war.

But for the sake of this present thrill that the book has provided, let us talk about it. And there are some, if not many, literary reasons also for its success. I will try my best to keep my cynicism away that the book does generate in me.

Estha shows signs of withdrawal right from the beginning. As a boy he is sensitive. He is inclined to keep the hurts to himself. Quite significantly, he is called a 'keeper of records' at one place. He keeps a record of all insults and injustice that he receives. The whole description of Estha is centred on inwardness, 'He retreated into further stillness. As though his body had the power to snatch its senses inwards (knotted, egg-shaped), away from the surface of his skin, into some deeper more inaccessible recess' (93). To match such an intensely introvert temperament, Estha faces extreme pain, insult, abuse, and injustice. He is held responsible for Sophie Mol's accidental death by his cruel, spinster aunt Baby Kochamma. Needless to add that he is not responsible for the death. He is sexually abused by Lemondrink man at Abhilash Talkies. More than that the man instills fear in Estha lest he might disclose the crime to anyone. As though this was not enough, he is separated from his mother and sister and sent to a drunkard father and a stepmother at Kolkata. Things could not have been worse for this unfortunate boy. Silence is his reaction, his revenge against this brutal world. It is as though the agony has over flown the danger level mark and there is nothing left to say. Verbal communication loses its meaning. Rahel cannot reach out to Estha except communicating through the body, the senses. That is how things have been portrayed in this novel. There is no let out, no vent, no room for Estha. The doors are shut. He is suffocated. After Abhilash Talkies experience, all that he could do was to vomit, 'He vomited a clear, bitter, lemony, sparkling, fizzy liquid. The acrid aftertaste of a Little Man's first encounter with fear' (119). It is fear that throttles Estha and finally chokes his voice. Arundhati, in a brilliant piece of analysis explains the tragedy, 'You're not the Sinners. You're the Sinned Against. You were only children. You had no control. You are the victims, not the perpetrators' (191). But there is no such help, no anger, no redress, no justice and no solution. Only, there is Estha who is quiet, who walks miles and miles, even in rain, getting drenched and who is obsessed with washing clothes. It is not clothes he is washing; he is trying to wash and clean his childhood. Childhood should be free, innocent and protected. But unfortunately there happened murky, ghastly things in his childhood, over which, he had no control. His responsive, communicative side is destroyed when he is separated from Ammu and Rahel, the two people in the world he loves and wants to live with.

Little Estha draws his own lessons, '(a) Anything can happen to Anyone, and (b) It's best to be prepared' (194). Perhaps he does not realize that there are certain things for which no amount of preparedness works. What follows is a very cruel and very touching description of Estha's departure. He is panicky. He does not want to go. The pages bear the pain of parting of a small son from his mother. Then the three of them start daydreaming together, 'I'll be a teacher. I'll start a school. And you and Rahel will be in it. And we'll be able to afford it because it will be ours! Estha said with his enduring pragmatism.... We'll have our own house, Ammu said. A little house, Rahel said. And our school we'll have classrooms and blackboards, Estha said' (325). With this sort of daydreaming, Estha parts. The school never happens. Ammu dies. Rahel goes to boarding schools, one after another. Estha loses his voice. He is silenced like death itself. His life goes waste. He is rightly compared to the wronged mythological hero, Karna. It is Estha's words that Kathakali man is voicing, 'Where were you...when I needed you most? Did you ever hold me in your arms? Did you feed me? Did you ever look for me? Did you wonder where I might be? Did you know how much I missed you?' (233).

The psychological dimension of Estha's case is only too glaring. Estha is sort of an enigma right from the beginning. His report card as a child says, 'Does not participate in Group Activities' (11). The seeds of looming silence were always there. Silence can be unnoticeable as also very loud and obstructive, 'Yet Estha's silence was never awkward. Never intrusive. Never noisy' (10). The whole tragedy can be summed up in the Darwinian law of survival of the fittest. For Estha, a flying bird signifies the fact that something so fragile, so unbearably tender had survived, had been *allowed* to exist, was a miracle' (12). The world with all its practical wisdom, cruel ways, prosaic thinking ruins the vulnerable, the delicate, the sensitive. This is exactly what happens with Estha. His eyes have been described as 'hunted.' Arundhati also points out the conditional love that Estha and Rahel receive from their mother. Ammu is a disciplinarian. If they behave according to the code, they get love; if they flout rules, they get less love. This type of mother terror weakens the twins internally, thereby making them less armed to face the world.

A kind of superhuman attachment has been suggested between Rahel and Estha throughout the novel. They may be two bodies but they have one soul. Communication need not be verbal between them. One knows instinctively what the other is feeling or going through. If one is standing at the door, the other knows even without any noise that the latch is to be undone. This feeling of oneness has been suggested and not concretely defined. This tells a lot about Arundhati's narrative techniques. The language is full of short, suggestive and pert remarks. Here and there shock treatment is given to the reader. Describing Ammu's huge pregnancy, she suddenly says, 'That was before they (Rahel's parents) were divorced and Ammu came back to live in Kerala' (3). While enjoying the scenario of birth and life, this sad sentence like a bitter pill is administered on the reader. As one reads the novel, one has the feeling of a great, big mystery being unfolded. It is like a ticking bomb that is about to explode any time. And explode it does when Sophie Mol dies, when Ammu mates with Velutha, when Velutha dies of police torture, when Estha stops speaking, and when sex is suggested between the twins. The bomb of human tragedy keeps exploding in this story. The whole book has a fateful tragic air. The oft repeated sentences (like, 'It's true. Things can change in a day.') are like tolling bells indicating impending disaster. These repeated lines are a symbol of fate, of unchangeable human destiny. Repetition of certain selected sentence throughout the novel is one of the major techniques of Arundhati. It is an effective technique as well. When nothing else makes an impression, mere repetition does.

Sorrow is an integral part of this novel. The story begins with the death of nine years old Sophie Mol, a cousin of Estha and Rahel. Her tombstone read, 'A Sunbeam Lent To Us Too Briefly' (7). It is at the funeral itself that the boundaries are drawn, 'Though Ammu, Estha and Rahel were allowed to attend the funeral, they were made to stand separately, not with the rest of the family. Nobody would look at them' (5). *Our* group is held responsible for a crime they have not committed. They have no role, no deliberate role at least in the tragic death but guilt is pressed on the tender minds of the kids. As the novel proceeds the tragic air sticks. The talk of punishment to kids is so painful. Pain comes almost as a person in different attires throughout the novel. When Margaret, Chako's ex-wife comes from England, Arundhati writes, 'But around her the air was sad, somehow. And behind the smile in her eyes, the Grief was a fresh, shining blue' (143). The book does not let you soar. With every joy, the hint of sorrow is intricately packed.

Similes are one lovely asset of Arundhati. The similes are the soul of her now legendary narrative skills. The similes are so impressive that one wants to remember them and preserve them. They are unusual, shocking, and yet so exact. Usually an abstract idea is clarified for the reader with the help of a concrete comparison. But here, there is no such pattern. The insects are like ideas (9), eyes are like a boat in the river (19), church swells like a throat with voices (6), when marrying, Rahel is like a passenger drifting towards an unoccupied chair in an airport lounge (18), the abandoned garden is like a circus whose animals have forgotten their tricks (27), Rahel's coming teeth are like words in a pen (37) and Ammu's bridal dressing is like polishing firewood (44). The similes of this book, in fact, deserve a separate, full length paper. They are simply beautiful. They evoke a deep feeling, a very profound, sad sentiment. They drive the message home. They are definitely the best part of Arundhati's linguistic arsenal. The cucumber becomes elderly, anything permanent is as permanent as a government job, eyes of an old lady are like butter spread behind specs, and television voices are noisy silence.

The prevailing conditions in India are another regularly hinted area of this novel. Nothing is articulated coherently yet much is conveyed. Right in the beginning, the role of police, and their attitudes are displayed when Inspector Thomas Matthew 'stared at Ammu's breasts as he spoke. He said the police knew all they needed to know and that the Kottayam Police didn't take statements from Veshyas or their illegitimate children.... 'If I were you,' he said, 'I'd go home quietly.' Then he tapped her breast with his baton.... Behind him a red and blue board said:

P oliteness
O bedience
L oyalty
I ntelligence
C ourtesy
E fficiency. (8)

Indian police is reduced to a cruel joke. Arundhati's political agenda (for which she is so famous now) has its seeds in this novel. Passing comments like giving reservation to converted Christians or the harm done by pesticides purchased from World Bank loans hint at the political agenda of the author. The tragedy of India is that even after five decades of political freedom she has not been able to realize its potential in any field. 'In the country that she (Rahel) came from, poised forever between the terror of war and the horror of peace, Worse Things kept happening' (19). The author's sarcasm is always there, ready to surface itself any moment at the slightest provocation. She says that 'we live(d) in a society where a man's death could be more profitable than his life had ever been' (281).

The bitter, comic taste comes when the people of Ayemenem receive Rahel and Estha back. The crudeness of perceptions is sharply brought out. 'It occurred to Comrade Pillai that his generation was perhaps paying for its forefathers' bourgeois decadence. *One was mad. The other divorced. Probably barren'* (130). The Indian concept of success is 'a house, and a Bajaj scooter. A wife and an *issue*' (134). This is how India is portrayed.

Rahel goes to America after marrying an American, Larry McCaslin. She gets divorced soon and returns. But a single word has not been dropped at or against McCaslin or American culture and way of life. As I hinted earlier, the narcissism of the author is only too obvious when she deals with Rahel. An uncommon beauty with speaking eyes when she is called a jazz tune, we know that Arundhati is talking about herself. Rahel is not held responsible for anything. Her decorating cowdung cakes with flowers in school or colliding with other girls to know whether breasts hurt—everything is described with narcissistic tenderness. The culmination of this self-love is reached when sex is suggested between Rahel and Estha without any tinge of guilt or regret as though it is the most natural thing to happen in the world!

Ammu's tale again is a self-indulgent extension of Rahel's narrative. She too is declared innocent in Arundhati's court. That is, of course, a child would describe her mother. Ammu begins her innings with a blunder a drunkard and liar. Things reach a tragic climax when Mr. Hollick, the English plantation manager offers to help the family if the extremely attractive Ammu 'be sent to his bungalow to be looked after' (42). Ammu's husband has no objection to the honourable proposal. Ammu returns to Ayemenem with her so vulnerable, so tender, so innocent 'frogs engrossed in each other's company, lolloping arm in arm down a highway full of hurtling traffic. Entirely oblivious of what trucks can do to frogs. Ammu watched over them fiercely. Her watchfulness stretched her, made her tout and tense. She was quick to reprimand her children, but even quicker to take offense on their behalf' (43).

Well, this lady, Ammu, has no time and no thought for herself. She knows that her chance at happiness is forever gone. Her abandoned sexuality, her emotional and physical needs emerge from her inner recesses at times. When she listens to soft, romantic songs on radio, something stirs within her. Her life is juxtaposed between two sad polarities—'The infinite tenderness of motherhood and the reckless rage of a suicide bomber.' This rage of a suicide bomber being her rejection of her sensual urges. When her longing for coziness gets unbearable, she walks wildly, swims at night, and wears flowers in her hair. She has been written off by the society. A divorced woman from an intercaste love marriage is dangerous indeed. She has nothing to lose. She becomes a woman with an unsafe edge. Finally, in a futile attempt to fight her cruel fate, this gloomy, beautiful, young woman falls in love with a low caste Paravan, named Velutha. He is also a man loved by her children during the day time. In the nights, it is her turn. Velutha too is portrayed as no ordinary man. He is quite a man—skilled, educated, and thoughtful in his own way. Above it all, he is acutely aware of the injustice of the caste tag. The chemistry between Ammu and Velutha is simply exploding. He loves her. She is loved by him. Together they refuse to budge to the love laws of the society as to who should be loved and how and how much. But then Velutha is just a man, no demigod. He has no magical power with which to fight society. He could do only one thing at a time. When he held Ammu with both hands 'he had no other arm with which to fight the shadows that flickered around him on the floor...in the shadows there were metal folding chairs arranged in a ring and on the chairs there were people, with slanting rhinestone sunglasses watching' (215). Velutha is killed by the police for flouting social laws, for being a Paravan, and still loving a Brahmin Syrian Christian. He is brutally, mercilessly, torturously killed by the police. The caring softness of his love is wasted, 'Ridges of muscle on his stomach rose under his skin like divisions of a slab of chocolate. He held her close, by the light of an oil lamp, and he shone as though he had been polished with a high-wax body polish. He could do only one thing at a time. If he held her, he couldn't kiss her. If he kissed her, he couldn't see her. If he saw her, he couldn't feel her' (215).

Velutha is the god of small things. This book is a rejection of all things that are big, great, dignified, correct, or perfect. It is imperfection that is portrayed here. Human weakness is celebrated with a bang. India with all her caste/class dividing consciousness has been targeted. With Velutha's death, the question of unethical treatment of lower castes is forcefully raised. Taboos are broken. If they are broken a little too far with Estha and Rahel, we can only say that much is to be forgiven to those who write well. I do not weigh Arundhati by any prize or 'copies sold' statistics. I can give her just one title, 'An Excellent Word Weaver.'

REFERENCE

Roy, Arundhati. 1997. *The God of Small Things*. New Delhi: Penguin Books (2002). All the page numbers in parentheses are from this edition.

Life's Hidden Patterns: A Thematic Study of *The God of Small Things*

16

BINAYAK RAY

> Live and let live, love and let love, flower and fade, and follow the natural curve, which flows on, pointless.
>
> —D.H. Lawrence, *The Letters of D.H. Lawrence*

Isolated things did not mean anything. As though the intelligence that decides life's hidden patterns—that connects reflections to images, glints to light, weaves to fabrics, needles to thread, walls to rooms, love to fear to anger to remorse was suddenly lost.—Arundhati Roy, *The God of Small Things*, 225-26.

Arundhati Roy's literary fame rests in the main on her only published novel to date *The God of Small Things*. Binoo K. John speculates that "For all we know, she might be a one-book marvel" (26). K.V. Surendran goes one better. He makes an undocumented claim that "Roy herself has remarked that *The God of Small Things* would be her first and last book" (248). A.N. Dwivedi considers Roy's one book not enough as a passport to fame. "A literary star ascending to the sky with a single shot," he thinks, "arouses doubts and distresses in the reader's mind" (1). By the some token, Dwivedi would have to deny greatness to such universally acclaimed one-novel novelists as Emily Bronte and Marcel Proust. Granted that as a one—novel novelist, Roy is in good company; her caliber, however, remains to be proved. For a starter, translation of her novel in forty languages and its bestseller status in several countries for several weeks testify to her popular success, her winning the Booker Prize for 1997 to critical recognition.

Roy has as many iconoclasts as enthusiasts. A.N. Dwivedi for one is so shocked by Roy's candid treatment of sex that he accuses her of deliberately writing down to the prurient west. His arguments become somewhat tangled as he concedes that Roy is "modernistic" and yet wishes her to have preserved India's ancient aesthetics and ethics intact, "...if a writer tries to negate the social and cultural ethics of a great nation (as ours is) and if he/she forgets the primary objective of Indian aesthetics and moral values, then he/she is committing a great blunder. And Arundhati Roy falls into the trap of this blunder" (11). No less outraged is J.P. Tripathi by same of the erotic scenes in the novel: "These are definitely marks of obscenity, even filth, the sop offered to the hungry common readers. These are the ugliest parts of the book" (23). In a similar vein, Mithilesh Kumar Pandey assumes as a matter of course that Roy "wrote the novel from the western point of view because erotic vulgar scenes as narrated in *The God of Small Things* do not seem to adhere to the boundary of Indian milieu" (136). First, Roy's public denunciation of the west does not go well with her presumed pandering to it. She says of the west: "These are people whose histories are spongy with the blood of others. Colonialism, apartheid, slavery, ethnic cleansing, germ warfare, chemical weapons—they virtually invented it all" (*The End of Imagination* 34). Second, she questions the very notion of "an Indian identity" and of the existence of "a single civilization that could call itself 'Indian civilisation.'" The utmost that she is willing to concede is that "we're an ancient people learning to live in a recent nation" (*The End of Imagination* 37-38). India's wholesale appropriation of Western Culture including the nuclear bomb, she insists, has hollowed out any claim to Indianness and authenticity. As she puts it sarcastically:

> We storm the heart of whiteness, we embrace the most diabolical creation of western science and call it our own. But we protest against their music, their food, their clothes, their cinema and their literature. That's not hypocrisy. That's humour. (*The End of Imagination* 45)

This leads her on to conclude that

> There's no such thing as an Authentic India or a Real India. There is no Divine Committee that has the right to sanction one single, authorized version of what India is or should be. There is no one religion or language or caste or region or person or story or book that can claim to be its sole representative. (*The End of Imagination* 49)

In order to get the right perspective on her novel, her self-identity needs to be understood: "I am a citizen of the earth. I own no territory. I have no flag. I'm female, but have nothing against eunuchs" (*The End of Imagination* 30). Anyway the facile invocation of the so-called authentic Indian ethics and aesthetics to excoriate *The God of Small Things* would be most inappropriate. An aggressive female individualist, Roy asserts her artist's inalienable right to personal vision.

As for the charge of pornography against *The God of Small Things,* Aijaz Ahmad shows up its flimsiness. He observes that "the problem with Arundhati Roy's handling of sexuality is not that it is pornographic but that it is so thoroughly conventional as not even to surprise anyone who reads English fiction with any degree of regularity" (104). Those who speak in the name of Indian ethics and aesthetics actually plead for the *status quo*. The postmodernist view is that literature is an instrument of interrogating and subverting received wisdom, of dismantling the old and the established. One of Roy's Booker Prize judges, Jason Cowley's rationale for plumping for her novel reflects this view:

> *The God of Small Things* fulfils the highest demand of the art of fiction: to see the world, not conventionally or habitually but as if for the first time. Roy's achievement, and it is considerable, is never to forget about the small things in life: the insects and flowers, wind and water, the outcast and the despised. She deserved to win. (28)

"Critical response to *The God of Small Things* ranges," M. Dasan justly remarks, "from total dismissal to near rapturous approval" (23). Even the exacting Aijaz Ahmad admits that "In *The God of Small Things* Arundhati Roy may well have written the most accomplished, the most moving novel by an Indian author in English." Not content with that fulsome praise, he further adds that "one can nevertheless safely think of it as possibly the most polished novel we have had in the language so far" (103). This apotheosis reaches the culmination with Mohit K. Roy hailing the novel as "a contemporary classic" (64) and Asha Choubey as "a classic" (121).

A pertinent question to ask at this stage is whether GST has an overarching theme. John E. Abraham holds that "Roy's vision expressed through this novel is blurred. The novel has no profound message to offer. It seems to be the result of the author's hatred and malice towards some people" (122). "Hatred and malice" alone are not exactly the stuff that can make "a classic." Aijaz Ahmad puts his finger right on the novel's thematic centre:

> The novel has a tight thematic unity, condensed in those wonderfully sparse sentences that come at the end of the first chapter but then haunt the whole novel, and which tell us that the book is really about certain oppressive social structures that "actually began thousands of years ago...in the days when Love Laws were made. The Laws that lay down who should be loved, and how much." (105)

Roy herself identifies in her interview with Praveen Swami an importunate intellectual quest as the impetus behind her novel: "Writing *The God of Small Things* was a fictional way of making sense of the world I lived in, and the novel was the technical key with which I did it" (106). Binoo K. John lends a universal dimension to Roy's personal concern, and calls the novel "a universal story of love and tragedy" (23). Roy too points to her book's universal appeal despite its Indian locale:

> My book doesn't trade on the currency of cultural specificity, even though the details are right. That is why, I think, it has been bought in so many countries, and why Americans come up to me and say, 'I've got an aunt like Baby Kochamma.' (Quoted by Jason Cowley 28)

Manifestly *The God of Small Things* is a love novel with socio-cosmic dimensions.

The God of Small Things is in the nature of a family saga. It traces the changing fortunes of a family over three successive generations and also of a few outsiders brought into the family circle through marriage, profession, politics, etc. That is its way of anatomizing self and love and all that perverts them. Thematically the story goes back "thousands of years": "That it really began in the days when the Love Laws were made. The laws that lay down who should be loved, and how. And how much" (*GST* 33). It, however, works out its theme through three generations of transgressors. This is how Rahel identifies the transgressors:

> Perhaps, Ammu, Estha and she were the worst transgressors. But it wasn't just them. It was the others too. They all broke the rules. They all crossed into forbidden territory. They all tampered with the laws that lay down who should be loved and how. And how much. (*GST* 31)

Pappachi and Mammachi, Baby Kochamma and Father Mulligan represent the novel's first generation of transgressors.

Pappachi is Shri Benaan John Ipe, son of late Rev. E. John Ipe of Ayemenem. An Imperial Entomologist at the Pusa Institute, he is designated Joint Director, Entomology, after Independence. He retires as Director. The moth he discovered should have been named after him but by a quirk of fate is named after his hated junior. The moth's "pernicious ghost" "tormented him and his children and his children's children" (*GST* 49). This loss of coveted professional fame only aggravates his chronic ill-humour. A measure of his innate human antinomy is that he invariably bullies in private and smarms in public.

The tyrannized Ammu devastatingly exposes his dual self:

> He was charming and urbane with visitors, and stopped short of fawning on them if they happened to be white. He donated money to orphanages and leprosy clinics. He worked hard on his public profile as a sophisticated, generous, moral man. But alone with his wife and

> children he turned into a monstrous, suspicious bully, with a streak of vicious cunning. (*GST* 180)

For his meticulously cultivated public image, he passes for "a wonderful husband and father," an object of other's envy and in reality his family's scourge. His sadism goes beyond the routine flogging of his wife and daughter. He once cut the nine-year-old Ammu's favourite gumboots to shreds in her very presence without losing his cool. His retirement from service further activates his latent roles as dominator and deifier.

Pappachi has all along been afraid of Mammachi's overshadowing him, and hence jealous. The young couple were in Vienna where Pappachi was doing his six-month course and Mammachi was taking her first lessons on the violin. The moment her teacher told Pappachi that his wife was exceptionally talented and was potentially concert class, her lessons were at once stopped. Seventeen years her senior, he bristles as an old man at his wife's comparative youth. So pompous is this retired government official that he thinks that to cooperate with his wife in her pickle venture is to demean himself. On the contrary, his jealousy goes on mounting as "he greatly resented the attention his wife was suddenly getting" (*GST* 47). The result is the increased frequency of his wife-beating. Chacko's intervention and warning to stop this brutality marks a turning point in Pappachi's life. His first act of revenge is to destroy his favourite mahogany rocking chair. His second: "He never touched Mammachi again. But he never spoke to her either as long as he lived" (*GST* 48). His passion to dominate balked, his passion to deify the English—his Anglomania—increases manifold. It was as a wife-beating patriarchist that he considered Ammu's college education "an unnecessary expense for a girl." It was as an Anglophile that he disbelieved that Mr. Hollick, the English manager, could lust after Ammu. So boundless is his faith in British propriety that "he didn't believe that an Englishman, any Englishman, would covet another man's wife" (*GST* 42). Under the spell of his intensified Anglomania, he buys a skyblue Plymouth from an old Englishman: "The Plymouth was Pappachi's revenge"

(*GST* 48). He drives in it alone in his three-piece suit sweating profusely. If he deifies the English, he also deifies himself. So immense is his self-love that he refuses to accept the reality of his advancing years and the accompanying physical changes. He clings to his vanished youth. That is why he keeps on his dressing table a picture of himself as a young man taken in a photographer's studio in Vienna. In his own devious way, Pappachi instantiates the narrator's maxim: "Man's subliminal urge to destroy what he could neither subdue nor deify" (*GST* 308).

The exact counterpart of the high-caste, affluent, Anglophiliac Pappachi is a low-caste, poor, superstitious Vellya Pappen, an Old World Paravan, who "had seen the Crawling Backwards Days" (*GST* 76). Roy seems to believe in some kind of sociocultural, if not biological, determinism. Anyway she remarks in her interview with Praveen Swami that "there are things which form you before you form yourself. And these things will never go away, for they constitute the deepest part of me" (107). Accordingly she shows most of her characters shaped by their world in the form of habit and custom, injunction and inhibition. Ammu attributes Mammachi's crying at Pappachi's funeral not to her love but to her broken habit: "She was used to having him slouching around the pickle factory, and was used to being beaten from time to time...human beings were creatures of habit, and it was amazing the kind of things they could get used to" (*GST* 50). A more convincing example of how a self is moulded by its interiorization of the society's image of it is affixed by Vellya. His two sons, the elder Kuttapen, a bed-ridden invalid creeping towards death, and the younger Velutha, a quick-witted, high-spirited rebel without the least trace of caste- and class-consciousness, represent the two extremes of human possibilities. Vellya thinks that the very self-assurance and self-respect that Velutha exudes is unbecoming of a Paravan. As it conflicts with his own self-abasing spirit instilled into him by society, he tries his utmost to tame his wilful son. When he has the ocular proof of his untouchable son Velutha's having sex with Mammachi's touchable daughter Ammu, he feels crushed. His sense of ingratitude to his benefactor's family combines with his overwhelming feeling of sacrilege. He volunteers the secret to Mammachi and wants to atone for fathering Velutha: "He asked God's forgiveness for having spawned a monster. He offered to kill his son with his own bare hands. To destroy what he had created" (*GST* 78). A long inherited taboo on intercaste sex has so constituted Vellya's psyche that he conceives love between his son and Mammachi's daughter inconceivable: "They have made the unthinkable thinkable and the impossible really happen" (*GST* 256). Convinced of Velutha's unforgivable sin, he cannot think of anything short of death as a fit punishment for the transgressor. So he goes on "sitting for hours at the door of their hut, still drunk, his glass eye and the edge of his axe glittering in the lamplight, waiting for Velutha to return" (*GST* 283). Vellya's determination to kill the intractable Velutha vividly illustrates "Man's subliminal urge to destroy what he could neither subdue nor deify" (*GST* 308).

Mammachi too with her oppositely oriented children, son Chacko and daughter Ammu, orchestrates the theme further. She is as caste- and class-conscious and swanky as Pappachi. Fellow victims of Pappachi's brutality and members of the same sex, Mammachi has no sympathy whatsoever for her daughter Ammu. Conversely she makes much of her son Chacko: "Mammachi often said that Chacko was easily one of the cleverest men in India" (*GST* 55). Her only basis for this extravagantly exalted opinion of her otherwise effete son is an Oxford don's opinion, of course relayed by Chacko himself, that "Chacko was brilliant, and made of prime ministerial material" (*GST* 56). The feminist Ammu's response to her mother's image of her pampered son is that "All Indian mothers are obsessed with their sons and are therefore poor judges of their abilities" (*GST* 56). On Ammu's view, the mess that Chacko makes of the family business, previously run very efficiently by Mammachi, and of the family property shows up his real mettle. In order to cease to be a burden to her parents and to escape an uncongenial parental home, Ammu enters into a loveless marriage with a Bengali Hindu. Since she marries without her parents' permission and outside her Christian community, she counts as a transgressor. Chacko in his turn makes a love match with an English waitress, of course without his parents' consent. Like Ammu, he is also a transgressor. After the birth of her twins, Ammu divorces her alcoholic, wife-beating husband when he wants to trade her for his job. Similarly Margaret gives birth to her daughter and divorces the feckless Chacko. So both the Oxford-educated brother and the school-educated sister are on the same footing as divorcees at the Ayemenem House. Ammu and her twins stay there on sufferance and Chacko as a privileged member. Ammu works as much in the factory as Chacko. She has, however, no legal claim to any of the family property. A beneficiary of patriarchy, Chacko gloats over his sister's plight: "What's yours is mine and what's mine is also mine." The indignant Ammu retorts "Thanks to our wonderful male chauvinist society" (*GST* 57).

Besides patriarchy, something more compelling prompts Mammachi's differential treatment of her children. It is not merely because she is a status-conscious snob that she despises Margaret as a "shopkeeper's daughter." She hates Margaret first for marrying Chacko and then for leaving him. But she would have hated her more if she had stayed. The riddle is that it is the Oedipus Complex in reverse that operates between the mother and the son. Chacko's prevention of Pappachi from beating Mammachi produces an unexpected consequence: "From then onwards he became the repository of all her womanly feelings. Her man. Her only Love" (*GST* 168). At Margaret's presence at the Ayemenem House, Ammu with a woman's instinct perceives "the undercurrent of sexual jealousy that emanated from Mammachi" (*GST* 329). As a victim of this incestuous love only in mind though, Mammachi too qualifies as a potential transgressor. Devasted as she was at the news of Chacko's marrying Margaret, she did not hesitate to pawn her jewellery to send him the much-needed money. When he returns home after his marriage breaks up,

> Mammachi joyfully welcomed him back into her life. She fed him, she sewed for him, she saw to it that there

> were fresh flowers in his room every day. Chacko needed his mother's adoration. Indeed, he demanded it, yet he despised her for it and punished her in secret ways. (*GST* 248).

Her defence of Chacko's libertine relationships with the women in the factory is that "He can't help having a Man's Needs" (*GST* 168). To facilitate the secret entry of the factory women into Chacko's room, she gets a separate entrance to it built. She even goes to the extent of bribing Chacko's Paravan (low caste) women. Conversely the outspoken, recalcitrant Ammu's clandestine satisfaction of her women's needs with the Paravan Velutha throws the same Mammachi into a frenzy. As her worked up imagination pictures Ammu in the act of sex with Velutha, her mounting revulsion reaches the flashpoint. Her casteism combined with her family pride, her animosity against Ammu combined with her double standard reduce the transgressors to a pair of animals:

> She thought of her naked, coupling in the mud with a man who was nothing but a filthy *coolie*. She imagined it in vivid details: a Paravan's coarse black hand on her daughter's breast. His mouth on hers. His black hips jerking between her parted legs. The sound of their breathing. His particular Paravan smell. *Like animals,* Mammachi thought and nearly vomited. *Like a dog with a bitch on heat.* Her tolerance of 'Men's Needs' as far as her son was concerned, became the fuel for her unmanageable fury at her daughter. She defiled generations of breeding...and brought the family to its knees. (*GST* 257-58)

The irony is that a mother in love with her son and jealous of his wife expects her divorced daughter in her late twenties to be a sexless angel. Mammachi gets Ammu locked up into her bedroom. The shiftless, libidinous Chacko hounds her out of the parental house. Mammachi's deification of the malleable Chacko and her destruction of the intractable Ammu go far towards universalizing the novel's overall theme.

Baby Kochamma, Pappachi's sister, is the novel's most formidable character. With her indomitable will and her unquenchable passion for domination, she looms large in it and propels most of its action. Even the consuming love of the eighteen-year-old fetching and vivacious Baby for the young, handsome Irish monk Father Mulligan is a form of the Nietschean will to power. So uncontrollable is her "sexual excitement" that at first she tries to "seduce Father Mulligan." Theirs is a case reciprocated love: "The young girl and the intrepid Jesuit, both quaking with unchristian passion" (*GST* 24). The religious taboo on a monk's sexuality and marriage obstructs their passion. The very reverse of a yielder that she is, Baby defies her father and becomes a Roman Catholic trainee novice "To love him just by looking at him" (*GST* 24). Frustrated in her love design, she comes out of the convent and goes to Rochester for a diploma in ornamental gardening. Time passes; she changes physically. Still she is "more in love with father Mulligan then ever" (*GST* 260). As a spinster at the Ayemenem house, she very conveniently forgets that Father Mulligan refuses to apostate for her sake. Self-flatteringly she manages to "persuade herself over the years that her unconsummated love for Father Mulligan had been entirely due to *her* restraint and *her* determination to do the right thing" (*GST* 45). The most egomaniac of the transgressors, she uses her love to satisfy her passion for possession, for domination. For long sixty-five years, she has been making the same entry in her dairy: "I love you I love you" (*GST* 297). Father Mulligan converts to Hinduism and becomes a devotee of Lord Vishnu. He stays in touch with Baby Kochamma; he writes to her every Diwali and sends her a greeting card every New Year. He sends her a photograph of himself as a saffron-clad monk addressing a gathering. It piques her vanity "It was the only thing he ever sent her that she hadn't kept. She was offended by the fact that he had actually, eventually, renounced his vows, but not for her" (*GST* 288). When he dies, she makes him over into her favourites image and possesses him completely: "If anything, she possessed him in death in a way that she never had while he was alive. At least her memory of him was hers. Savagely, fiercely, *hers*" (*GST* 288). In Freudian theory, the process of internalizing a lost or dead person as a way of coping with separation or (especially) bereavement is called "incorporation" (Jeremy Hawthorn 171).

In a reaction against her youthful renunciation of the world, Baby Kochamma turns in her eighties into a compulsive materialist. She has developed an abnormal passion for material possessions and so a morbid fear of dispossession. Hence her paranoia about the marauding Naxalites. More striking is in Rahel's phrase "*living her life backwards*" (*GST* 22). At eighty-three, she has her hair bobbed and dyed, her face made-up and is always bejewelled.

Her governing passion for domination has Father Mulligan as its first target; it varies its object with her age and mood. As a thwarted maiden, she becomes an enthusiastic ornamental gardener. With all the virulence of a sex-starved maniac, she sets herself to denaturing nature: "Like a lion-tamer she tamed twisting vines and nurtured bristling cacti. She limited bonsai plants and pampered rare orchids. She waged war on the weather" (*GST* 26-27). Her passion for domination remains unabated throughout the whole length of her long life. The real significance of her old-age TV addiction is that "She presided over the world in her drawing room on satellite TV" (*GST* 27).

When the ever domineering Baby Kochamma begins to use her human pawns to satisfy her will to power, she degenerates into a full-blown sadist. She would seem to dislike Ammu's twins Estha and Rahel for being life's victims. She detests them for being "doomed, fatherless waifs," for being "Half-Hindu Hybrids" and most of all for being interlopers at their grandmother's house. Her suspicion of even the grown-up twins is so pathological that she thinks that "They might even steal their present back" (*GST* 29). In her grand design to receive Chacko's daughter Sophie in style, she reduces the little twins to a pair of puppets. For any deviation from her stern injunction to speak in English, they forfeit their pocket money. They are subjected to word-perfect rehearsal for an English car song. Estha is sick, but Baby Kochamma's demand is that "Estha has to be well for Sophie Mol" (*GST* 111). Rahel's mumbled protest puts her back up. A combination of her exhibitionism and Anglophilia prompts her to appoint the twins "Ambassadors of India" to receive Chacko's English ex-wife Margaret and their daughter: "You're going to form their First Impression of your country" (*GST* 139). These are nothing compared to her heartless manipulation of the little things to extricate herself from her false charge against Velutha of abducting the children. It is to save her own skin that she begins her step-by-step blackmail of the innocent, helpless, bewildered twins. First she accuses them of murdering Sophie, and then draws vivid pictures of prison life for them and for their mother. Frightening them out of their wits and telling them that Velutha is dying, she requires them to say "Yes" to the Police Inspector's question that Velutha is their abductor, which is a blatant lie. She selects "the more tractable" Estha for this mission. Her motiveless malignity comes through in her unalloyed sadism towards the twins. Thirty-one-year-old Rahel returns from America to meet the re-returned Estha after a gap of twenty-three years. Baby Kochamma "was delighted that Estha had not spoken to Rahel" (*GST* 20). Even when the twins were children, "she grudged them the comfort they drew from each other. She expected from them some token unhappiness" (*GST* 46). She succeeds in making them unhappy; she machinates to get Estha sent back to his estranged father.

It is the indomitable spirit of the husbandless Ammu that affronts the resigned Father Mulligan-less Baby Kochamma: "Baby Kochamma resented Ammu, because she saw her quarrelling with a fate that she, Baby Kochamma herself, felt she had graciously accepted" (*GST* 45). She has an added reason for her ill feelings towards her niece. Holding as she does to some form of patriarchy, she believes that a married daughter has no position in her parents' home. As for a divorced daughter, she has no position anywhere at all. As for a divorced daughter from intercommunity love marriage, whose victim is Ammu, Baby Kochamma leaves the extent of deprivation unspecified perhaps because unspecifiable. No less groundless and virulent is her animus against Velutha. She treats him as the representative of the Marxist processionists who stalled the family car and heckles and humiliated her in particular. "Baby Kochamma focused all her fury at her public humiliation on Velutha.... She began to hate him" (*GST* 82). In the novel's scheme, Baby Kochamma with her ornamental gardening, Anglophilia and Culture-mongering stands on the side of civilization. On the contrary, the free-spirited Ammu and her soul mate Velutha are creatures of impulse and instinct, are so to say children of nature. Hence Baby Kochamma's common animosity towards them. Fate conspires with her to put her bugbears into her clutches. Divulgence of Ammu's secret affair with Velutha coincides with the disappearance of the children. It is a godsend for the vindictive Baby to kill two birds with one stone:

> She saw it as God's way of punishing Ammu for her sins and simultaneously avenging her (Baby Kochamma's) humiliation at the hands of Velutha and the men in the march.... She set sail at once. A ship of goodness ploughing through a sea of sin. (*GST* 257)

The sanctimonious Baby ordains Velutha's immediate dismissal and banishment, and works on Mammachi's anger to get Ammu imprisoned into her bedroom. Not content with that, she goes to the police station and lodges an FIR. She complains that a dismissed Paravan with Naxalite connections Velutha attempted to molest her divorcee niece with twins, and perhaps had a hand in the kidnapping of the children. She thus seals the innocent Velutha's fate. To complete her design, she insinuates into the grief-stricken Chacko's mind that Ammu was "the person actually responsible for Sophie Mol's death. Ammu and her two-egg twins" (*GST* 322). It can therefore be said of Baby Kochamma that she is "Impelled by feelings that were primal yet paradoxically wholly impersonal" (*GST* 308). She harms the tractable twins and ruins the intractable Ammu and Velutha out of sheer malice.

Roy explores all through the novel the capacity of "Human Nature" for "Love. Madness. Hope. Infinite joy" (*GST* 118), demonstrates how an "edifice constructed by the human mind" is "decimated by human nature" (*GST* 287), and how the economy of the human mind relates "love to fear to anger to remorse" (*GST* 226). She puts to an adroit use the three generations of characters, who modulate the novel's obsessive theme and dramatize one generation's impact on the other and the consequential differences. A member of the second generation, Chacko is a hybrid in more senses than one. Surprising his father in the act of thrashing his mother, he catches Pappachi's vase-hand and twists it around his back. "I never want this to happen again, he told his father" (*GST* 48). Evidently wife-beating is not in Chacko's line. After his English wife Margaret divorces him, Chacko returns home to be deified by his mother: "Chacko needed his mother's adoration. Indeed, he *demanded* it, yet he despised her for it and punished her in secret ways" (*GST* 248). The divorced Chacko pines for his mother's adulation to regain his lost self-image and self-love. The fact that she so obligingly puts him on a pedestal and thereby demeans herself inevitably earns her the idol's contempt. Sadomasochism is inseparable from any kind of one-sided or romantic love and has many forms. Exempt from the obsession with caste and class distinction, Chacko, however, fully shares his parents' Anglophilia or "cultural colonialism" (Leela Gandhi 19). In his very important discourse on Anglophilia, he confesses: "They were a family of Anglophiles. Pointed in the wrong direction, trapped outside their own history, and unable to retrace their steps because their footprints had been swept away" (*GST* 52). As any adorer despises himself and exalts his idol, so any Anglophile detests his own culture and apes a foreign and supposedly superior one. He opts out of his own history but cannot enter the chosen one. At best he can only imitate its externals but cannot capture its spirit. Ridiculous is his attempt to re-dream the dreams of his idols. The irony of Anglophilia is that it "has made us adore our conquerors and despise ourselves" (*GST* 53). The culturally rootless, homeless Anglophiles live an imitative life that lacks substance, authenticity, intensity and significance. Chacko's realization of the primordeality of the earth, antiquity of life and the very recency of civilization does not accord with the exclusive pursuit of culture, foreign or native. Despite all that, his father's Anglophilia and his mother's mollycoddling profoundly affect his marriage choice. With her passion for balance, Roy very cleverly indicates "The troubling reciprocity between the metropolitan centre and the colonial periphery" (Leela Gandhi 134). When at the airport Estha greets Sophie Mol in the Western style, she responds in the Indian: "'Just like a ladoo one piece two,' Sophie Mol whispered to Estha. She had learned this in school from a Pakistani classmate" (*GST* 150).

If Chacko is a living contradiction, it is because he cannot integrate his mind and his nature. By birth and upbringing a feudal, "Chacko was a self-proclaimed Marxist" (*GST* 65). His way of practicing Marxism is to entice the pretty girls in his factory into his bedroom more for reason of sex than politics. His exploitation of his employees justifies Ammu's acid remark: "An Oxford avatar of the old zamindar mentality—a landlord forcing his attentions on women who depend on him for their livelihood" (*GST* 65). The dilemma of the Marxist Chacko is that he owns a factory that does not break even. Though he has the employees' interests at heart, he is forced to underpay them and deny them their legitimate benefits. In case of a real crisis, it is Mammachi who has to face upto it. The pragmatic Margaret correctly sizes Chacko up when she discerns that "a tortured Marxist was at war with an impossible incurable Romantic" (*GST* 245). Like his father, he escapes ostrich-like from life's reality and antinomy into the world of dreams or sweet memories. As his father used to keep on his bedside table the most flattering of his photographs, so does he: "On the bedside table there was a silver-framed black-and-white wedding picture of Chacko and Margaret Kochamma taken outside the church in Oxford" (*GST* 239).

It is the romantic Chacko who comes to the fore in his role as Margaret's lover and husband. Chacko as a slovenly Rhodes Scholar from India and Margaret as a tidy waitress are polar opposites. He admires her self-sufficiency, her intellectual independence, her level-headedness. He is grateful to him "For not being his cloying mother. He grew to depend on Margaret Kochamma for not depending on him. He adored her for not adoring him" (*GST* 246). Chacko abhors his mother for adoring him; he adores Margaret for being undemonstrative. This psychological puzzle is the hub of sadomasochism. Chacko actually does not love Margaret the woman. Perhaps without knowing it himself, "he was deeply in love with his love for Margaret" (*GST* 246). Which is why when she deserts him for Joe, his love for her increases rather than diminishes. Chacko is a sadist in relation to his masochist mother; he is a masochist in relation to the sadist Margaret. So complete is Mammachi's self-identification with Chacko, her idol, that anything he says in dispraise of himself and in praise of Margaret mortifies her. In a trademark masochist vein, he belittles himself and extols Margaret and his rival Joe: "'She traded me in for a better man,' he would say to Mammachi, and she would flinch as though he had denigrated her instead of himself (*GST* 249). The egocentricity of Chacko's love for Margaret becomes manifest in his use of his ex-wife as a source of extra prestige and pride for him: "Anybody could see that Chacko was a proud and happy man to have had a wife like Margaret White" (*GST* 143). No wonder the very presence of Margaret induces "Chacko's proud, tennis-trophy smile" (*GST* 329). Chacko loves Margaret with his mind and showers all his feelings on her. But his nature, his needs, and his sensuality find their outlet with the Paravan working girls in his factory. Even as a lover, he shows all over again his ambivalence as an Anglophile and a Marxist. He cannot overcome the contradiction between his "Marxist mind and feudal libido." And he has to accept the stark reality of "Disjuncted sex from love. Needs from Feelings" (*GST* 168-69). It is the trauma of his daughter Sophie's accidental death that ends his play-acting, crushes his dream and exposes him to life's reality: "Like a child touched by tragedy, who grows up suddenly and abandons his playthings, Chacko dumped his toys. Pickle Baron dreams and the People's War joined the racks of broken airplanes in his glass-paned cupboard" (*GST* 281). The intensity of the grief strips away the thin veneer of his imitation British culture and selective respect for women, and whips up the sleeping bully. He thunders at his divorced, shelterless, twins-saddled sister Ammu:

> 'Pack your things and go,' Chacko would say, stepping over the debris. Looming over them. A chrome door handle in his hand. His bullying power. The enormity of his own terrible grief. (*GST* 226)

Here is another spectacle of human nature demolishing the human mind.

No less selfish is Margaret's love for Chacko. Before she met him, she had a very low self-esteem; "She had always thought of herself as a somewhat uninteresting, thick-waisted, think-ankled girl." Chacko's passionate love refurbishes her self-image. He liberates her so much from the glare of self-scrutiny and cramped spirit that "she discovered a little magic in herself, and for a while felt like a blithe genie released from her lamp." The narrator ruthlessly points out that "what she assumed as her love for Chacko was actually a tentative, timorous acceptance of herself (*GST* 245). It is to her interest to continue to think of "herself as an ordinary woman, and him as an extraordinary man" (*GST* 249). For only then she can banish all qualms for ditching him for a more practical man. The real significance of Chacko's being in love is that "It is not directed at a woman; it is directed at anima, at a man's ideal his dream, his fantasy, his hope, his expectation, his passion for an inner being whom he superimposes over the external woman" (Robert A. Johnson 141). Anyway the thoroughly romantic love of Chacko and Margaret is not at all based on their acceptance of each other's intrinsic worth. It feeds on their mutual projections of each other for their own selfish needs. They serve as a foil to the human lovers that Ammu and Velutha are. Careful counterpointing of character and theme is an important feature of the novel. The "unfriendly jewelled bear," "the Orangedrink Lemondrink Man" satisfies his "needs" when he gets Estha to masturbate him. His "needs" and "feelings" like Chacko's are obviously "disjuncted." In pointed contrast is the Englishman who goes native, speaks Malayalam, wears mundus and commits suicide when his boyfriend is taken away from him. He is the very reverse of the Anglophiliac Chacko who marries an Englishwoman for love and exploits the native girls for sex.

The colonized Pappachi and his decolonized progeny deify the English. Margaret's father has a colonizer's superciliousness. Not only does he disapprove of the wedding, he also demonizes the Indians as a whole: "He disliked Indians, he thought of them as sly, dishonest people. He couldn't believe that his daughter was marrying one" (*GST* 240). In a manner of speaking, Margaret too would belong with the transgressors.

Now the focus shifts to a pair of characters who embody the novel's positive values. Even as a child, Ammu turns into a rebel in revulsion against the bully of a father and the doormat of a mother: "As a child, she had learned very quickly to disregard the Father Bear Mother Bear stories she was given to read. In her version, Father Bear beat Mother Bear with brass vases. Mother Bear suffered those beatings with mute resignation" (*GST* 180). Belonging as she does to an entirely different breed of self-respecting and self-asserting woman, she shows her rebelliousness in action when she takes on her drunken, bullying husband. She retaliates by hitting him into unconsciousness. A measure of her fundamental difference from Chacko is her response to her wedding photographs: "When she looked at herself in wedding photographs, Ammu felt the woman that looked back at her was someone else" (*GST* 43). Without this unblinkered vision, she could not develop her free spirit. Of course she has her share of the fight between "the human mind" and "human nature," between history in the form of civilizing ideas and biology in the form of primal instincts. It is this internecine battle that makes her unpredictable:

> It was what she had battling inside her. An unmixable mix. The infinite tenderness of motherhood and the reckless rage of a suicide bomber. It was this that grew inside her, and eventually led her to love by night the man her children loved by day. (*GST* 44)

She fights her husband to preserve her exclusive right to her body. She even shakes off the twins playing with her body: "She wanted her body back. It was hers" (*GST* 222). She is no Baby Kochamma living for the spirit in her youth and for the flesh in her old age. She believes with the Kathakali Man that her body is her soul (*GST* 230). She deludes herself into thinking that her egregious mistake in choosing the life partner has atrophied her capacity to dream. Her body keeps alive her inclination to dream.

The sequence of events building upto Ammu's ultimate explosion is a tribute to the novelist's architectonic skill. Two "Plays" are being staged simultaneously. The subject of one is civilization, its occasion the ceremony welcoming Margaret and Sophie, its participants almost all the characters except Rahel and Velutha. The subject of the other play is nature or human nature at its most innocent, at its most frolicsome. Sophie's welcome calls forth the most elaborate display of formality, artificiality, downright hypocrisy. As English guests, they are the cycosure and object of adulation. In this ritual, make-believe passes for truth, and so hypocrisy creeps in. For instance, neither the mother nor the daughter is a raging beauty, but they are praised as such by everybody except the blind Mammachi and the sulky Ammu. From within this play circle, Ammu, exasperated with its play-acting, finds a great relief in watching the other play. In this Rahel and Velutha are improvising just to exercise their inventiveness and with no intent to deceive each other. Ammu fixes her attention on the bare bodied Velutha's fatless, ribbed, athletic body. She has known him since his boyhood. What strikes her is that "His smile was the only piece of baggage he had carried with him from boyhood into manhood" (*GST* 175). That her attraction for him is purely instinctive is underlined by its suddenness:

> Suddenly Ammu hoped that it *had* been him that Rahel saw in the march. She hoped it had been him that had raised his flag and knotted his arm in anger. She hoped that under his careful cloak of cheerfulness, he housed a living, breathing anger against the smug, ordered world that she so raged against. (*GST* 175-76)

It is important to note that Ammu proceeds from Velutha's body to his mind. Already physically attracted towards him, she wants to discover in him a kindred soul. For her part, she herself has developed since her childhood "a lofty sense of injustice and the mulish, reckless streak that develops in

Someone Small who has been bullied all their lives by Someone Big" (*GST* 181-82). That the sight of Rahel and Velutha's carefree frolicking excites in Ammu "a delicate, purple tinge of envy" shows that human emotion is never either simple or pure. In Roy's vocabulary, history and civilization are interchangeable terms as they are in Hegel's (Leela Gandhi 170). Caught in the grip of an instinctive seizure, Ammu travels in an instant beyond the pale of civilization into the natural state of man:

> Centuries telescoped into one evanescent moment. History was wrong-footed, caught off guard. Sloughed off like an old snake-skin. Its marks, its scars, its wounds from old wars and the walking backwards days all fell away. (*GST* 167)

Thus dropping out of history and society, she develops her autonomous self, absolutely unconditioned by anything outside it. Instinct now, as before their first ever nocturnal meeting, facilitates their telepathic communication. Velutha too becomes simultaneously dehistoricized and deconditioned: "In that brief moment, Velutha looked up and saw things that he hadn't seen before. Things that had been out of bounds so far, obscured by history's blinkers" (*GST* 176). They have no other identity except as man and woman, united by affinity and mutual desire. Their momentous self-discovery and mutual recognition last only a minute. They backtrack into the straitjacket of history:

> It only took a moment.
> Ammu saw that he saw. She looked away. He did too. History's fiends returned to claim them. To rewrap them in its old, scarred pelt and drag them back to where they really lived. Where Love Laws lay down who should be loved. And how. And how much. (*GST* 177)

Ammu has tasted, even though for a moment, the ineffable joy of being natural and authentic. She has at the back of her mind the image of the lecherous English manager Hollick, who has turned her into an Anglophobiac. The prim Margaret seizes on "sniffing" as a substitute for "kissing" and attempts an innuendo: "Do the men and women do it to each other too?" This provokes Ammu to snap at her: "Oh, all the time!" Then she proceeds to rip the mask off civilization: "That's how we make babies" (*GST* 178). With this bombshell, the "suicide bomber" Ammu makes her public appearance.

In her afternoon dream, Ammu sees Velutha. She could touch him as he could touch her. But they refrain from doing so because "there were people, ..., watching" (*GST* 215). That clearly shows the extent to which Ammu has internalized the Love Laws and their forbidding keepers. This inhibition from within has to contend with the dawning knowledge of the inevitabilities of aging and dying. The withered, embittered Baby Kochamma prefigures her future. It is not so much the fear of death as the fear of creeping towards it with her life unlived that injects into her an element of desperation. In the bathroom where she engages in a thorough scrutiny of her body "the fates conspired to alter horribly the course of their mysterious mother's road" (*GST* 224). She yet needs a decisive push which comes in the form of an English song on her transistor, a song that sings her own life and goads her on to do what she wants to. "The cheap coincidence of those words" (*GST* 332) precipitates her plunge. Driven by her irresistible instinct and banking on its telepathic assurance, she rushes to the river-bank. As her spiritual double, Velutha just duplicates her:

> That knowledge had slid into him that afternoon.... When history had slipped up..... That she had gifts to give him too, that in return for his boats, his boxes, his small windmills, she would trade her deep dimples when she smiled. Her smooth brown skin. (*GST* 332)

It is as pure children of nature, as creatures of instinct and impulse that they finally meet: "They weren't thinking any more. The time for that had come and gone" (*GST* 334). Still the vestiges of old fear cloud Velutha's mind. She takes the initiative and offers herself. And then only his body triumphs over his mind: "Despite his fear his body was prepared to take the bait. It wanted her." In her case too "her body existed only where he touched her. The rest of her was smoke." They celebrate the victory of "human nature" over "the human mind," of biology over history (Civilization): "Once he was inside her, fear was derailed and biology took over" (*GST* 336). Mini Nanda thinks that "Twins carve their own space in a Marvellian Carp Diem" (182). This is more true of Ammu and Velutha, who anticipate the twins. The novel fully substantiates Roy's claim in her interview with Alok Rai that "The God of Small Things probes biology" (3). As for the "human love" of Ammu and Velutha, as distinct from the "romantic love" of Margaret and Chacko, it is both, precipitate and short-lived. It is born and is consummated on the very day of Sophie's arrival and ends almost with her funeral. The novelist's dialectical vision thus correlates love and death. The quintessence of the "human love" of Ammu and Velutha inheres in mutual recognition, acceptance and fulfilment. In contradistinction to "romantic love's" selfishness is "human love's" selflessness: "Love is distinct from my ego: love was here before my ego came into the world, and love will be here after my ego departs. Yet love is something or 'someone' who lives within me. Love is a force that acts from within, that enables my ego to look outside itself, to see my fellow humans as something to be valued and cherished, rather than used" (Robert A. Johnson 189). As the transgressors of all Love Laws, Ammu and Velutha incite anarchy: as the children of nature, they menace civilization itself. For their own survival, society and history have to exterminate them as quickly as they can.

The God of Small Things is replete with twins of the most amazing variety. To begin with the recondite pair: Ammu and Velutha. To call them soul mates or kindred souls is to acknowledge them as spiritual twins. To underline their status as such, the novelist has them react to an identical situation in the same way and with the same phraseology. The overbearing, abusive Police Inspector Thomas Mathew's contemptuous dismissal of Ammu's plea elicits her dignified response "she'd see about that" (*GST* 284). The equally imperious and abusive Mammachi's threat to have Velutha castrated and killed extorts his defiant retort "we'll see about that" (*GST* 284). They have served their turn and are replaced, to represent the third generation, by Estha and Rahel, Ammu and Baba's biological twins. They are central to the novelist's design for the book, "which is not about what happened but about how what happened affected people" (the website on Roy 5). That accounts for the novel's psychological preoccupation and for the biological twins' role as scapegoats paying for the sins of their elders. Nakula and Sahadeva (*GST* 233) are mere inactive mythical twins. Not so Velutha's playfully invented "Long-lost Twin brother" (*GST* 177) Urumban. This creature of imagination comes to acquire a grim reality with a devastating ironic effect. To counterpoint this is Chacko's funny story of "the Man with Twin Sons," the optimist Pete and the pessimist Stuart (*GST* 242).

The relationship between the twins Estha and Rahel is an intricate one. Despite all their physical differences, these "two-egg twins" think in their childhood, when memory begins but not individuation, "of themselves together as Me, and separately, individually, as We or Us." With their "single Siamese soul" (*GST* 41), they are "physically separate, but with joint identities" (*GST* 2). An early instance of their joint identities is offered by the Velutha episode. After the impulsive Rahel claims to have sighted Velutha in the procession, Chacko demands her to affirm her claim. She continues to falter until she gets the required signal from the cautious Estha, her senior by eighteen minutes but sagacious by nature. Such is the symbiosis between them that Rahel can intuit Estha's dream, his experience with the Orangedrink Lemondrink Man, even the taste of his food. This empathy can function as telepathy. Upset by the vice done to him by the Orangedrink Lemondrink Man, which he has not breathed to anybody, he comes at dead of night to Rahel's hotel room and waits without knocking. "Rahel stood on a chair and unlatched the door for him" (*GST* 119). Similarly Ammu and Velutha reach the river-bank with the certainty of meeting each other but without any communication to that effect. Evidently the novelist presents instinct as a means of telepathy. Anyway the narrator not only emphasizes the twins' spiritual oneness but also their prescience: "A hot twin and a cold one. He and She. We and Us. Somehow, not wholly unaware of the hint of doom and all that waited in the wings for them" (*GST* 122). Quite consistent with their shared mutuality is Rahel's refusal to communicate to Estha in Calcutta the news of Ammu's death. It would be, she argues, "like writing letters to a part of yourself (*GST* 164). On the eve of Estha's being "returned" to his father in Calcutta, Ammu binds the twins by the promise to love each other always. The seven-year-old twins find the promise superfluous because "for them there was no Each, no Other" (*GST* 225). This one soul in two bodies survives intact when they are thirty-one-year-old: "He and She. We and Us" (*GST* 237). Traumatized and estranged in childhood, they develop into two complementary adults. The empty Rahel and the quiet Estha are a perfectly matching pair: "That the emptiness in one twin was only a version of the quietness in the other. That the two things fitted together. Like stacked spoons. Like familiar lovers' bodies" (*GST* 20). The novelist thus subtly prepares for the twins eventual incest.

Ammu's relationship with her twins is fraught with grievous consequences. The irony is that with her mother's boundless love and solicitude for her children, she contributes not a little to their ruination. As a divorces mother, she loves her children double; she is their mother and father all in one. Her maternal Love, however, is leavened by an element of cruelty: "Ammu loved her children (of course), but their wide-eyed vulnerability, and their willingness to love people who didn't really love them, exasperated her and sometimes made her want to hurt them—just as an education, a protection" (*GST* 43). Her overprotectiveness and her pride in them, reminiscent of Mammachi's in regard to Chacko, strain her a lot. It is no less a strain for the children to avoid doing anything that would lessen her love for them and to do everything to earn it. The novelist interweaves the strand of maternal-filial love with that of transgression and punishment to create a complex web. She uses the children to demonstrate once again what incites transgression and what transgression brings in its train. The repetitive pattern working through three generations acquires an air of eternity and universality.

Impelled by his irresistible instinct, Estha bursts out singing in the theatre to the audience's extreme annoyance. He tries hard to control himself but fails. The novelist drives home Estha's utter helplessness through repetition: "He couldn't help it" "the song came back, and Estha couldn't stop it" and "Estha couldn't help it" (*GST* 100-01). He comes out into the lobby and gives vent to his overmastering instinct through full-throated singing. The roused "jewelled bear," the Orangedrink Lemondrink Man orders Estha to stop his singing, which is a theatre offence and merits "a Written Complaint." On top of that, he has offended the Man himself. Since "you've *disturbed* me, at least come and have a drink" (*GST* 102) as a punishment. Estha's not having pocket money changes the form of punishment. The Man mesmerizes Estha, imposes his will on him and has him masturbate him. The man wipes his semen off Estha's hand, but Estha would spend the whole of his life wiping that irremovable remembered semen off his mind. The result is his lifelong mania for washing and cleanliness. The narrator calls the masturbation incident "a Little Man's first encounter with Fear" (*GST* 119). It is much more than that. The hellish experience becomes his obsession that recurs at regular intervals. This miasma blights all his joy of life. The possibility of that evil Man's getting at him any moment turns Estha into a permanent paranoiac. The final upshot is the seven-year-old's fatalism, encapsulated in his maxim "Anything can Happen to Anyone" and a countervailing pragmatism: "It's Best to be Prepared" (*GST* 198). These are, however, subsequent developments, and so belong to the future. The reason for his immediate anguish is the fear of forfeiting Ammu's love in case she comes to know of his encounter with his polluter: "He knew that if Ammu found out about what he had done with the Orangedrink Lemondrink Man, she'd love him less as well. Very much less" (*GST* 113).

Ammu very sensibly explains to "Estha and Rahel that people always loved best what they *Identified* most with" and that "When you hurt people, they begin to love you less"

(*GST* 98 and 112). Nevertheless she is so obtuse that despite her children's obvious revulsion against the Orangedrink Lemondrink Man, she goes on praising him extravagantly. The exasperated Rahel blurts out: "So why don't you marry him then" (*GST* 112)? As Estha's song, so Rahel's outburst is designed to show how instinct overwhelms the conscious self. It works from within the unconscious. So Rahel "didn't know where those words had come from. She didn't know that she'd had them in her" (*GST*). Rahel shares Estha's gnawing fear: "A little less her Ammu loved her" (*GST* 112). Estha is punished for his transgression. Rahel punishes herself for hers by abstaining from her dinner. Such is Ammu's maternal pride in her children that she wants them always to be a credit to her, to put in "a smooth performance." Any lapse on their part causes her anger and their anguish. She even threatens to banish them by way of punishing their disobedience: "'If ever,' Ammu said, 'and I *mean* this EVER, ever again disobey me in Public, I will see to it that you are sent away to somewhere where you will jolly well learn to behave" (*GST* 148).

When Ammu's affair with Velutha becomes public, she is locked into her bedroom. The innocent twins come to her door and ask why she has been locked up. Mad with anger, she calls them "the millstones round my neck." Then she follows it up with virtually ordering their banishment: "Why can't you just go away and leave me alone" (*GST* 253)? Ammu's love has been all through the sole determinant of the twins' lives. Now that they have lost it, they feel that they have no reason to stay any more with her. The sagacious Estha draws the obvious conclusion that "the Time Had Come for them to run away, because Ammu didn't want them any more" (*GST* 264). Ammu's affair with Velutha indirectly and her angry words to the twins directly contribute to the tragedy that overtakes the children and in which Sophie dies. Baby Kochamma with her gratuitous malice and Ammu with the best of intentions affect the twins in the same way. This is the height of irony.

The novelist's strategy appears to be to show first the traumatized adult twins and then the child twins being exposed to successive traumas and developing fixations. Estha is inveigled by Baby Kochamma into identifying Velutha before the Police Inspector as their abductor. Police action leaves Velutha so much mangled and misshapen as to be hardly recognizable. Rahel has reason enough to misrecognize him as his twin brother: "It's his twin brother. Urumban" (*GST* 311). Estha is required to identify the disfigured, dying Velutha as Velutha the kidnapper. When confronted with him, Velutha fixes his wandering eyes for a moment on Estha. Estha gives the damning testimony against an innocent, funful, loving friend. His betrayal at once kills his childhood: "Estha's mouth said Yes. Childhood tiptoed out" (*GST* 320). As a sop to his outraged conscience, he confides to Rahel immediately after the testimony: "It wasn't him. It was Urumban" (*GST* 320). Nevertheless the image that continues to haunt him is that of Velutha's battered skull and gory face. And the consciousness that does not give him a moment's respite is that of his collusive lie. When Baby Kochamma contrives to pack him off to Calcutta to prevent his lie being exposed, "He left his voice behind" (*GST* 326). No wonder he turns into a mute isolate. An eyewitness to the brutality on Velutha, Estha develops special sympathy for small things such as the old dying dog Khubchand at his father's house. He nurses him during his long-drawn-out death with all the affection and care of a mother. That the snuffing out of the young, vital Velutha is the direct cause of Estha's new tenderness is made quite explicit: "To Estha—steeped in the smell of old roses, blooded on memories of a broken man—the fact that something so fragile, so unbearably tender had survived, had been allowed to exist, was a miracle" (*GST* 12). After the death of his pet, he becomes a compulsive walker.

The twins' childhood identity and their adult complementarity leave their mark on the different stages of their life. It is "the Loss of Sophie Mol" that "ushered Rahel through childhood (from school to school) into womanhood" (*GST* 16). Estha becomes a recluse at his father's home intent on domestic chores. Rahel becomes after Ammu's death a recusant, a rebel and ultimately a drifter. In contrast to Estha's settled philosophy of life, she undertakes an inquiry into "life and how it ought to be lived" (*GST* 17). Because of her ingrained flippancy, "Rahel drifted into marriage" (*GST* 18) with a strange American Larry McCaslin. Larry treats her in the same way in which Estha treats the old dog: "Something still and small. Unbearably precious" (*GST* 19). This contrasts sharply with Chacko's brutality towards his own divorced sister Ammu whom he hounds out of their paternal house: "Get out of my house before I break every bone in your body." This incident impacts on the seven-year-old Rahel in the form of a permanent nightmare: "After that for years Rahel would dream this dream: a fat man, faceless, kneeling beside a woman's corpse" (*GST* 225). Rahel is privy to the disease-ravaged, jobless Ammu's overflowing love for her twins and of her pathetic dream of a bright future. The memory of the dead mother with her "marble eyes" and more poignantly that of the young Velutha haunt Rahel even in far-away America: "A young man with an old man's mouth" (*GST* 72). Estha and Rahel were "an under-age audience" to the drama of police brutality on Velutha. That it "was a clinical demonstration in controlled conditions...of human nature's pursuit of ascendancy" (*GST* 309) was beyond their comprehension. The reason why Velutha's death weighs so heavily on them is their confusion over their own role in it. Baby Kochamma gave them option between saving Ammu and courting prison life: "In the years to come they would replay this scene in their heads. As children. As teenagers. As adults. Had they been deceived into doing what they did? Had they been tricked into condemnation" (*GST* 318)? They swallow Baby Kochamma's bait with so much alacrity precisely because their interest in saving Ammu and themselves coincides with Baby Kochamma's interest in saving her own skin. So they cannot escape all moral guilt for their action. Be that as it may, they are definitely unwitting "midwives" of Ammu's dream, her secret affair with Velutha. The lovers pay for it with their lives, and the children with their "childhoods" (*GST* 336).

In their innocence and ignorance of the extent of Ammu's responsibility for the disaster that ruined them all, the child twins "held themselves wholly culpable for her grief" (*GST* 324). With the benefit of hindsight, they realize how they have been convenient instruments in others' hands, how undeserved are their sufferings and their death in life. The child Estha blames himself for Ammu's premature death: "His fault that she died alone in the lodge with no one to lie at the back of her and talk to her" (*GST* 325). The adult Rahel, however, accuses their exploiters: "As though that was what twins were meant for. To be borrowed and returned" (*GST* 156). Much of the action of the novel is presented as "play" and "performance," and most of the characters engage most of the time in play-acting. The adult twins are no exceptions: "A pair of actors trapped in a recondite play with no hint of plot or narrative. Stumbling through their parts, nursing someone else's sorrow. Grieving someone else's grief" (*GST* 191). It is, however, not easy for them to blame their predicament on anyone in particular. For many human agents and fate or chance have collaborated to bring it on, including of course themselves: "Esthappen and Rahel both knew that there were several perpetrators (besides themselves) that day. But only one victim (Velutha)" (*GST* 191). What is more troubling is that play and reality go on changing places. This idea is driven home to the adult twins when they sit watching the Kathakali dancers enact Bhima's dismemberment of Dushasana:

> It was no performance. Esthappen and Rahel recognized it. They had seen its work before. Another morning. Another stage. Another kind of frenzy (with millipedes on the soles of its shoes). The brutal extravagance of this matched by the savage economy of that. (*GST* 235)

What Bhima is doing to Dushasana in play the policemen did to Velutha in earnest? Only an intensely felt emotion in the form of sorrow and death, love and happiness can resolve the appearance-reality dichotomy. Thus for the child twins, "Ammu's tears made everything that had so far seemed unreal, real" (*GST* 8). Taking Ammu's dead body to the crematorium, Rahel feels that "Real life was inside the van. Where real death was" (*GST* 162). It is Ammu's prerogative to show the twins love as the way to self-discovery and reality: "She could feel herself through him (Velutha). Her skin. The way her body existed only where he touched her. The rest of her was smoke" (*GST* 335). The empty Rahel and the silent Estha resort to incest to purge themselves of their accumulated traumas, to resolve all their dichotomies and to regain their lost identity.

The relations between any two generations in the novel are marked by identity and difference. Accordingly Rahel and Estha of the third generation at once resemble and differ from Ammu and Velutha of the second. Rahel keeps on watching the barebodied Estha with the same intentness with which Ammu watched the barebodied Velutha: "Rahel watched his stomach suck inwards and his ribcage rise as his T-shirt peeled away from his skin, leaving it wet and honey-coloured." Where, however, Estha differs from Velutha is that he is "A fisherman in a white-tiled bathroom, with sea-secrets in his eyes" (*GST* 92-93). Similarly Rahel "appeared to have grown into the skin of her mother." Mother and daughter have a number of shared features. "Only her (Rahel's) eyes were incontestably more beautiful. Large. Luminous" (*GST* 92). The adult Rahel and the adult Estha are presented, in preparation for their eventual incest, not as simple but as composite beings: "Rahel watched Estha with the curiosity of a mother watching her wet child. A sister a brother. A woman a man. A twin a twin" (*GST* 93). Significant in this context is Ammu's impression of Velutha, and this in the midst of making Love to him: "At the moment that she guided him into her, she caught a passing glimpse of his youth, his youngness, the wonder in his eyes at the secret he had unearthed and she smiled down at him as though he was her child" (*GST* 336). And the fact that Rahel and Estha are biological twins lends a special aura to their relationship:

> He was a naked stranger met in a chance encounter. He was the one that she had known before Life began. The one who had once led her (swimming) through their lovely mother's cunt.

> Both things unbearable in their polarity. In their irreconcilable far-apartness. (*GST* 93)

Estha on his part discerns in Rahel their mother's image: "Grown into their skin.... Their beautiful mother's mouth" (*GST* 300).

Through their actual physical union, Estha and Rahel return to the prenatal condition from which they have emerged, and in the process resolve all multiplicities to a bare simplicity. They unite sex and love, needs and feelings. They go one better than their rebellious mother. Ammu had transgressed caste and class taboos: they transgress the ultimate taboo on incest. Rahel has improved on Ammu inasmuch as she has extruded the "Watcher" from within her mind. And she has also outgrown the far-away look in her eyes that so exasperated her American husband. In other words, the twins have developed absolutely autonomous selves. At the same time, the verbal similarity between the two love scenes accentuates the identity between the two generations of lovers. The Estha-Rahel scene is described thus: "Except perhaps that it was a little cold. A little wet. But very quiet. The Air. But what was there to say?" (*GST* 328). These very words occur in the Velutha-Ammu scene as well: "It was a little cold. A little wet. A little quiet. The Air. But what was there to say" (*GST* 338)? Ammu and Velutha's ecstatic joy at fulfilled love is interlaced with an uneasy sense of foreboding, if not utter helplessness. In contrast, victims of searing memories and desiccated emotions as they are, what the twins "shared that might was not happiness, but hideous grief" (*GST* 328).

Man is at the mercy of blighting chance, liberating instinct and fettering history or civilization. Antinomy is of the essence of human emotion as unpredictability is of his life. Generational relationship is marked by identity and difference. Random events interlock and complete life's hidden pattern. In this vision of life, revolutionary Marxism has no positive role to play. "Human love" as distinct from "romantic love" can serve at best as a palliative to the inevitable sufferings man is born to. Hence the paramount importance of love in life.

THE TITLE OF *THE GOD OF SMALL THINGS*

> To me the god of small things is the inversion of God. God's a big thing and God's in control. The god of small things...whether it's the way the children see things or whether it's the insect life in the book, or the fish or the stars—there is a not accepting of what we think of as adult boundaries. This small activity that goes on is the under life of the book.
>
> Arundhati Roy on the website 3

That the title of a work of art gives it a distinct identity is the least important of its functions. It is the first point of contact between a work of art and its audience. It offers the artist the first opportunity to orient the audience, to alert it to the work's import. Constrained by the title's obligatory pithiness, he scrupulously chooses subtle and suggestive naming words. More often than not, the title of a work of art serves as a pointer to its theme. The title of *The God of Small Things* is no exception to this rule.

As a testimony to their "joint identities," Rahel remembers at the outset of the novel a number of Estha's experiences to which, however, she has no direct access. The first of these is Estha's horrifying experience with the Orangedrink Lemondrink Man, the second is the taste of tomato sandwiches Estha consumed on the Madras Mail. The comment that "And these are only the small things" (*GST* 3) is rich in irony. Estha becomes fixated on the emotional wound inflicted on him by the Orangedrink Lemondrink Man. The Madras Mail is the symbol of his first ever separation from Rahel. These two experiences go on retroacting on him and scar him for life. They are therefore the very opposite of "small things"; they are momentous enough to turn Estha into a morbid youth. This ironic reversal of values informs the novelist's deft use of many of the so-called small things in the novel. Separated at seven, the twins meet again at thirty-one. Gone are their childhood "joint identities." They have separated out into two distinct individuals, each enclosed within his own psychic cocoon. The result is that "Edges, Borders, Boundaries, Brinks and Limits have appeared like a team of trolls on their separate horizons. Short creatures with long shadows, patrolling and Blurry End" (*GST* 3). A troll is "a supernatural being in Scandinavian legends depicted as either a dwarf or giant and living in caves or under bridges" (*Encarta* 1999). The novelist packs a lot of significance into the pregnant oxymoron "short creatures with long shadows." Mental boundaries are invisible, and so are like "short creatures." At the same time, they are impregnable, and so are capable of casting "long shadows." Evidently small things and big consequences are not incompatible.

The novel's ostensible "God of Small Things" Velutha is liquidated unceremoniously, but produces far-reaching, long-lasting consequences. He lives for decades in the minds of the twins, of course not as a pleasant memory. Estha "carried inside him the memory of a young man with an old man's mouth" (*GST* 32). That precisely is Rahel's haunting memory: "A young man with an old man's mouth" (*GST* 72). The gruesome killing of the low-caste, low-class, defenceless Velutha convinces Estha that this world denies the small, delicate things even the right to exist. That is why the natural death of his long ailing dog makes him feel "that something so fragile, so unbearably tender had survived, had been allowed to exist, was a miracle" (*GST* 12). Like Estha, Rahel's American husband Larry has the sensitivity to appreciate the worth of a small thing that Rahel is to him: "Something still and small. Unbearably precious" (*GST* 19). The narrator uses Larry's inability to understand the reason for Rahel's abstracted look as an excuse to present an ironic picture of India. Overridden as individuality is in India by collectivity, personal despair or personal turmoil counts for nothing in the face of "public turmoil of a nation." The context makes it fairly clear that "Big God" is the nation or an institution, "Small God" a private individual. Roy's idea of "God" which means "Big God" is that of a bully, of a fascist. Exercising as he does power and control, he demands obedience and denies freedom: "That Big God howled like a hot wind and demanded obeisance." "Small God" is a private individual, fortified by the knowledge of his own absolute insignificance. He has no expectation, and therefore no disappointment. No despair can touch him because there are worse unfortunates than he. His insouciance is rooted in his irrepressible spirit. Significant is Roy's image of "Small God" with the emphasis on his insignificance and his indifference:

> Then Small God (cosy and contained, private and limited) came (away) cauterized, laughing numbly at his own temerity. Inured by the confirmation of his own inconsequence, he became resilient and truly indifferent. Nothing mattered much.... Because Worse Things had happened. (*GST* 19)

All the bad characters in the novel model themselves on "Big God," the good on "Small God." Roy's "Small God" looks like a cross between an existentialist and a stoic. He shows his sangfroid through his eyes. The novel dramatizes the dialectic between "Big God" and "Small God," between Big Men and Women on the one hand and Little Men and Women on the other, between power and love.

A measure of the perfect reciprocity between the novel's theme and its technique is the double demonstration they offer of the novelist's life vision. The action of the novel begins with Sophie Mol's arrival at Ayemenem, and dates from that day. The action climaxes with her accidental death and its cascading consequences. The disappearance of the children coincides with Velutha's dismissal from service for his affair with Ammu. This enables Baby Kochamma to implicate him in the children's kidnapping, which results in his killing by the police. To get rid of Ammu and Estha who can expose her false charge against Velutha, Baby Kochamma presents them to the heart-broken Chacko as Sophie's murderers. Estha is returned to his father in Calcutta, Ammu is hounded out of the house. Death of her only child coming on the heels of the death of her second husband renders Margaret a lonely woman. The failed and bereaved Chacko seeks solace in Canada. Sophie's death causes the break-up of the entire household. As for the mental repercussions of the deaths of Sophie, Velutha and Ammu, they become Estha and Rahel's haunting memories and overcast their youth. Sophie's arrival in itself is a small event. But her death causes reverberating consequences affecting a host of lives. Estha and Rahel recur again and again to a few traumatic moments from their childhood. The structure of the novel parallels their obsessions in the very process of their formation: "Little events, ordinary things, smashed and reconstituted. Imbued with new meaning. Suddenly they become the beached bones of a story." The novel also deals with love between Mammachi, Pappachi and Chacko, between Baby Kochamma and Father Mulligan, between Chacko and Margaret, between Ammu and Velutha, between Estha and Rahel. And the lovers are in some way or other transgressors. In one sense, the story is strictly temporal, beginning with Sophie's arrival. In another sense, it is timeless: "That it really began in the day when the Love Laws were made. The laws that lay down who should be loved, and how. And how much" (*GST* 32-33).

Like Big God, a Big Man is one who stifles his instincts and emotions, and goes in for will and authority, division and distinction, injunction and inhibition. A Little Man is the direct antithesis of a Big Man. He believes in the sanctity of his instincts and emotions, in the holiness of the heart's affections. He is as much against authority and tyranny as he is for humility and equality. A Bihari coolie uses ambition as a criterion of differences: "There are big dreams and little ones. "Big Man the Laltain sahib, Small Man the Mombatti" (*GST* 89). The implication is that in order to realize his big dreams, a Big Man steels himself to all interfering instinct and impulses, and pursues single-mindedly his set goal. In this respect, he resembles the steady flame of the well-protected lantern. In the absence of any such stabilizing ambition to keep him anchored to a chosen course, a Little Man wavers as much as a flickering candle. Anyway one's high ambition contrasts with the other's lack of it. Some of these differences come through in the audience's behaviour towards Estha, caught singing in the theatre:

> 'Get him out of here!' the Audience said, when they found him.
> Shutup or Getout. Getout or Shutup.

> The Audience was a Big Man. Estha was a Little Man, with the tickets. (*GST* 100)

It is Pappachi who exhibits all the features of a Big Man. A big government official with a big dream to have a moth named after him, he goes on beating his wife and daughter mercilessly. When his son Chacko, "a big man," restrains him, he starts playing a Big Man in public in his Plymouth. It is his tyranny that turns Ammu into an explosive rebel.

> As she grew older, Ammu learned to live with this cold, calculating cruelty. She developed a lofty sense of injustice and the mulish, reckless streak that develops in Someone Small who has been bullied all their lives by Someone Big. (*GST* 181-82)

Pappachi's snobbism and casteism complete his picture as a Big Man. Treated as a Little Woman by her overbearing husband, Mammachi plays to the hilt the role of a Big Woman. She punishes Ammu for humbling her proud family, and Velutha for presuming above his caste and class through their love for each other. Chacko too becomes his father's son when he thunders at Ammu his order of expulsion for her transgression: Normally not a blusterer, he is "Surprised at his own strength. His bigness. His bullying power" (*GST* 226). Baby Kochamma's bigness consists in her Machiavellianism. She plays on the Police Inspector Mathew to dispose of Velutha whom she hates. She works up Chacko's grief to get rid of Ammu and Estha whom she fears. She turns a defeat into victory by spiritually possessing the dead Father Mulligan. She vicariously presides over the world through her TV. She is a woman of formidable will and intellect, altogether devoid of emotions and softer feelings.

There is a totally different kind of bigness that deserves mention. A big occasion would seem to demand everything big: big speeches, big ideas, big emotions. The novel presents a number of big occasions but without the expected big things. Chacko is receiving his ex-wife and daughter. The situation is tailor-made for gushing. The characters concerned instead engage in mere formalities. The narrator wryly comments:

"And the Air was full of Thoughts and Things to Say. But at times like these, only the Small Things are ever said. The Big Things lurk unsaid inside" (*GST* 142). The narrator repeats this comment verbatim on all the big occasions. The novel features lovers of various kinds, but it scrupulously avoids courtship scene of the conventional kind. Lovers do not engage in love talk: they do not even emote. Estha and Rahel make love and they do it silently: "But what was there to say? (*GST* 328). However tempestuous Ammu's and Velutha's love for each other may be, they not even declare their love. Even their ecstatic love-making cannot make them eloquent. The same question is repeated here too: "But what was there to say?" (*GST* 338) And the reply is another repetition: "The Big Things ever lurked inside" (*GST* 338). The implication seems to be that deep thoughts and emotions do not need explicitly verbal communication especially between intimates. Eloquent silence is enough for them. Articulation is not the only means and the only forms of communication. Instinct has been shown repeatedly as effecting telepathy.

Going by Roy's own explanation of the phrase "the god of small things," one may think that the god in question is not so much an individual character in the novel as a mindset. It is specifically, in the very words of Roy, "a not accepting of what we think of as adult boundaries" (Roy on the website 3). Velutha and Estha are Little Men, Ammu and Rahel are Little Women. All the four are equally unaware of any caste or class distinction, or for that matter any barrier to camaraderie anywhere. This is because they are loyal to the instinct within them, and not to any institution outside. The twins are asked not to visit the Paravan Velutha's house. They have a compelling reason for flouting this injunction. Made to feel unwanted at their grandparents' house and openly humiliated, they are in their element and at their ease in Velutha's hut. They spend their happiest time in the company of the child-like Velutha whose genuine love for them makes him, and not their unfeeling uncle Chacko, their surrogate father. They in turn love him so much that his death brings on their death in life. These four free spirits or transgressors constitute a circle of their own, a circle of love and interlinked fate. All of them suffer intensely and suffer for each other. They are votaries of love and victims of power.

The fullest embodiment of Roy's idea of "Small God" with his characteristic insignificance and insouciance, with his instinct for bonhomie and love is Velutha. Ammu finds in him her dream man and anoints him "The God of Small Things." It is only after Ammu and Velutha have discovered their instinctive love for each other that Ammu dreams of him as "The God of Small Things." This not-yet-named dream lover's description is as follows: "Ridges of muscle on his stomach rose under his skin like divisions on a slab of chocolate" (*GST* 215). This tallies fairly with Ammu's previously observed image of Velutha: "She saw the ridges of muscle on Velutha's stomach grow taught and rise under his skin like the divisions on a slab of chocolate" (*GST* 175). So the fact that Ammu's "God of Small Things" is Velutha is beyond any doubt. One teasing question is that the real Velutha is not one-armed as the dream Velutha is. But why? A wild guess is that the novelist wants to indicate some kind of affinity between Velutha and Estha who most often stiffly holds his polluted hand away from his body. First, in the dream scene, a parenthesis pictures Estha thus: "Tangerine-shaped too, was the Thing that Estha carried into *The Sound of Music* in his sticky Other Hand" (*GST* 217). Second, Ammu in the thick of love-making "smiled down at him (Velutha) as though he was her child" (*GST* 336).

As a marginalized Paravan and a factory hand at that, Velutha is a social lightweight, a man of no consequence. Hence he leaves no footprints in sand, no ripples in water, no image in mirrors. It is worth remembering that his lack of importance and ambition is the source of his perpetual carefreeness and of his angelic smile. He is the God of Loss because his love for Ammu causes the loss of job and of his life, the loss of Ammu's home, of her children and finally of her life. It causes the twins the loss of their childhoods. A sweet smile always rippling on his lips earns him the sobriquet "The God of Sudden Smiles." It is not for nothing that he is also "The God of Goose Bumps." On the night of Sophie's arrival, beautifully dressed Ammu sits facing Velutha. "She touched him lightly with her fingers and left a trail of goose bumps on his skin" (*GST* 339). Last of all, he is the "God of Small Things" because Velutha and Ammu do not look to anything beyond their self-fulfilling, secret love. They have nowhere to go, nothing to look forward to except the hope of meeting tomorrow. "So they stuck to the small things" (*GST* 338). Their "joint identities" are their shield against life's evils. As the novel celebrates loving-kindness, the principal attribute of "The God of Small Things," it has been very aptly named.

WORKS CITED

Abraham, John E. "A Broad Study on Arundhati Roy's *The God of Small Things.*" *The Indian Journal of English Studies* Vol. XXXVII, 1998-99.

Ahmad, Aijaz. "Reading Arundhati Roy politically." *Frontline*, August 8, 1997.

Choubey, Asha. "The Magic Wand of Arundhati Roy: The Strategy of Words in *The God of Small Things.*" *Arundhati Roy's Fictional World*. Ed. A.N. Dwivedi. Delhi: B.R. Publishing Corporation, 2001.

Cowley, Jason. "Why we chose Arundhati." *India Today,* October 27, 1997.

Dasan, M. "Arundhati Hits the Socio-Political Ball." *The Critical Studies of Arundhati Roy's The God of Small Things*. Ed. Jaydipsinha Dodiya & Joya Chakravarty. New Delhi: Atlantic Publishers, 2001.

Dwivedi, A.N. "Reversing the Gear: A Critique of Arundhati Roy's *The God of Small Things.*" *Arundhati Roy's Fictional World.* Ed. A.N. Dwivedi.

Gandhi, Leela. *Postcolonial Theory: A Critical Introduction.* 1998. Rpt. New Delhi: 2002.

Hawthorn, Jeremy. *A Glossary of Contemporary Literary Theory.* London: Arnold, 2000.

John, Binoo K. "The New Deity of Prose." *India Today*, October 27, 1997.

Johnson, Robert A. *The Psychology of Romantic Love.* 1984. Rpt. London: Arkana, 1987.

Nanda, Mini. "Is There a God of Small Things?" *Contemporary Indian Literature: Position and Expositions*. Ed. Santosh Gupta. Jaipur: Rawat Publications, 2000.

Pandey, Mithilesh Kumar. "The Erotic Scenes in *The God of Small Things*." *The Indian Journal of English Studies*. Vol. XL, 2002-03.

Roy, Arundhati. *The End of Imagination*. Kottayam: D.C. Books, 1998.

——. *The God of Small Things* (abbreviated to *GST*). New Delhi: IndiaInk, 1997.

——. "A million dollars is the least interesting part of the story" (Interview with Alok Rai). *The Times of India*, 6 April, 1997.

——. "When you have written a book, you lay your weapons down" (Interview with Praveen Swami). *Frontline,* August 8, 1997.

Ray, Mohit K. "Locusts Stand I: Some Feminine Aspects of *The God of Small Things*." *Arundhati Roy's Fictional World*. Ed. A.N. Dwivedi.

Surendran, K.V. *The God of Small Things: A Saga of Lost Dreams*. New Delhi: Atlantic Publishers, 2000.

Tripathi, J.P. "*The God of Small Things:* Behind the Veneer of Popularity—The Ephemeral and the Eternal." *Arundhati Roy's Fictional World*. Ed. A.N. Dwivedi.

Disastrous Synthesis of Desire and Duty in Manju Kapur's *Difficult Daughters*

17

DEVIKA

Manju Kapur's desire to give an outlet to her deep buried thoughts and feelings of imaginative impulse resulted in *Difficult Daughters*. This work bares various whims in newly woven pattern that establish its worth as a work abounding in certain novelties. No wonder, the novel has grabbed the critical acclaim so soon because it involves hard work of eight years. She remains humble about her book as she says in *Rashtriya Sahara Magazine*, "Nothing is planned in a big way, but eventually things may take a grand shape. Writing this novel was not very difficult for me, but it took eight long years before the book finally saw the light of the day" (1999: 112).[1] Indubitably, the work won Commonwealth Writers' Prize for Best First Book for its valuable contribution to the field of literature. Earlier as B.K. Das puts it that women have been "presented in literature from their (male's) viewpoint" but now women have taken the reins in their hands and they are nowadays "presented in the writings of female writers from their point of view" (1998: 143).[2]

Manju Kapur takes delight in the presentation of the psyche of two or more generations to highlight the parities and disparities lurking in-between. She commences the novel introducing Ida as her mother Virmati's funeral only to unfold their lives in the ensuing pages. Virmati presents a contrast to her mother as well as her daughter. She etiolates in the effulgence of her mother and daughter. The desire on her part to come out of the fetters of household periphery rams her on such a path where she goes astray. To give a new meaning to her life she trudges ahead on the path of rebellion but her tragedy is that being new to the field of unbridled freedom she does not know what to do with this newly acquired liberty. Lack of sound power of judgment doesn't allow her to invite anybody to guide her through. The focus gets blurred and her attention is caught by trivial happenings of her life that devastate her and leave her parched.

Gradually, the futile and lackadaisical struggle on her part, stemming from her deep roots in her own culture, that are diametrically opposed to that of the professor, to cut professor from her life ends in a fiasco. Her agonizing downfall lacerates the soul of this victim of indecisions. She loses her virginity to professor and too benumbed to react blurts it out as "an outdated morality" (1998: 114)[3] to get ahead in life. The traumatic experience of abortion makes her forgive him, but the daughter reacts vehemently when caught in the same situation. The comparison between the two makes her daughter appear more mature and strong-willed. Ida, though she also endures the harrowing experience of abortion, never forgives her husband for forcing her to remain deprived of the bliss of motherhood. The idea to deify the husband never comes to her mind; in fact, the lack of virtues in him helps her walk out of that relationship. She does not want to maintain a relationship that is fake and hollow. She acts like Ammu who prefers to die at "a viable die-able age" (1997: 3)[4] discarding a husband who is insensitive to human values. Both present a contrast to Nalini of *Circles of Silence*. Nalini, "a grown woman who had a right to look for her own happiness" (2002: 330)[5] gets into a relationship and wants to get married to the person whom she finds a good human being despite his bearing the stigma of a murdered wife; for her the stamp of relationship is not important, completion is craved and accordingly vital decisions are taken.

Comparison between two generations highlights Virmati's and Harish's mother in an altogether different light. Their outlook towards life has been entirely different, as subconsciously they all seem to be aware of the affairs of life.

Kishori Devi's observation aptly sums up her deep agonizing understanding of the limitations of her gender:

> In this life we can do nothing but our duty. Serve our elders, look after our children, walk along the path that has been marked for us, and not pine and yearn for those things we cannot have. Since our destiny is predetermined, that is the only way we can know any peace. Duty is our guide, and our strength. How can we control the things outside us? We can control ourselves. (194)

Alikeness in their thinking may be accredited to the time they belong to. Unmindful of their opinion regarding society, they try their level best to keep family values intact, sometimes even at the cost of their dignity; Ganga in her whole-hearted endeavour to maintain that dignity belongs to the earlier generation. Giving a damn thought to break the shackles of marriage they continue carrying on their responsibilities irrespective of their respectable or otherwise status in family, something rarely done by their daughters.

The shift in thinking regarding the status of women comes to the fore with the advent of fledglings like Shakuntala and Virmati. Shakuntala gives a stripped sketch of the current trend, "Here we are, fighting for the freedom of the nation, but women are still supposed to marry, and nothing else" (15). Their respective mothers, quite worried, fail to imagine that a girl is liable to do anything else except getting married and bearing children. Elder generation cherishes and exercises an entirely different viewpoint; for marriage and wife a subtle and subdued streak of reverence permeates, "A wife was not for show after all" (61). Like the mother of Uma in *Fasting, Feasting* by Anita Desai, both the mothers feel like saying, "Our daughter does not need to go out to work" (1999: 143).[6] But these mothers lack control over the wishes of their daughters. Shakuntala's open and aspiring views not to consider marriage the ultimate goal of every girl's life give Virmati's imagination new wings, "It was possible to be something other than a wife" (17). Eventually, when she does indulge in an objectionable relationship morality pangs make

Virmati uneasy: "As for me, I know I have failed in my duty and I will be punished one day. Nobody can escape their karma. Maybe what is happening to me now is part of it, and there is no use protesting" (85).

Manju Kapur ventures into a less trodden realm of presenting vulnerable characters as the central figures and spins her yarn around weak characters like Virmati and Harish. Harish, a professor by profession lives in an idyllic world quite ignorant of the mundane realities. Rather insensitive to the needs of his faithful and dutiful wife whose worth he never realizes, he wants to have Virmati not as his wife but as a woman to gratify the cerebral spark of his personality. His temptation to have Virmati physically is so strong that as soon as he is with her he wants to have sex with her. Whenever his physical hunger pangs don't disturb him he desires her to appreciate his intellectual capabilities, which he rarely uses or displays. His insatiable desire for undiluted adoration as an intellect makes him grope for Virmati.

Virmati, a victim of ineffectual will power, struggles a lot to get out of the rut of domesticity but fails to land anywhere Virmati doesn't know what does she want from life; she moves forward irrespective of being right or wrong. She displays courage only for shattering the shackles only to be shackled again. Her desire to gain academic lore gets her entangled in an affair with Harish; studies take a back seat, only to let the affair blossom according to the convenience of the professor. A quisling desire to be independent allows her to become merely the second fiddle to Harish, a crippling. This man of seemingly sublime and sober nature, in verity, turns out to be a sycophant who spoils the life of Virmati to satisfy his thirst for keeping a woman in his awe.

Over the years, the subjectivity of Indian women writers has become diminutive and objectivity has come to the fore. Earlier, on the basis of characters it has been easy to gauze the work or character. This thing is visible in the works of writers like Shobha De and Anita Desai. Now writers like Preeti Singh and Manju Kapur cover a wide range of traits of characterization. In *Difficult Daughters* if there is a dangling character like Virmati, who remains a constant sufferer then there is a powerful character like Swarna Lata, who is assertively triumphant in her tone:

> I wrote and told my parents. There was not a moment to lose.... 'They had no choice.... I was very clear that I wanted to do something besides getting married. I told my parents that if they would support me for two more years I would be grateful. Otherwise I would be forced to offer satyagraha along with other.... But they agreed because they knew I meant what I said.... Thank God all this is over,' said Swarna Lata. 'It was quite unpleasant while it lasted. I prefer not to quarrel with my parents, but sometimes there is no alternative.' (107-08)

The description clarifies that she is not a weak character. Her vision of life is quite pellucid, as she knows what does she want from life. Immorality or shamelessness is not her pet; lofty aims for higher studies make her quarrel with her parents and they give way to her wishes because they know she means what she says. She even does not like the idea of quarreling with her parents. It's not that she doesn't get married at all, she does get married but when she considers herself fit to shoulder the responsibilities of a wife and later on a mother. There is no place for scandalized tempest in her married life; the idea of becoming second wife never occurs to her. Thriving on the sap of her positive points she leaves no scope for strain in her marriage. It's not that she merely becomes a housewife and stops living for her own self, she continues indulging in activities she deems fit to get involved in. Her name Lata that means 'creeper' fits well. Though creeper can't stand on her own and needs proper support but her full name is Swarna Lata, the 'golden' element in her name bestows her with the qualities to give vitality and exuberance to those she clings.

The desire to intervene in the affairs of others is utterly amiss; hand of help is extended when helpless Virmati needs it the most. She never forces Virmati to divulge her secrets to her and when Virmati needs Swarna's help for abortion she helps her in the best possible way. She doesn't let her go to a '*dai*' because she finds it dangerous for her to undergo such an unsafe means to get her unborn aborted. With the help of some acquaintance she attempts to get appointment with one of the best doctors. Not only that she makes it a point that Virmati faces no problem whether it is related to money or public shame, she also emotionally supports her and psychologically makes her feel better. Virmati never feels the threat from her side and has full confidence that Swarna will never betray her trust.

Her own younger sister presents a contrast to Virmati. When Virmati refuses to get married to Inderjit despite his being a good match, Indu creates no scene and willingly gets into that abrupt relation keeping in mind not her welfare, likings and interests but the prestige of her family. She, however, shows no ill will towards her elder sister and always remains polite to her. She does not mind much the "pressures and oppressions of patriarchal culture" as Mohanty Sachidananda says in *The Hindu* (2000: 14).[7]

Characters like Kasturi and Lajwanti share similarities as well as dissimilarities. This novel gives shelter to characters like Virmati, Swarna, Ida, Ganga, Kasturi, Shakuntala, Indu, Chhotti, etc. who show no resemblance to one another and yet all are the creations of one writer only. Similarly Harish, Giridhar, Lala Diwan Chand, etc. have emanated from the imagination of the same lady writer, yet Lala Diwan Chand is the pillar of strength of his family and makes sure that all the members face no problem, on the other hand, Harish, the intellectual professor who guides none except Virmati who never forgives herself for whatever she has done in her life, is unable to provide support to anyone and himself thrives on both of his wives. Ganga takes care of all his needs and he is shameless to announce to Virmati that Ganga doesn't do much. This cripple who purely dances to the tunes of his needs uses Virmati unreservedly but gets married to her very reluctantly.

The emotional void exercises a great influence over the incidents and decisions in the lives of these characters. The professor, so to say, is married and his wife is quite a competent housewife, a very nice host, a great cook, a very gentle daughter-in-law, an affable neighbour, a loving mother, and also a very caring wife. She handles all the household chores perfectly but when fails to fill the emotional void in her husband's life it turns out to be her misfortune because that void gets filled by Virmati and no wonder, he gets attracted towards her. When Virmati tries to snap ties with him after he makes his wife pregnant, he tightens his snare around her calling her an indispensable part of his life, 'There is a void in my heart and in my home that you alone can fill' (112). The magnetic charm draws her closer to the man because, "It was the first time a man had called her sexy, and when she closed her eyes she could still feel his whisper drifting through her body, under her skin" (1999: 93).[8]

Similarly the emotional void in Virmati victimizes her, "At times Virmati yearned for affection, for some sign that she was special" (6). But she is disappointed to get none. They want her to do in life what they find good and respectable for her but the problem begins when the question of marriage is raised and Virmati retaliates. She has always been a very good, caring and obedient daughter and has never wished to insult her parents. But the emotional void has settled in her because the role of the surrogate mother deprives her of her childhood care and affection and unfortunately, she lands in the hands of an already married professor. The idea of being an intruder time and again makes her snap the ties but fails because the professor fills the emotional void in her and for that she brings a bad name to her family.

She suffers tremendously while undergoing the tragic experience of an abortion, bears the shame and stigma of the second wife and intruder, and feels frustrated with herself for spoiling the life of professor's first wife. Pangs of guilt continue haunting her even when she and professor get along very well. She harbours the sense of repentance to such an extent that even after her death she wants to repent for her action:

> When I die, she said to me, I want my body donated. My eyes, my heart, my kidneys, any organ that can be of use. That way someone will value me after I am gone.... And she went on, when I die I want no shor-

> shaar. I don't want a chauth, I don't want an uthala, I want no one called, no one informed. (1)

Along with marriage, affairs, and children Manju Kapur sets her story of love, struggle and betrayal against the background of pre-independence days. The struggle is in its full swing and all the characters irrespective of being male or female get affected by it. The struggle though in the background is not utterly neglected and certain parts of novel depict the delicate condition prevailing at that particular period of time. The description is very accurate and the facts conform to the situation. Manju Kapur deals with the sensitive issues with great precision and nowhere we get the idea that some tampering has been done to use the background merely for the purpose of it. Her accounts sound genuinely appropriate:

> It is 1943, and the strain of being the colony of a warring nation shows. There are shortages and the costs of living are rising. In the market-place, bureaucratic procedures multiply. The government seeks to introduce fixed prices as profiteering spirals. The dark face of control emerges, the black market, hoarding, raids, and punishment. (216)

When the movement is at its peak then families move ahead to help the needy. The family of Virmati does help according to their position and status. They donate whatever extra they have; they arrange food for freedom fighters who are on their way to achieve freedom for the country. Virmati also donates all the belongings of Ganga to the needy people though she does it with a different purpose. This hectic period also shows the unsafe way of life at that period of time. How the streets remain deserted and how benignly the houses are plundered and looted is also highlighted.

Not only the scenario is depicted, the involvement of people is also shown. When Harish is with his friends, the talks inadvertently turn to the political upheavals. Not only the males but females also are acutely aware of the need of the hour and where girls like Swarna actively participate in the movement, girls like Virmati though they don't actively participate in the movement are aware of its urgency. The communal hatred, landing of money, donation for the freedom fighters, etc. remain the active issues, and people remain aware of it.

The movement for freedom also takes symbolic significance, as it is the period when women have started shedding their inhibitions. Like the country they inhabit they are also fed up of the ways they are attuned to by others and they have to really struggle hard to break the manacles. It takes time on their part to get established on their own. Shakuntala, Swarna, etc. are the first freedom fighters who sow the seeds of independence in Virmati and others to help them move ahead and achieve something else as well except husbands.

Virmati, who has always lived for others never gets the pleasure of being the center of attention and when in her life she manages to get Ganga out of it she feels that this is the only thing she has been craving throughout her life. Harish is there to give all his undisputed attention to her:

> In the evening, Virmati would sometimes fill the tank with a little water, climb down the steps, and lie down. Her mind was drained of all emotion. Her limbs were heavy with torpor. Harish would sometimes join her. Submerged in the depths of the tank all they could see was the far-away sky and the grey walls. Often they made love. There was no one to see them, no one to mind anything they did. Virmati had never had so much space around her. Maybe this was really what she had fought for all along, space to be. (253)

Throughout her life she has never been given attention, she is there to carry out certain responsibilities. And nobody has considered it odd or wrong. The first generation considers it just a normal routine and nobody else but Virmati feels a bit uneasy:

> Ever since Virmati could remember she had been looking after children. It wasn't only baby Parvati to whom she was indispensable, to her younger siblings she was second mother as well.... At times Virmati yearned for

> affection, for some sign that she was special.... Why did she need to look for gestures when she knew how indispensable she was to her mother and the whole family? (6)

Her own existence never gets individualized by anyone in the elder generation. It's her cousin Shakuntala who jolts Virmati out of her incumbency. She apprises Virmati of the current scenario in Lahore where women have crossed the threshold of domesticity to live for themselves. She cherishes the freedom of being independent because for her marriage is not the eventual finale of life. Her education and intelligence enable her not to bank on the male members of her family. No wonder, she becomes Virmati's role model because Shakuntala voices her opinion of giving females the right to choose and lead independent life where they can wield the power to decide for themselves:

> ...how much satisfaction there can be in leading your own life, in being independent. Here we are, fighting for the freedom of the nation, but women are still supposed to marry, and nothing else. (14-15)
>
> But for my mother, marriage is the only choice in life. I so wish I could help her feel better about me. (15)
>
> It was useless looking for answers inside the home. One had to look outside. To education, freedom, and the bright lights of Lahore colleges. (15)
>
> ...times are changing, and women are moving out of the house. So why not you? (16)

In this novel thus, the elder generation seems to be very particular about marriage, which according to them is the only door to happiness and satisfaction for women. Lajwanti is unable to do anything with her daughter's choice of not getting married, has it been in her power to do something then she would have never allowed her daughter to do the job and live away from the home. Kasturi also thinks on the same line and when Shakuntala is there to see her convalescing aunt, her aunt is quick to remind her that marriage is the only path for girls to have bliss in their lives:

> 'Still, it is the duty of every girl to get married,' remarked Kasturi mildly...'Beti,' said Kasturi, in a mild scolding voice, 'how can family disturb? You are getting very modern in your thinking.... What is the need to do a job? A woman's shaan is in her home. Now you have studied and worked enough. Shaddi.' Here Kasturi's eyes glistened with emotion. 'After you get married, Viru can follow.' (13)

But Shakuntala thinks otherwise and shows her displeasure at the idea of being forced into a marriage. Not only Shakuntala, Virmati also protests against her marriage though for another reason. Along with studies it is also the charm of professor that keeps her away from arranged marriage. She makes it clear that she wants to 'Study...I don't want to marry.... I do not like the boy' (80). Along with Shakuntala and Virmati, Swarna who does not want to make a mess of her life by getting married right now shows her penchant to study further:

> My mother wanted me to marry. She said I had done my BA and that was enough.... I love Lahore. All my friends are here, all my activities. I had to stay here, and so I decided to do an MA. I wrote and told my parents.... They'd already begun to send me photographs of prospective husbands! Each looking uglier than the last.... I was very clear that I wanted to do something besides getting married. (107)

Harish may have influenced Virmati because of his education and sophistication but he fails to influence his kids with his learning. The kids rebel and find a way on their own. Ida pays her mother in the same coin by not listening to her pleas to study properly. Giridhar and Chhotti also decide the course of their lives irrespective of the wishes of their father. Giridhar marries against the wishes of his parents and gets into the business much to the chagrin of Harish. Chhotti excels in studies merely to get her father's attention but refuses to get married and instead of getting into the field of humanities, books or music, joins the IAS to accommodate her mother and grandmother. She does it perhaps to show her father that she is doing his duty by providing home and protection to her mother and grandmother. Likewise, Ida is also not far behind in the race to decide things on her own:

> Ida refused to show any signs of intellectual brightness. 'There are other things in life,' she told her mother.
> 'Like what?' asked Virmati.
> 'Like living.'
> 'You mean living only for yourself. You are disappointing your father.'
> 'Why is it so important to please him?' Ida protested to her mother. She wanted to please herself sometimes, though by the time she grew up she was not sure what self she had to please. (257-58)

Mothers think alike irrespective of age. Virmati's mother has expected her daughter to remain happy in her life. Her vision has been restricted to family, marriage, and kids; accordingly she has always desired her daughter to feel the delight of being a wife and a mother. When Virmati becomes mother of Ida she wishes her the best and wants her to get whatever she and Harish deem the best for her. Again the younger generation decides against the wishes of the parents. They ricochet and move ahead irrespective of the expectations of their parents. Ida does not find studies the ultimate goal of life and simply wishes to live for herself, something which younger Virmati herself has done. Ida sums up her resentment in one line, "I grew up struggling to be the model daughter. Pressure, pressure to perform day and night" (258). Inadvertently, Virmati becomes the same mother with whom she herself could not accommodate when she has been young. Her reins tauten around her daughter and likewise her daughter starts looking for escape routes to remain away from such smothering environment. As Virmati has tried in her life to get along with her mother so does Ida though to please her mother she does get married to a person who is an academic but walks out of that relationship the way Virmati has turned her back to the boy chosen by her parents. As per the meaning of her name 'a new slate, and a blank beginning' (256) she leaves her mother and her past behind and wants to make a new beginning afresh.

The issue of second wife is also focused on. Ganga is shown as a typical Indian wife who lives only for her husband. She never finds faults with her husband; it is only Virmati who gets subjected to "an accusing, protesting silence..." (1997: 10)[9] of his wife and others. She curses her for her intrusion in her life. The difference between the first and second wife is very strikingly presented. She is never given the right to meddle with the household affairs. When Virmati shows her displeasure to Harish regarding his work still done by his first wife, Harish bypasses the issue by asking her to remain with him and tries to cajole her to forget about everything else and make him the center of her attention. The very next day she tries to get up early in the morning so that she can wash his clothes, Harish requests her not to intervene in the usual routine of his house because first his mother takes bath, then his wife takes bath because otherwise she can't enter the kitchen and kids are also important because they are not supposed to be late for the school. She is not allowed to do any work not because she is special because she is a forced member and undoubtedly unwanted too.

The relationship she shares with the children of her husband is also not a healthy one. They hate her without knowing the proper reason. Even when they grow up, no signs are shown of their liking; instead they become indifferent to her presence. Even her sister-in-law who says nothing indecent to her, feels uneasy in her presence, prefers not to stay with her and takes the leave on one or another pretext. Virmati never gets admiration from his kids. Even her parents never forgive her. Her father dies without forgiving her, so does her grandfather. When she goes to see her grieved mother, she reacts vehemently. She wishes to remain in touch with her siblings and invites her younger sister to come and see her. Her visits from once a week extend to once a month and then stop altogether. She dares not even ask the reason of her not coming.

Ganga reacts in a natural way by not accepting her because Virmati herself finds it hard to accept Ganga in Harish's life despite her being his legally wedded wife. Though all the rights are with Ganga yet the poor soul craves for her husband and fails to get his love and admiration. She cries her heart out when she gets to know about Harish's involvement with Virmati. Her mother-in-law who finds her daughter-in-law a perfect housewife feels sorry for the poor soul. Ganga gets the sympathy of Virmati's mother also because all the rights, being his wife, solely belong to her. Virmati manipulates to send Ganga away from Harish's house but fails to snatch away Harish from her heart. Even when she is not with her husband, she wears bindi, sindoor and never does anything without the consent of her husband; ironically, he remains her god.

It is not that her mother, her mother-in-law, or his first wife spurn her, even her daughter does not want to lead life the way her mother has done. Curiosity on her part to peep in the past of her mother urges her to visit the relatives of her mother but they maintain a respectable silence about the deeds of her mother. Initially, she gets to know about her mother in tits and bits, but when everything gets known to her, she wishes that the memories of her mother should not haunt her and spare her to lead her life in a way she finds suitable, "This book weaves a connection between my mother and me, each word a brick in a mansion I made with my head and my heart. Now live in it, Mama, and leave me be. Do not haunt me anymore" (259).

An immaculate expose of the plight of an unmarried girl involved in an extramarital affair resulting in secret meetings, unwanted pregnancy, harrowing experience of abortion and the sense of guilt and shame is projected by Manju Kapur. When Virmati gets to know that she is pregnant she can think of nothing else but shame and humiliation. She gets angry at Harish for not being careful and depends not on her near and dear ones but her roommate Swarna. She gets the child aborted because of her unmarried status. Whereas on the other hand when Ganga gets pregnant, it is a matter of great pride. The news is spread around and all are happy for her; even Virmati's mother is happy and guesses are made that perhaps she will be blessed with a son this time. Motherhood is very respectable in society provided one is legally married. When Virmati gets married and becomes pregnant, the stance of her mother-in-law becomes soft towards her. Extra care is taken of her. She is given milk with almonds and sugar instead of tea.

The inequity between unwedded pregnancy and wedded pregnancy is prominently highlighted. Society approves only the socially acclaimed relationships otherwise all the relations are looked down upon. Virmati gets a bitter taste of it when she gets pregnant without getting married and tastes the other flavour of it when after getting married she gets pregnant. It is her pregnancy that softens even her mother towards her. When she gets to know that Virmati is pregnant and the situation is too delicate she sends for her. Though not completely but her mother forgives her for bringing disgrace to her family. A mute forgiveness works though the scar remains intact. Only Ganga is not happy with her pregnancy because Virmati's kids will share what is the sole right of her kids.

Manju Kapur, brushing aside the trace of a social critic or social reformer, writes as an artist whose aim is to present life and its nuances the way she perceives it. No character is portrayed in larger than life image; no attempt has been made to give a role model, none is blessed with the abundance of virtues. Characters, sometimes strong and sometimes weak, are presented as common human beings capable of making mistakes.

After getting married Kasturi gives birth to eleven children in quick succession, a thing over which she has no control. Virmati being the eldest never gets her share of love, care and affection. Lala Diwan Chand gives full freedom to his granddaughter who returns disgrace to him. His faith is awarded by disgrace of his family. Ganga, a very dutiful and faithful wife, fails to win the heart of her husband. Harish, a ventriloquist, a victim of unforeseen forces, himself suffers and makes others suffer because of reasons over which he has no control. Ida does not hate her father despite his being a weakling. Ida is not intellectually bright, but gives a damn care to it. Chhotti is very brilliant but gives preference to the need and care of her mother and grandmother and shows no interest in music or humanities. Giridhar also does the same thing; he gets married according to his choice. Ida is divorced and childless, but it is not her fault. Virmati takes the bold step of being the second wife of an already married man but suffers throughout her life. She dares not let any other male come into her life, a trend she subconsciously keeps in mind. Professor wants a companion and not *a washerwoman*. This shows that some inscrutable designs engulf all sans letting them know of its presence.

Manju Kapur in her *Difficult Daughters* blatantly scoffs the societal setup when it blocks the way of her desired course. The very first sentence is enough to give the piquant taste of the mindset of Ida where she states in a matter of fact way that she hardly wishes to be like her mother—quite a bold statement on the part of an Indian girl where mothers are considered the role model: "The one thing I had wanted was not to be like my mother" (1).

With Shakespeare the reins of life have remained in the hands of glorified personalities of great magnitude; this type of tyranny got challenged by Russian authors like Leo Tolstoy, Anton Chekhov, Maxim Gorky, et al. who made common man the tragic hero of this drama of life. Likewise Manju Kapur also takes a bold step to introduce her characters as weaklings. The professor, whom Virmati adores to the point of deification, is just a bundle of deficiencies. He spoils the life of his first wife by considering her a mere commodity.

In Manju Kapur's *Difficult Daughters* the explanation of the affairs of life is not very rhetorical or lengthy but very succinct and subtle as is clear from the incident when Virmati is about to decide about the professor or when she is going to commit suicide. The fanciful flight of independence and economic liberation drive her to tread on a path considered least honourable in society. Her desire to unearth the literary treasure ends in a fiasco, as instead of being a true judge she emerges as a woman who falters and fumbles to make her life a faded affair where she neither gets nor gives satisfaction to any of her family members.

It is a story of an ordinary girl who is extraordinary only in her rebellion not to marry the boy chosen by her elders. She costs her elders the loss of their invaluable honour, breaks the heart of so many members of her family and the family of the professor only to do nothing extraordinary but to lead a life, which is hardly considered dignified. She shows her free spirit where it is not at all required and acquiesces where she should rebel. The rebellion on her part is phony as she hardly tries sincerely to gain something valuable or if she desires anything worthy then she hardly strives to achieve that. The desire on her part to become worthy makes her unworthy bit-by-bit and ultimately she becomes disgusted with her own.

To reprise, *Difficult Daughters* is a work, which abounds in details regarding the lacerating friction between desire and duty. All the characters irrespective of their age or generation are caught in the intricate jumble of cross currents. The attempt to break free as an individual or remain tethered to the customs makes them oscillate from one end to another one. While others take life as a continuity involving their share of contribution, Virmati and Harish tend to nurture a relationship that snaps their mite to the whole. The hurricane they bring in the lives of others smashes everything in their lives. Their act alienates their children from them, brings them a bad name in society, and fails to bring them the peace desired. The congenial combination of desire and duty makes life balanced whereas antagonistic amalgamation of the two leads to inexorable doom.

NOTES AND REFERENCES

1. *Rashtriya Sahara Magazine*. April 1999, 112.
2. Das, B.K., *Twentieth Century Literary Criticism,* New Delhi: Atlantic Publishers, 1998, 143.
3. Kapur, Manju, *Difficult Daughters,* New Delhi: Penguin Books India (P) Ltd., 1998, 114. All the subsequent references for *Difficult Daughters* have been taken from the same edition of the, hereafter cited, within the text along with page numbers in particular.
4. Roy, Arundhati, *The God of Small Things*. New Delhi: India Ink Publishing Co. Pvt. Ltd., 1997, 3.
5. Singh, Preeti, *Circles of Silence*. Great Britain: Hodder & Stoughton, 2002, 330.

6. Desai, Anita, *Fasting, Feasting.* London: Chatto & Windus, 1999, 143.
7. Mohanty, Sachidananda, *The Hindu,* 6 Feb. 2000, xiv.
8. Lahiri, Jhumpa, *Interpreter of Maladies.* New Delhi: Harper Collins Publishers, 1999, 93.
9. Roy, Arundhati, *The God of Small Things.* New Delhi: India Ink Publishing Co. Pvt. Ltd., 1997, 10.

Feminism: A Perspective

MALLIKARJUN PATIL

18

Jane Freedman says there are many feminisms of concerns with women's inferior position in society and with discrimination encountered by women because of their sex. Feminists call for changes in the social, economic, political or cultural order, to reduce and eventually overcome this discrimination against women.

The term feminism is relatively a modern one. It was first used in 1871 in a French medical text to describe a cessation of development of the sexual organs and characteristics in male patients, who were perceived as thus suffering from feminization of their bodies. The French writer-republican and anti-feminist—Alexandre Dumas used the term 'feminism' on the subject of adultery to describe women behaving in a supposedly masculine way. G. Fraise thinks the term was used in medicine to signify feminization of men, while the same in politics for describing the virilization of women. It is a clear gender confusion prevailing in regard to differences between men and women even today. The term feminism was used for claiming liberty and equality when American Declaration was expedited in 1776 and when Elizabeth Cady Stanton and Susan B. Anthony founded the National Women Suffrage Association. The same reflected in the mid 19th century Britain. It is said even before this, Olympe de Gouges and Theroighe de Mericourt in France and Mary Wollstonecraft (in her work *A Vindication of the Rights of Women*) tried to argue for liberty and justice for women. Ironically, the women organizations did not call themselves as feminists. Delmer observes 'feminist' *does* not mean a woman working for her social emancipation and empowerment essentially. Accordingly a man can also be a feminist. That is to say feminism is a field itself with its own *locus standi* (ideas, history and practice).

In another way, feminism refers to feminists' movements that took place in the late 19th and the early 20th centuries, generally called the 'First Wave.' The 'Second-Wave' feminism refers to the resurgence of feminist activity in the late 1960s and 1970s. Jane Freedman argues that feminism is also a continuum of thought and action. Some theorists divide feminism as liberal feminism, Marxist (social) feminism and radical feminism. Liberal feminists think of social injustice based on man-woman divide basing their thought on capitalism; and radical theorists think of women's depending as a result of patriarchy. Recent classifications include psycho-analytical feminism, post-modern and post-structuralist feminism, black feminism, Western feminism and Eastern feminism.

What makes feminist theme is 'equality-difference' debate over the divide between the two. Women's biological difference mattered most. Sherry Ortner argues man-woman difference is a matter of pan-cultural fact. She says 'man is closer to culture,' while woman is 'closer to nature.' It is true 'equality-difference' debate is one that has remained central to feminism. Feminists argue "women can be equal to men." Some of them even say "they are better than men." The reasons of this group are not biological but socio-cultural: "as outsiders and nurturers, women do things differently from, and better than, men."[1] The central factor for 'equality-difference' debate is the question of the relevance of biological differences between men and women. Most men argue, even many women admit, that women because of mothering and breast-feeding have lesser physical strength. They cannot equal men in many spheres. Woman is judged to be less reasonable than man, more ruled by emotion, and thus incapable of higher and tougher decisions. Even biologists attest this. Robert Wights is of the opinion, "women lack men's genes for competitiveness and risk-taking behaviour."[2] This led feminists to question man's superiority and for formulating ways for overcoming biological problems. As a result, concepts like 'biological sex' (female) and 'social gender' (feminine) came into being. But Simone de Beauvoir's

Le Deuxieme Sexe (The Second Sex) published in 1949 exerted a lot of influence on feminism. She said, "One is not born a woman: one becomes one."[3] Jane Freedman says of Simone de Beauvoir that "One may be born as a 'female' of the human race but it is civilization which creates 'woman,' which defines what is 'feminine,' and prescribes how women should and do behave. And what is important is that this social construction of 'woman,' has meant a continued oppression of women. The social roles and modes have kept them in an inferior position to that of men."[4] Jane says the gender inequality or saying that woman is 'an eternal feminine' is a social construct. Ann Oakley speaks of sex and gender, the latter just as an attribute. She writes, "'Sex' is a word that refers to the biological differences between male and female: the visible difference in genitalia, the related difference in procreative function. 'Gender,' however, is a matter of culture: it refers to the social classification into 'masculine' and 'feminine.'[5] Delphy talks of gender and sex difference, saying the former is the constant (variable) and the latter, container (invariable). Even sex is thought of as a construct. Thomas Laqueur says people did not distinguish men from women, just because, women bore children but because, she had different sex organs. Delphy says gender precedes sex.

Interestingly Freud, it is said, argued that man's morality is higher than woman's. Because man's morality is based on notions of justice, while woman's on the notion of care.

Feminists are trying to get full socio-political citizenship for women. As W. Brown argues politics is viewed more as a man's domain world-wide. Political philosophers like Plato, Aristotle down to Hobbes, Locke and Rousseau argued that woman is not as rational as man for decision-making. As for the public and private domains of life, man belongs to the former and woman, to the latter. This 'public-private divide' is a traditional view. Fraisse argues that democratically woman is not given citizenship from the point of republican thought, she is denied representation, and feudally, it is said, political power is masculine.

Olyme de Gouges, a French revolutionary published her *Declaration of the Rights of Woman and Citizen* in response to *Declaration of the Rights of Man and Citizen* in 1789. She said, since women were men's equal, they must get all that men get. But Olyme de Gouges was guillotined for her radicalism. The pressure for women's right took an air with the 19th century Suffrage Movement, in Europe and America. Jane Freedman says this was not the question of women's right but the question of human rights. Stacey and Price think, "If women wish to make changes in the societies they live in, they must seek and achieve power positions. It is essential that women should enter the political arena since the societies are all male dominated, for men certainly cannot be relied upon to initiate or carry through the necessary changes."[6] Women organizations such as Emily's List in the USA and UK supported women by financing them for the sake of participation in politics. Women got a quota in Scandinavian countries. The French women went to the court in 2000 for ensuring gender parity. Today India is also debating legislation on women's equal representation in elected assemblies. Feminists argue that equal representation for women is a matter of justice. Secondly they say only women can represent women's interests. Thirdly though less important is that women can make the process of governing smooth. Anne Phillips calls the second reason as 'politics of presence.' As for citizenship T.H. Marshall speaks of three groups of rights granted to individuals by the state, these rights being civil, political and social. Jane Freedman says, "Civil rights are those 'necessary for individual freedom-liberty of the person, freedom of speech and thought and faith, the right to own property and to conclude valid contracts, and the right to justice.' Political rights are the rights to elect and take part in the bodies invested with political power. Social rights comprise the whole range from the right to a modicum of economic welfare and security to the right to share to the full in the social heritage and to live the life of civilized being according to the standards prevailing in the society."[7] Marshall adds that women have been struggling for these rights from time immemorial.

Employment and the Global Economy

Many French feminists fought for gender-parity in wages. What more? As Rowbotham explains, "Women workers did not simply say homework should be banned. It was a vital means by which women with children could support themselves. Instead, they proposed that homework be paid the same rate as work in the workshops. They also demanded state child-care, laundries, and restaurants, along with training for women workers, they began to form their own cooperative associations to secure employment, improve conditions, and enable them to run their work places democratically. These cooperative associations extended beyond the workplace. They provided housing and welfare services and they imagined communal housing with gardens and schools and health services for workers on a large scale."[8] What a wonder, even Marx could not think of women's problems whole-heartedly. He said the struggle for women's emancipation was subsumed within the class struggle. German Socialist Clara Zetkin spoke of protective legislation for women. Others thought of women's unpaid work within the family. Today Globalization has given an international colouring to the feminist problems.

Job-segregation and sexual harassment explain the low status of women as ever before. Hartman argues that capitalism and patriarchy ('dual-system theory') have done much harm to women. Jane Freedman speaks of men's control of women's access to well-paid jobs. There is an argument that women should not continue doing household work for the sake of paid work on parity with men. Dalla Costa suggests if women do not get recognition for domestic work, childbearing and caring, they should go on strike. But Marxists find this idea as theoretically untenable. Jane Freedman thinks Globalization, in its way, has oppressed women as did colonialism. Interestingly some feminists like Vandana Shiv argue for eco-feminism. Shiv says, the western colonialism and science have destroyed man's harmonious relations with the natural world. Women say natural environment must be cared for and used carefully. Women's knowledge is vital to the maintenance of biodiversity.

Sexuality and Power

Feminists have hotly thought over sexuality. In 1918, a US feminist Crystal Eastman wrote, "Feminist are not nuns. That should be established. We want love and to be loved, and most of us want children, one or two at least, but we want our love to be joyous and free—not clouded with ignorance and fear. And we want our children to be deliberately, eagerly called into being, when we are at our best, not crowded upon us in times of poverty and weakness. We want this precious sex knowledge not just for ourselves, the conscious feminists; we want it for all the millions of unconscious feminists that swarm the earth,—we want it for women."[9]

Feminists want women control their sex and mothering. So the use of abortion and contraception came into being. Catharine Mackinnon argues sexuality constitutes gender, allowing men dominate women. She says it is the linchpin of gender inequality. Walby adds women need a great control over their bodies. This leads to heterosexuality. Feminists blame men for thinking of their own satisfaction in intercourse. Some suggest women must go for lesbianism or think of some mutual sexual enjoyment. Bunch says women then cannot be true sexualists without being lesbians, as "the very essence, definition and nature of heterosexuality is men first."[10] Leeds Revolutionary Feminist Group states heterosexuality proves male superiority. By the by Robin Morgan who says pornography also contributes to women's misery argues, "Pornography is the theory and rape is the practice."[11] Jane Freedman says, "Feminist have argued against pornography on three counts: first that it encourages sexual violence and rape against women, second that in its humiliation of women it is itself a form of sexual violence, and third that women are hurt and economically and sexually exploited in the production of pornography."[12] Accordingly as pornography arouses desire in men, the latter humiliate women. In Andrea Dworkin's view men colonilize women by way of using institutions like law, marriage, prostitution, pornography, health care, the economy, organized religion and systematic aggression against women (for instance rape). Mackinnon even went to the extent of opposing or banning pornography, while the other feminists want it for sexual expression.

Susan Brownmiller says all women are victims of rape or the threat of it which finally makes women subordinate to men. She compares rape to Myrmidons who served Achilles with loyalty. It is an 'anonymous agent of terror.' So it is a system of male control of women. Some feminists think that reproduction and mothering are a burden on women, part of the oppression which must be lifted; these feminists see new technology that will take the burden of reproduction away from women as the key to women's liberation. Whereas the same is a great pleasure for many women and other feminists.

Ethnicity and Identity

It is commonly known that the so-called feminism is represented by a dominant white, middle-class, often, understanding the differences of race, class, ability and sexual orientation of others. Jane Freedman says there are many feminisms. For ex: the popular Eurocentric feminism has overlooked the working classes and negroes and the women living in the Third World. Black women are called 'fallen women, wares and prostitutes.' Black feminists, for ex, think that family for many of them is not a site of oppression but a site of protection from racism. They think white women suppress black women. The popular feminists think that feminism is a Western Ideology. Whereas Kumari Jayawardena says feminism was born in the Third World. Uma Narayan argues that Third World feminism is a response to particular problems in Third World countries. She writes, "Issues that feminist group in India have politically engaged with include problems of dowry-murder and dowry-related harassment of women, police rape of women in custody; issues relating to women's poverty, health and reproduction; and issues of ecology and communalism that affect women's lives. Indian feminist political activities clearly make feminists and feminism part of the national political landscape of many Third World countries. I am arguing that Third World feminism is not a mindless mimicking of 'Western agendas' in one clear and simple sense—that, for instance, Indian feminism is clearly a response to issues specifically confronting many Indian women."[13] Cynthia Enloe thinks colonization made women subservient to the west.

Now we have the so-called post-modernist and post-structuralist theories of feminism. These two concepts being the same in the context of feminism, focus upon specific aspects of sex in terms of race, geography, culture and the like. Jane Flax challenges the natural, fixed and universal definitions of gender relations. Chris Weedon writes, "A post-structuralist feminism, on the other hand, committed as it is to the principle of difference and deferral never fixes meaning once and for all. For post-structuralism femininity and masculinity are constantly in process and subjectivity, which most discourses seek to fix, is constantly subject to dispersal."[14] In sum, Jane Freedman argues for a feminism for some kind of collective identity of women, while at the same time acknowledging differences.

REFERENCES

1. Hester Eisenstein and Alice Jordine, *The Future of Difference.* New Brunswick, NJ, Rutgers University Press, 1988, xxv.
2. Robert Wights qt. by Jane Freedman, *Feminism.* New Delhi: Viva Books, 2002, 13.
3. Simone de Beauvoir's *Le Deuxieme Sexe* qt. by Jane Freedman, *Ibid.*, 14.
4. Jane Freedman, *Ibid.,* 14.
5. Ann Oakley, *Sex, Gender and Society.* London: Temple Smith, 1972, 16.
6. Stacey and Price, *Women, Power and Politics.* London: Tavistock, 1981, 35.
7. T.H. Marshall, *Citizenship and Social Class.* Cambridge: CUP, 1950, 10-11.
8. Rowbotham, *Women in Movement: Feminism and Social Action.* New York: Routledge, 1992, 61.
9. Crystal Eastman, qt. by Rowbotham, *Women in Movement: Feminism and Social Action.* New York: Routledge, 1992, 224.

10. C. Bunch, "Lesbians in revolt," in Marshall (ed.) *Women and Values*. Belmont, CA: Wadsworth, 1986, 131.
11. Robin Morgan, "Theory and Practice: Pornography and Rape," in L. Lederer (ed.) *Take Back The Night: Women on Pornography*. New York: William Morrow, 1980, 139.
12. Jane Freedman, *Ibid.*, 64.
13. Uma Narayan, *Dilocating Cultures: Identities, Traditions and Third World Feminism*. New York: Routledge, 1997, 13.
14. Chris Weedon, *Feminist Practice and Poststructuralist Theory*. Oxford: Blackwell, 1987, 99.

'O, Those Extraordinary Women!'

It is fatal for a woman to lay the least stress on any grievance; to plead even with justice any cause; in any way to speak consciously as a woman.... Anything written with that conscious bias is doomed to death...it cannot grow in the minds of others.

—*Virginia Woolf*

When a man becomes an author, it is probably merely a change of employment to him.... But no other can take up the quiet, regular duties of the daughter, the wife, or the mother...; a woman's principal work in life is hardly left to her own choice; nor can she drop the domestic charges devolving on her as an individual, for the exercise of the most splendid talents that were ever bestowed.

—*Elizabeth Cleghorn Gaskell*

And yet she must not shrink from the extra responsibility implied by the very fact of her possessing such talents. She must not hide her gift in a napkin; it was meant for the use and service of others. In an humble and faithful spirit she must labour to do what is not impossible, or God would not have set her to do it.

—*Elizabeth Gaskell*

We dwell with satisfaction upon the poet's difference from her predecessors, especially her immediate predecessors: we endeavour to find something that can be isolated in order to be enjoyed. Whereas if we approach a poet without this prejudice we shall often find that not only the best, but the most individual parts of her work may be those in which the dead poets, her ancestors, assert their immortality most vigorously.

—T.S. Eliot

I think I may boast myself to be, with all possible vanity, the most unlearned and uninformed female whoever dared to be an authoress.

—Jane Austen

The appearance of Woman in the field of literature is a significant fact.... The advent of female literature promises woman's view of life, woman's experience: in other words, a new element.

—George Henry Lewis in 1852

Of all departments of literature Fiction is the one to which, by nature and experience, women are best adapted.

—George Henry Lewes

...and while before
The world thou burnest in a poet fire,
We see thy woman heart beat evermore
Through the large flame.

—Elizabeth Barrett to George Sand

What is a Poet? To whom does she address herself? And what language is to be expected from her?—She is a woman speaking to women.

—Wordsworth

If men could see us as we really are, they would be a little amazed; but the cleverest, the acutest men are often under an illusion about women: they do not read them in a true light: they misapprehend them.... If I spoke all I think on this point; if I gave my real opinion of some first-rate female characters in first rate works....

—Charlotte Bronte

One generally finds in the writings of even ingenious men that they take up the characters of women too easily...the two sexes are too much considered as different species. He or she who soars not above simplicity is most likely to understand the human heart best in either sex, especially if he can make allowance for different modes of education, constitution, and situation.

—*Samuel Richardson*

The life of woman rolls forth like a stream from the fountain, or it spreads out into tranquility like a placid or stagnant lake.

—*Walter Scott*

These chosen few, wish to speak for themselves, and not to be an echo—even of the sweetest sounds.... The paradise they ramble in, must be of their own making.

—*Mary Wollstonecraft*

Was not the world a vast prison, and women born slaves?

—*Mary Wollstonecraft*

Has paterfamilias, with his Oriental traditions and veiled female faces, very successfully dealt with a certain class of evil? What if materfamilias, with her quick sure instincts and honest innocent eyes, do more towards their expulsion by simply looking at them and calling them by their names?

—*Elizabeth Browning to Thackeray [who rejected her poem for dangerous frankness]*

Contributors

Santwana Haldar, F.M. Auto College, Balasore, Orissa [R]Ranipatana, Bank Colony, Balasore, Orissa.

Devika, Lecturer, Languages Group, BITS Pilani, Rajasthan.

Binod Mishra, Department of Languages, Birla Institute of Technology and Science. Pilani, Rajasthan.

Rashmi Gaur, Associate Professor, Department of Humanities and Social Sciences, IIT, Roorkee, Uttar Pradesh.

Rano Ringo, Research Scholar, Department of Humanities and Social Sciences, IIT, Roorkee, Uttar Pradesh.

Madhu Joshi, Department of English, Kumaun University, Nainital, Uttaranchal.

Mallikarjun Patil, Lecturer, Department of English, Gulbarga University, Gulbarga, Karnataka.

Binda Sharma, Head, Department of English, C.M.D. Postgraduate College, Bilaspur, Chhattisgarh.

G.A. Ghanshyam, Assistant Professor, Department of English, Govt. Autonomous Science P.G. College, Bilaspur, Chhattisgarh.

Sadhana Agrawal, Assistant Professor of English, Govt. Maharaja Autonomous P.G. College, Chhatarpur, Madhya Pradesh.

S. **Ambika,** Research Scholar, Department of English, Noorul Islam College of Engineering, Kumaracoil, Kanyakumari District, Tamil Nadu.

Ram Sharma, Lecturer in English, Janata Vedic College, Baraut, Baghpat, Uttar Pradesh.

Narinder Kumar Neb, Lecturer in English, D.A.V. College, Jalandhar, Punjab.

Shubha Tiwari, Sr. Lecturer, Department of English, A.P.S. University, Rewa, Madhya Pradesh.

Binayak Ray, Research Scholar, C/o K.K. Roy, Prof. of English [Retd.], Ramkrishna Sarani, Shiv Mandir, North Bengal University, Raja Rammohunpur, Dt. Darjeeling, Siliguri, West Bengal.